CISTERCIAN FATHERS SERIES: NUMBER THIRTY-THREE

Idung of Prüfening: Cistercians and Cluniacs
The Case for Cîteaux

© Copyright, Cistercian Publications Inc., 1977
All rights reserved

A translation of *Dialogus duorum monachorum* and *Argumentum super quatuor questionibus* by Idung of Prüfening. Translated by Jeremiah F. O'Sullivan, Grace Perigo, and Joseph Leahey from the edition of R. B. C. Huygens, 'Le moine Idung et ses deux ouvrages: "Argumentum super quatuor questionibus" et "Dialogus duorum monachorum" ', *Studi Medievali*, 3rd series, XIII, 1, 1972.

cistercian publications

Editorial Offices
The Institute of Cistercian Studies
Western Michigan University
Kalamazoo, Michigan 49008-5415

*The work of Cistercian Publications is made possible in part
by support from Western Michigan University to
The Institute of Cistercian Studies.*

Cistercian Publications books are available
through the following addresses:

The United States: Liturgical Press
Saint John's Abbey Collegeville, MN 56321-7500
sales@litpress.org

The United Kingdom and Europe: Alban Books Ltd
14 Belford Road West End
Edinburgh EH4 3BL
sales@albanbooks.com

Canada: Bayard Books
49 Front Street East, Second Floor
Toronto Ontario M5E 1B3
cservice@novalis-inc.com

Library of Congress Cataloguing in Publication Data

Idung of Prüfening.
  Cistercians and Cluniacs.

  (Cistercian Fathers series : 33)
    Translation of Dialogue duorum monachorum and De quatuor quæstionibus.
    Bibliography : p.
    Includes index.
    CONTENTS: A dialogue between a Cistercian and a Cluniac monk. — An argument over four questions.
    1. Cistercians. 2. Cluniacs. 3. Monks. 4. Nuns
I. Idung of Prüfening, De quatuor quæstionibus. English. 1977. II. Title.
BX3406.2.13513 255'.1   77-9289

Book design by Gale Akins
Typeset at Humble Hills Press, Kalamazoo, Michigan 49004

Printed in the United States of America

CISTERCIAN FATHERS SERIES: NUMBER THIRTY-THREE

CISTERCIANS AND CLUNIACS
THE CASE FOR CÎTEAUX

A Dialogue between Two Monks
An Argument on Four Questions

by

Idung of Prüfening

CISTERCIAN PUBLICATIONS INC.
KALAMAZOO, MICHIGAN
1977

After retiring in 1967 from a distinguished teaching career at Fordham University, Jeremiah F. O'Sullivan continued his life-long work in medieval Cistercian history by translating twelfth-century Cistercian treatises for Cistercian Publications. He donated his time, his expertise, and his labor to the Publications, and he enlivened the correspondence of the editors with his thoughtful and witty comments on scholarly and monastic life, medieval and modern.

The margins of the books and photocopies he worked from are liberally decorated with uniquely expressive marginalia *which comment in words or cartoons on the obscurities of the passage, the glee of the translator at solving a difficult turn of phrase, or his impatience with a pedantic writer. In themselves they are collectors' items.*

The editors of Cistercian Publications regret deeply that circumstances prevented them from publishing any of Professor O'Sullivan's translations before his death in 1975. He would have enjoyed sharing his work with his former students and with his many friends. In the Dialogue between a Cluniac and a Cistercian Monk, the insights of a lifetime of study, his innate generosity, and his Irish humor have combined to produce a lilting and colloquial rendition of an entertaining, and colloquial, twelfth century polemic.

The companion piece, An Argument on Four Questions, has been dedicated by one of his students, Joseph Leahey, to Professor O'Sullivan and to his wife.

In appreciation for the encouragement
the counsel
the labor

he generously gave to us
and to his students,

the editors of Cistercian Publications
join Professor Leahey in dedicating
this volume to the
memory of

Jeremiah F. O'Sullivan
and to his wife
Claire

Errata

page	line	for	read
vii		Leahy	Leahey
13	B-11	though	through
13	7	dispensations	dispensation
16, n. 15		*Thesauris novis*	*Thesaurus novus*
16	B	now have been	nor has been
26	B-12	personification of	personification or
49	16	forgeting	forgetting
51	21	can be impediment	can be an impediment
52	23	to available	to avail
58	22	abhorrant	abhorrent
73	9	on that I had	on that day I had
83	25	become enemies	became enemies
87	22	this several chapters	this in several chapters
88	B-3	preaching the very	preaching by the very
105	9	not to be overborne	not be overborne
106	26	Those which exists	Those which exist
110	7	of a gold coin	a gold coin
115	[III,27]	mCistercian	Cistercian
119	B-19	Geizi	Giezi

TABLE OF CONTENTS

Cistercians and Cluniacs: The Case for Cîteaux
    Introduction 3
    Author's Preface 21
    Part One 25
    Part Two 61
    Part Three 101

An Argument Concerning Four Questions
    Introduction by Joseph Leahy 145
    The Argument. 151

Notes 193

Abbreviations 223

Bibliography 227

A DIALOGUE BETWEEN A CLUNIAC AND A CISTERCIAN

A DIALOGUE BETWEEN A CLUNIAC AND A CISTERCIAN

INTRODUCTION

HE SEEDS OF MONASTIC RENEWAL had been long germinating before ripening into fruit in the eleventh century.[1] This was a century of spiritual quest by individuals and groups for soul-satisfying outlets. New monastic Orders had their origins in these enthusiasms, as did also the growth of Europe's new affective spirituality. Devotion was becoming more personal and more outgoing. This new European spirituality was itself an essential element in the development of the eleventh century monastic renewal.

The new Orders had in common one outlook on the religious life—an outlook somewhat akin to that prevailing in the fourth and fifth centuries—a longing for the silence and austerity of the desert and for a renaissance of the ideals of the *ecclesia primitiva*. It is not an accident of words that the Camaldolese, the Carthusians and the Cistercians referred to their original settlements as 'the desert'. Of the religious communities formed during this period, the best known and ultimately the most influential was that group of monks who departed in protest from the monastery of Molesme and settled in the soggy swampland of Cîteaux.

The monks in the New Monastery, as the settlement at Cîteaux was called by contemporaries, gave living form to the desert ideal and to affective spirituality through a life of physical deprivation and through devotion to the Passion of Christ and to the Virgin Mary. They were not content with patching and shoring up current monastic practices. Instead, they peeled off the layers of liturgical accretions which were the legacies bequeathed to monasticism by centuries-long development and the influence of Romans, Teutons, and Celts. In giving of itself to western civilization, monasticism had received from the different ethnic bodies it had molded some gifts which were ultimately not to its advantage. The men at Cîteaux wanted to clean house and go back to basics.

Conservative prelates, in addition to monastic administrators who did not want to see either the delicate equilibrium of *Rule* and *Custom* shaken in the slightest, or the *status quo* of the monastic institutional structure disturbed, gave voice to their disapproval of the living conditions prevailing at Cîteaux. In what may very well be regarded as an affluent society, especially insofar as the greater monasteries were concerned, the way of life at Cîteaux was considered completely out of order by many lay and ecclesiastic persons. Cîteaux was the monasticism of the poor, with its peasant black bread and beans, personal manual labor in the recovery of swamp land, and liturgical simplicity. A socially conscious feudal-minded world found it very difficult to accept the fact that freemen were doing the work of serviles. Accordingly, lay and cleric alike were inclined 'to look before they leaped,' that is, before they accepted the ways of the New Monastery. Society passes its own judgments on the transgressors of its mores,[2] and the early paucity of postulants at Cîteaux's doors likely stemmed from this disapproval.

Cîteaux's viability was assured by the arrival of St Bernard, accompanied by a goodly number of relatives and their friends. St Bernard became the dominant personality of twelfth-century Europe. As he propagated the Order, the shadow, or the reality, of his presence was simultaneously to be found in the councils of the papal curia, in archiepiscopal and episcopal palaces, in episcopal and abbatial elections, in discussions on social problems, in church councils, and in the new schools of philosophy and of theology which constituted the intellectual fibre of twelfth-century cultural renaissance. Throughout his ministry he dealt dynamically with questions that troubled all elements of twelfth-century society.

From the very outset Cîteaux had made clear its position on the current monastic malaise and in 1134 put it on public record in its *Instituta*.[3] By implication, these regulations proclaimed other monasteries to be fatted exemplars of monasticism as a feudal institution and violators of the integrity of the *Rule of St Benedict*. While maintaining silence on the subject, some of the monks of Cluny must have been concerned about the document's implications and its pointed applications to their way of life. This concern must have been heightened when Bernard effectively propagated the Order of Cîteaux. Ultimately— with much washing of dirty linen—a family quarrel between Cîteaux and Cluny flared into the open.[4]

Around 1122 Cluny's Grand Prior,[5] taking advantage of St Bernard's momentary absence from Clairvaux, personally induced Bernard's cousin, Robert, who was a monk there, to accompany him to Cluny. Cluniacs claimed that Robert had been offered to them as an oblate by his parents. Bernard countered this argument by declaring that Robert had never lived at Cluny as an oblate and thus was free to enter the Order of Cîteaux. Cluny lost no time in taking the case to Rome for adjudication; there and then Bernard came face to face with the Cluniac influence in Rome. In late 1124 or early 1125,[6] when no doubt was left but that he had lost his case, Bernard wrote a letter, not to the Lord Abbot of Cluny or to the Grand Prior, or even to the community of Cluny, but to Robert himself.

Ostensibly it was a private letter. Bernard's expressions of love and compassion for his young cousin were movingly tender and personal, yet the abbot wrote the letter primarily as a public propaganda pamphlet.[7] As such, the letter became the opening shot in the twelfth-century controversy between Cluniacs and Cistercians.

The saint drew a striking contrast between the luxury of Cluniac life and the austerity of Cistercian monasticism. He contended that the soft clothes of Cluny were the luxuries of the weak, not the arms of fighting men. The exotic spices used at Cluny might indeed please the palate, but they also inflamed lust. Among the Cistercians salt with hunger was seasoning enough and hard work made their simple vegetables, beans, roots, and bread taste delicious. Bernard's overdrawn charges against the Cluniacs probably bordered on libel.[8] What must have been especially galling to the monks of Cluny was Bernard's inference that Robert courted eternal damnation by remaining at Cluny.

Over the course of the next two decades, the abbot of Clairvaux followed up and expanded the theme of this manifesto in two treatises, *Apologia ad Guillelmum* (1125) and *De praecepto et dispensatione* (between 1141 and 1144),[9] and in a number of more or less private letters.[10]

Monks of both Orders felt impelled to make public their offerings to this controversy. Although the conflict produced a great many public recriminations, it was not without charity[11] and positive results.[12] Finally the affair ended, probably with mutual sighs of relief, for lack of sustenance. But before the arguments had subsided, a number of tracts had been penned by monks of both parties;[13] even secular clerics entered the controversy.[14] One of the most important treatises to come out of the controversy was the *Dialogue between a Cluniac and a Cistercian.*[15]

THE AUTHOR

Who was the author of this tract? Nowhere in the *Dialogue* does he reveal his identity. Only once does he provide a direct clue to his name by referring to himself as 'I. a sinner monk.'[16] Philibert Schmitz identified him as Iring of Aldersbach in Bavaria.[17] Actually, his name was Idung.

Eberhard Demm and R. B. C. Huygens have both recently established Idung's identity beyond any reasonable doubt,[18] and Huygens, through careful investigation of existing archival materials, has been able to sketch a biography of this shadowy monk.[19] Even if we did not have Huygen's fine study, we would be able, on the basis of information furnished by the *Dialogue* alone, to hazard certain guesses about its author's life: this tract's Cistercian disputant is no fictional character; he is the author. Through a careful exegesis of the *Dialogue* we can surmise his ethnic background; we can learn of his spiritual struggles as a Cluniac *conversus*; we can vaguely guess his education prior to entering religion, and we can make several judgments about his interest in law—roman and canon—and his acquaintance with patristics.

The *Dialogue* leaves little doubt that ethnically its author was a German. As Martène and Durand pointed out in the early eighteenth century, his spelling Cluny as Clony, Rupert as Roudpert, and Anselm as Anshelm indicate his Germanic background. When in spiritual difficulties, he sought out German counsellors, Dom Gebhardt of Admont[20] and a monk of Reichersberg.[21] He also dedicated his tract to Abbess K. of Niedermünster, of whom he requested the favor of having her nuns transcribe it for presentation to the world.[22] Indeed, each of its five known extant manuscripts has a German connection.[23]

The author of the *Dialogue* gives the impression of being a spiritually intense man, who grasped thoroughly the meaning of the Cistercian movement. We learn that he became a monk, professed *ad succurundum*,[24] at a Cluniac monastery.[25] After ten years as a *conversus*,[26] he discovered that his life as a Cluniac monk no longer satisfied his spiritual needs. That is, he now needed for fulfillment the abnegation and discipline delineated in the *Rule* in its original form. In that frame of mind he passed over to a Cistercian monastery.[27] The *Dialogue* hints that later his case was discussed at Rome, with the possibility that he would be ordered to return to the house of his original profession.[28] Apparently nothing came of it.

The *Dialogue* gives the impression that its author was a well-educated man—a product of the schools—and secure enough in his education to make it the butt of a gentle joke. The Cluniac, with feigned inferiority, says to him: 'With your trained mind and your ersatz words, which you learned long ago in the schools, you are trying to muddle my uneducated mind.'[29] He was certainly acquainted with dialectics and aristotelian logic, as he shows in one dazzling display of verbal gymnastics.[30] In many respects this middle-to-late-aged monk appears simply an elderly, cloistered aspirant to the new learning. But he was more than that. As Huygens has shown, prior to entering the Cluniac house at Prüfening, he had been a schoolmaster at Regensburg.[31] He was one of the new breed of scholars of the twelfth-century renaissance.

At some time in his life, perhaps while he was a Cluniac, he became a student of patristics. Undoubtedly, during his ten years at Prüfening he used its patristic library. His knowledge of the Fathers may be questioned but his acquaintance may not. He quotes the Desert Fathers, but for the most part he places his reliance for authoritative proof on Saints Jerome, Augustine, Basil, Ambrose, and Gregory the Great. His quotations from the Fathers are of interest because he may very well have been quoting from memory; this probably accounts for the many inaccuracies which crop up in his citations. In Idung's case, this will to quote accurately must be accepted *in lieu* of the accomplishment. The following are a few random quotations from the *Dialogue* compared with the patristic originals:

St Jerome, Homilies on the Psalms
(Ps 145:7)

IDUNG	ST JEROME
'He who gives food to the hungry.' He [St Jerome] says to the monks, 'Monk, pay attention, you who give food to the hungry and not to the regurgitating: you who are surfeited, take your food, but do not take the bread which is to be given to the hungry. Take what you can put in your stomach, not what you can put in a bag. Take what you can put on your back, not what you can put into a chest.'[32]	'He gives food to the hungry.' He feeds the hungry, not the bloated. Let the monk who does not have confidently receive; let him who has and is surfeited not receive. You know if you are poor. If you are hungry and have nothing, you do a greater service by receiving than does he who gives.[33]

Prosper of Aquitaine, *On the Contemplative Life*

IDUNG	PROSPER OF AQUITAINE
Prosper, in his *Rules for Canons*, agrees with St Jerome when he says: 'To give to those who already have is nothing other than to lose it.'[34]	The pastor of a church should not give anything to persons who are sufficiently well-off, since such generosity is simply wasteful.[35]

St Ambrose, *On the Duties of the Clergy*

IDUNG	ST AMBROSE
St Ambrose . . . says: 'How can we usurp something as ours for which we do not have the written authority of Scripture?'[36]	Although at times jests may be proper and pleasant, still they are unsuited to the clerical life. For how can we adopt those things which we do not find in the holy Scriptures?[37]

St John Chrysostom, *Six Books on the Priesthood*

IDUNG	ST JOHN CHRYSOSTOM
This is what St John Chrysostom said: 'The soul of the priest should be more resplendent than the rays of the sun so that never is it forsaken by the Holy Spirit and can say, "I live; no, not I, but Christ lives in me!" '[38]	Indeed, the soul of the priest should be purer than the rays of the sun lest the Holy Spirit ever desert him and so that he can say 'I live; no, not I, but Christ lives in me!'[39]

Three of these examples closely *paraphrase* an original text. One is almost totally dissimilar from the passage which is supposedly being quoted. We can only conjecture about the reason for this lack of textual accuracy. Very likely, Idung, on being received by the Cistercians, was sent to a monastery far distant from his former Cluniac house. Here he may have lacked adequate library facilities. Remembering the essentials of what he wanted to say, and who said it originally, he did his best to reproduce the text from memory.

With the exception of texts on liturgy and chant, the first Cistercians had demands which exceeded the collection of library materials. Idung's quotations have a sense of urgency to convey the meaning of what he had to say and to cite who in authority said it rather than one of concern for literal textual accuracy. Apparently, he did not have on hand even a copy of one of the many handbooks of quotations which abounded in his day.

He does, however, quote one source with a good degree of accuracy —Gratian's *Decretum*—indicating that he had direct access to this textbook of canon law. He utilizes the *Decretum* (published around 1140) in seventeen instances as supporting documentary evidence. In addition, the language of the *Dialogue* allows us to infer that Idung was familiar with roman legal terms, the *Etymologiae* of Isidore of Seville, and probably the *Decretum* of the great French canonist, Ivo of Chartres. Evidently law—roman and canon—was of more than passing interest to him. He is a good example of the resurgence of legal studies in the Schools, in which he probably pursued this branch of studies prior to entering a Cluniac monastery as a man-turned-late-in-life-to-God—a *conversus*.

The *Dialogue* also gives evidence of Idung's personal involvement in the then heated controversy between segments of the monastic orders and the orders of canons on the questions of Holy Orders, preaching, and the cure of souls in parishes. Idung was interested enough in this argument to treat the topic at some length, even though it was wholly extraneous to the central theme of the *Dialogue*. It is apparent that Idung looked with greater suspicion upon the new Orders of Canons Regular than he did upon the whole Order of Cluny. If there is animosity anywhere in the *Dialogue* it is in the author's attitude toward the Norbertine canons, whom he even denies the status of canons, arguing that, because they live according to a *Rule*, they are monks.[40]

Yet, happily, Idung had a healthy ability to see his own foibles and prejudices as others must have seen them and to treat them with some objectivity. Therefore, during the Cistercian's (i.e., Idung's) attack on the Norbertines, the author poses a question through the Cluniac and offers himself a bit of advice, providing thereby a valuable clue to his identity. The Cluniac says: ' . . . why do you . . . make yourself obnoxious to three Orders: [a] the Black Monks [Benedictines], [b] the Canons Regular, and [c] the habited Norbertines? Stop your foolish arrogance, lest you be branded with the mark of the detractor.'[41]

Until recently, studies of the *Dialogue* could only speculate how the author had made himself obnoxious to three orders. Now, thanks to Demm and Huygens, the answer is known. The same man who composed the *Dialogue* also authored the *Argumentum super quatuor questionibus*.[42] That treatise dealt with the lively question of Holy

Orders for monks in a manner which would make its author odious to the canons and the black monks.[43] Its author is known to be Idung of Prüfening.

THE *DIALOGUE'S* PURPOSE AND DATE

Idung's purpose in composing the *Dialogue* is not difficult to fathom. In his prefatory dedication to Abbess K. of Niedermünster he remarks:

> ... I do not please some who were also bound to me in brotherly love [in religion] because I deserted the monastery and order of my first conversion. For this reason I have authored this *Dialogue* that, through the reasons and authoritative evidence collected therein, it may serve as my exculpator and legal counsel against those who accuse and censure me.[44]

The *Dialogue*, therefore, is his defense against the charge that by leaving his Cluniac house he has broken his vow of *stabilitas* and has become that most worthless type of monk—the *gyrovagus* or wanderer.[45] By extension, the treatise is also his defense of the whole Order of Cîteaux against those who argue that the Order in origin,[46] spirit, and daily action violated stability.

His argument revolves around the premise that a monk's profession is to Christ and the *Rule*, and not necessarily to a particular monastic house. Therefore, a monk's stability and constancy are to be judged in the light of his strict adherence to God and the *Rule*. In Idung's own words:

> The monastery to which a monk is called is one thing; the monastic calling is something quite different. The monastic calling consists in promising to obey the *Rule* in its integrity; provided [a] it be kept, it knows no one location and provided [b] the professed remains in that calling to which he was called. If it is not kept, even if the monk never leaves the monastery he first entered, he is ... outside it .... They accuse us of having violated our primary pledge of faith, we, the monks who entered the Order of Cîteaux because our main purpose was to keep the *Rule*, even though both charges can be lodged against them ... , since they have turned to one side from keeping their pledge and likewise from observing the *Rule*.[47]

There was nothing new about such arguments. St Bernard, whom Idung quotes and cites freely, had made the same defense of Cîteaux. Indeed, the content and implications of the *Dialogue* are best understood when read in the context of both the *Apologia ad Guillelmum* and *De praecepto et dispensatione.*

It is obvious that Bernard had already died when Idung composed the *Dialogue,* since the saint is referred to as 'Dom Bernard, abbot of Clairvaux of happy memory.'[48] Therefore, the tract was written after 20 August 1153. Also, since nowhere in the *Dialogue* is Bernard given the title 'Saint,' we can further infer that Idung composed his work before St Bernard's canonization in 1174. Of these dates and only these dates can we be reasonably certain, yet we can make further speculations. R. B. C. Huygens has argued that Idung probably composed this treatise shortly after leaving Prüfening and entering a Cistercian house. At this point he would have been full of the first ardor of conversion and in the greatest need of justifying his actions, both to himself and to others. Huygens has further shown that Idung probably became a Cluniac in 1144 and a Cistercian ten years later, in 1154 or early 1155. Therefore, he dates the composition of the tract around 1155.[49]

If Huygens' dating is correct, it would mean that the *Dialogue* was written toward the end of the first generation of the Cluniac–Cistercian squabble. This is significant, since it would show that already by the mid-fifties the quarrel was beginning to go stale and much of the holy anger of the first days was giving way to other concerns.

The *Dialogue* has somewhat the tone of two friends who meet, have a friendly, at times even witty, debate and who on occasion, because onlookers expect it of them, raise their voices in mock anger. This is not to say that the friends do not disagree over some rather fundamental issues. But they respect one another's sincerity and seem to feel that already too many angry, hasty words have been shouted by both sides. The Cluniac best sums up their attitudes and to all intents ends the discussion on the relative merits of both orders when he says: 'After giving full consideration to your presentation, I have, in sum, concluded that the very weapons we hurl at you, you, in order to justify yourself, hurl back at us, forgetting the Lord's precept, "Revenge is mine, I will repay".'[50]

THE USE OF LAW IN THE *DIALOGUE*

The *Dialogue* belonged to the twelfth century not only as an example of the Cluniac–Cistercian controversy but also as an integral part of the twelfth-century renaissance's interest in law.[51] Its central theme, argued by the Cistercian disputant, is that for monks professed in that order, the *Rule of St Benedict* is *law,* law in the sense that law was regarded in imperial Rome; it is a plea for the *Rule*'s strict and literal observance, thereby to insure the rule of law in religion. While Idung recognizes custom as an implementation of what is absent from the original *Rule*,[52] he maintains that customary enactments are of a lower grade in legal status, and as the Law of Rome emanated from one strong central point (the emperor and senate), so the Law for religious had its being in one central document—the *Rule of St Benedict*. As customary law in Rome was derived from the will of the people and thus was suspect, so custom in monastic Orders originates in the body at large and is thereby suspect.

According to Idung, the *Rule of St Benedict* has its source in the Highest of all Authorities: 'Wherefore St Benedict ordered us to follow the Master, the *Rule*, in all things, because, since we are men, there are times when we deceive and are deceived. Following the precepts laid down in the *Rule*, we do not deceive nor are we deceived, since they have their source in God, inasmuch as the Holy Spirit instituted them by means of St Benedict, in addition to the protection afforded by St Gregory the Great.'[53] The Cistercian on several occasions leaves no doubt about the place of monastic Custom, especially as practised by the Cluniacs,[54] *vis-a-vis* the *Rule*:

¶This indeed is *your* custom and is contrary to the *Rule of St Benedict* and the canons . . . [55] Tell me, I ask you, do you know of any reason for this strange custom of yours?

¶I [the Cluniac] cannot tell you of one for the simple reason that I know of none, nor do our superiors give any other than quoting from the authority of our own Custom.[56]

¶Rash, indeed, is custom; indeed, your Custom is more rash, because it is not only without, but even contrary to, authority; . . . [57] Usage which goes contrary to reason and sacred authority is ab-use rather than use.[58] . . . the Customs of Cluny are a deviation from the law given us by God, i.e., from the *Rule*, and thereby they bring dishonor on the Giver of the law, St Benedict.[59]

In other words, the *Rule* is Law. It is the Law of the Order and the rule of law; it is there for all to see and is authenticated by Scripture. Since it has its source in God, it is a guarantee, when followed faithfully, that one neither deceives nor is deceived. They who have professed it are not permitted to leave undone what it commands, nor are they to do what it forbids. Accordingly, let no one dare to express doubts about the *Rule* given by St Benedict, and let nobody dare to sit in judgment thereon.[60]

Yet, the *Rule* in its entirety has precepts which are not to be found in the original *Rule* of St Benedict. Following Benedict's advice,[61] these were culled from the Fathers.[62] What of those precepts incorporated into the *Rule*, but not in the original? In that case, 'all things are lawful, but all do not edify; all are lawful, but not all are expedient; no man is to seek his own but another's good.'[63] This scriptural conclusion parallels the teaching of the father of Latin canon law, the monk Gratian of Bologna, who some fifteen years earlier had written that man is governed in two ways, by natural justice and by custom. Natural justice, by which each is ordered to do to another what he wishes done to himself, is contained in written law and in the Gospel, while custom is a kind of law instituted by common usage, which is accepted as law when law is lacking.[64] It also runs side by side with that part of Chapter 4 of the *Rule of St Benedict* which states: 'Each is to do to another what he wants done to himself.'[65]

The full implication of the Cluniac-turned-Cistercian's arguments is that Cluny's sin lies not so much in its customs *per se* as in its having turned custom into an instrument for permanent dispensation from the *Rule*. To him the word 'dispensation' in this sense has unsavory overtones, and he defines it within narrow limits:

> Dispensation should not and cannot be had unless great indeed is the necessity which demands it, so that when the need ends, what was done for necessity's sake for some compensatory good to the community should also end . . . . A dispensation is nothing more than a permitted discontinuation of what has been ordered. And who is it who can bestow upon himself permission for discontinuation of the *Rule* unless it be one who is irrationally presumptuous?[66]

The Cistercian has given what he considers a definition of dispensation, and has followed it immediately by a comment which casts doubt on the validity of dispensation from any precept of the *Rule,* a way of life so perfectly constructed that it carries within itself its own dispensations though the discretionary powers granted to the abbot.[67] 'All monks,' he continues, 'are subject to the *Rule* which teaches that the abbot is to do everything, but he is to keep in mind the observation of the *Rule* . . . what dispensation is necessary from those precepts which are remarkable for their built-in discretionary powers?'[68]

In Idung's eyes the Order of Cluny had gone beyond the legal exercise of abbatial discretion allowed by the Rule. They had no scriptural authority to dispense themselves from the *Rule* except within the limitations defined by the *Rule*. For the *Rule* as Law is nothing if not the sum total of all its precepts and, conversely, all its precepts constitute the Law.[69] He issues a full and final indictment of

Cluniac transgressions when he writes: 'Once the dispensation behind which you hide as a shield protecting your departures from the *Rule* is removed, there remains only the violation of the *Rule,* the dishonoring of God and of St Benedict and, according to Pope Damasus, your blasphemy against the Holy Spirit.'[70]

In all this Idung reveals himself as a convinced Cistercian, but not as a keen observer of social evolution. The dispensation from the *Rule* as practised at Cluny were a visible expression of a monastic society which had evolved from peasant status to a non-menial, non-hand-labor *stratum* of society: from the peasant tiller of the soil to the legally free feudal *persona*. These were the men who forced their will upon the *Rule* to so great an extent that they lived more according to a monastic custom tailored to their needs than to the needs of those who had lived some four hundred years before them. Custom was king, and queen, in the medieval secular world, and it echoed in monastic chapter rooms. However, a basic question about the validity of these customs and their effects arose in the minds of the eleventh and twelfth century reformers.

The question was: what was Cluny's authority for substituting custom to so great a measure that it practically degraded and sat in judgement on the *Rule*? Cluny had no proper answer to give, beyond appealing to the antiquity of its own tradition. If one emphasizes the *Rule* as law, however, Cluny's answers appear quite lame, its position legally weak. It had become an empire in subjects and a power-house in secular and ecclesiastical politics, but when men akin in mind to those of the New Monastery began to ask basic questions about its claim to be a monastic institution according to the integral *Rule of St Benedict,* its weakness was revealed and its decline accelerated.

†Jeremiah F. O'Sullivan

Edited with
additional material by A. J. Andrea
University of Vermont

NOTES TO INTRODUCTION

1. Bede K. Lackner, *The Eleventh Century Background of Citeaux,* CF 8 (1972).

2. On the other hand, certain clerics such as Guibert de Nogent and William of Malmesbury understood the import of what they saw and what it portended; they were strong in their praise and admiration, thereby publicizing the life and ideals of Citeaux.

3. Juliano Paris, ed., *Nomasticon cisterciense seu antiquiores ordinis cisterciensis constitutiones* (Solesme, 1892) 212-233. On the intentions of the founders of the Order of Citeaux see: M. Basil Pennington, ed., *The Cistercian Spirit: A Symposium,* CS 3 (1970); M. B. Pennington, 'Towards Discerning the Spirit and Aims of the Founders of the Order of Citeaux,' *Studia Monastica* 11 (1969) pp. 405-420; and Louis J. Lekai, 'Rule and Constitution,' in *The White Monks* (Okauchee, Wisconsin, 1953) pp. 23-33. For English translations of some of the earliest Cistercian documents see the *Exordium Parvum,* trans. R. E. Larkin in Lekai, pp. 251-266 and *The Charter of Charity,* trans. D. Murphy, *ibid.,* pp. 267-273.

4. The quarrel between Cluny and Citeaux has been succinctly presented by Philibert Schmitz, *Histoire de l'ordre de St Benoit* (Maredsous, 1942-1949) 3: 27-36. Studies in English on this topic include: Adrian Morey, 'The Conflict of Clairvaux and Cluny,' *Downside Review* 50 (1932) 87-107; Edmund Bishop, 'Cluniacs and Cistercians,' *Downside Review* 52 (1934) 48-70 and 209-230; David Knowles, 'Cistercians and Cluniacs: the Controversy between St Bernard and Peter the Venerable' in *The Historian and Character* (Cambridge, 1963) 50-75; and W. Williams, 'Peter the Venerable: a Letter to St Bernard,' *The Downside Review* 56 (1938) 344-353.

5. We follow here the dating of Adriaan H. Bredero, 'Cluny and Citeaux au XIIeme siecles: les origines de la controverse,' *Studi Medievali,* 3^{a} Serie, 12, 1 (Spoleto, 1971) 135-175. Bredero has identified the Grand Prior as Matthew, later cardinal bishop of Albano. An older opinion maintained that Robert departed around 1117 at the instigation of the Grand Prior, Bernard d'Uxelles. For this traditional view see A. H. Bredero, 'The Controversy between Peter the Venerable and Saint Bernard of Clairvaux,' *Studia Anselmiana* 40 (1956) p. 59.

6. So dated by Damian van den Eynde, 'Les premieres lettres de Saint Bernard' in J. Leclercq, *Recueil d'etudes de Saint Bernard et ses ecrits* (Rome, 1969) 3: 395-396. The critical text of this letter may be read in PL 182, and in *Sancti Bernardi Opera,* VII, edd. Jean Leclercq and H. Rochais (Rome, Editiones Cistercienses). An English translation is available in Bruno Scott James, ed. and trans., *The Letters of Saint Bernard of Clairvaux* (London, Chicago, 1953) 1-10. A new translation with notes will appear in the Cistercian Fathers series.

7.   Bredero, 'Cluny,' pp. 143 ff. and Leclercq, *Recueil* (Rome, 1962) 1: 202.
8.   For a more balanced and objective evaluation of twelfth century Cluniac practices, see Knowles, 'Cistercians.'
9.   SBOp 3: 63-103 and 243-295 respectively; translated with introductions in *Bernard of Clairvaux, Treatise I*, CF 1: 3-69 and 73-150.
10.   For example, see Ep 91 to the local chapter of Benedictine abbots gathered at Soissons to consider reforms modeled after Cistercian practices; Ep 96 to Richard, Abbot of Fountains, and his brethren upon the reformation of this house according to Cistercian observance. (These letters are translated in James, pp. 139-141 and 240-241 respectively.)
11.   The deep friendship which developed between Peter the Venerable, Abbot of Cluny, and St Bernard has been studied by a number of scholars. See J. Leclercq, *Pierre le Vénérable* (Saint Wandrille, 1946) p. 84; Bredero, 'Controversy,' pp. 56 and 69-71; J. B. Auniord, 'L'ami de S. Bernard, quelques textes,' Coll. 18 (1956) 89-99; and Ann Proux Lang, 'The Friendship between Peter the Venerable and Bernard of Clairvaux,' in *Bernard of Clairvaux: Studies Presented to Dom Jean Leclercq*, CS 23 (1973).
12.   Cistercian examples and criticisms did influence Cluniac reforms. See note 10 above and David Knowles, 'The Reforming Decrees of Peter the Venerable,' *Studia Anselmiana* 40 (1956) 1-20.
13.   The major documents of the Cluniac-Cistercian controversy are listed in C⁻¹ 1: 184.
14.   The two most famous were Walter Map and his friend Gerald the Welshman. Walter's attacks upon Cistercian avarice and hypocrisy can be read in his *De nugis curialium*, ed. by M. R. James (Oxford, 1914) 35-54. The *De nugis* has been translated by M. R. James and John E. Lloyd, *Walter Map's "De Nugis Curialium"* (London, 1923) and by Frederick Tupper and Marbury B. Ogle, *Master Walter Map's Book, De nugis curialium (Courtiers Trifles) Englished* (London, 1924). The satirical poem 'De Clarevallensibus et Cluniacensibus' in *The Latin Poems Commonly Attributed to Walter Mapes*, ed. Thomas Wright (London: Camden Society, 1841) 237-242, was probably not written by Walter Map but by an anonymous cleric who shared his attitude of 'a curse on both houses'. Gerald (Giraldus Cambrensis, also known as Giraldus de Barri, and called by his enemies Sylvester) liberally attacked the White Monks in his *Speculum Ecclesiae* in *Opera*, ed. J. S. Brewer (London, 1873) 4, *passim*. See also David Knowles, 'Some Enemies of Gerald of Wales,' *Studia Monastica* 1 (1959) 137-141 and P. Bruno Griesser, 'Walther Map und die Cistercienser,' *Cistercienser-Chronik* (1924) 137-167.
15.   Originally published by E. Martene and V. Durand, *Thesauris novis anecdotorum* (Paris, 1717) 5: cols. 1570-1654. R. B. C. Huygens has produced the first critical edition in 'Le moine Idung et ses deux ouvrages: "Argumentum super quatuor questionibus" et "Dialogus duorum monarchorum" ' in *Studi Medievali*, 3ª Ser., 13, 1 (Spoleto, 1972) 375-470. See Watkin Williams' analytical synopsis of the tract, 'A Dialogue between a Cluniac and a Cistercian,' *The Journal of Theological Studies* 31 (1930) 164-175. Neither Elisabeth Kernau's dissertation, *Ein Dialogus duorum monachorum Cluniacensis et Cisterciensis aus dem 12. Jahrhundert. Der Gegensatz zwischen Kluniazensern und Zisterziensern* (Diss. phil. Mss., Vienna, 1941), nor Josef Storm's thesis *Untersuchungen zum Dialogus duorum monachorum Chuniacensis et Cisterciensis. Ein Beitrag zur Ordensgeschichte des 12. Jahrhunderts* (Diss. theol., Munster, 1926) have been available to us.
16.   Prefatory dedication to Abbess K. of Niedermunster.
17.   Schmitz, *Histoire de l'ordre de St Benoit* 3: 33. He is not mentioned by Oliver Kapsner, *A Benedictine Bibliography* (Collegeville, Minn., 2nd ed., 1962) 2 volumes, or by A. Potthast, *Bibliotheca Historica Medii Aevi* (Berlin, 1896) 2 vol.

18. Eberhard Demm, *Reformmonchtum und Slawen-mission im 12. Jahrhundert* (Lubeck and Hamburg, 1970) 99-106, was the first to provide positive evidence linking Idung to the *Dialogue*. R. B. C. Huygens, 'Zu Idung von Prufening und seinen Schriften, "Argumentum super quatuor questionibus" und "Dialogus duorum monachorum," ' *Deutsches Archiv fur Erforschung des Mittelalters* 2 (1971) 544-555, established Idung's authorship beyond any shadow of a doubt.
19. Huygens, 'Le moine Idung,' pp. 295-308.
20. II, 19.
21. I, 2.
22. Preface.
23. Huygens discusses the manuscripts in 'Le moine Idung,' pp. 309-334. The only one of the five *mss* which did not originate in a German or Austrian abbey came out of Morimond, whose orientation was decidedly German rather than French, Archdale A. King, *Citeaux and Her Elder Daughters* (London, 1954) 329-387, gives a short history of Morimond.
24. Literally, 'for relief [of his soul].' That is, he made his profession to insure his soul's salvation at a moment when he appeared at the point of death. In this way he would die as a monk. See II, 17.
25. Huygens identifies the monastery as Prufening and dates Idung's entry around 1144. 'Le moine Idung,' p. 297. Prufening had originally been a benedictine abbey built by Bishop Otto of Bamberg but it was colonized by the Cluniac house of Hirschau in 1109. See L. H. Cottineau, *Repertoire topobibliographique des Abbayes et Prieuries* (Macon, 1939) 2: cols. 2369-2370. See also H. G. Schmitz, *Kloster Prufening in 12. Jahrhundert* (Diss., Giessen, 1969).
26. A *conversus* was a monk who entered religious life at an advanced age. See Lackner, pp. 67-68, for a description of Cluniac *conversi*.
27. Huygens, 'Le moine Idung,' p. 298, believes that he entered an Austrian Cistercian abbey.
28. III, 1, 2.
29. II, 29.
30. III, 24.
31. Huygens, 'Le moine Idung,' p. 296.
32. I, 32.
33. *CC Series Latina* (Turnholt, Belgium, 1953-   ) 78: 325-326.
34. I, 32.
35. *Decretum Gratiani*, C. 1, q. 2, c. 7.
36. I, 51.
37. PL 16:58-59.
38. II, 57.
39. PG 48:679.
40. II, 32. On the whole, however, twelfth century relations between the Norbertines and the Cistercians were friendly enough. See Alfons Zak, 'St Bernard und St Norbert und die Freundschaft ihrer Orden,' *Cistercienser-Chronik* 31 (1919) 177-188.
41. II, 32.
42. See Demm's study of the parallels in argument and phraseology which exist between the *Dialogus* and the *Argumentum*, pp. 101-106 and Huygens' further contributions in 'Zu Idung,' pp. 545-546.
43. The tract is edited by both Demm, pp. 113-133 and Huygens, 'Le moine Idung,' pp. 343-374. The *Argumentum* was probably composed around 1144-1145.
44. Preface.
45. In Chapter 1 of the *Rule*, Benedict characterized gyrovagues as the worst sort of monks, who spend their lives wandering from province to province, totally slaves to their own wills. On the virtue and vow of stability, see RB Chapters 5, 58, 60, and 61. There can be no doubt that stability was, along with obedience, one of the twin cornerstones of benedictine monasticism. See

Douglass A. Roby's unpublished doctoral dissertation, *STABILITAS and TRANSITUS: Understanding Passage from One Religious Order to Another in Twelfth Century Monastic Controversy* (Yale, 1971), for a study of the various twelfth century concepts of *stabilitas*.

46. The Cistercian Order began with the flight of St Robert and some companions from the abbey of Molesme to the wilderness of Citeaux. See Lackner, pp. 217-276.
47. I, 47.
48. I, 8.
49. Huygens, 'Le moine Idung,' pp. 297-298.
50. I, 48.
51. Christopher Brooke, *The Twelfth Century Renaissance* (London: Thames and Hudson; New York; Harcourt, Brace, and World paperback, 1970) 75-89, and Charles N. Haskins, *The Renaissance of the Twelfth Century* (Meridian paperback, 1957 [original ed., 1927]) 193-223.
52. Compare Gratian's statement: 'Custom is a kind of law instituted by common usage, which is accepted as law when law is lacking.' *Decretum* D. 1, c. 5.
53. I, 57.
54. See Lackner, pp. 48 ff., for a survey of the evolution, compilation, and standardization of Cluny's customs.
55. I, 50.
56. I, 44.
57. I, 51.
58. I, 45.
59. I, 28.
60. II, 21.
61. RB 73.
62. I, 54.
63. I, 46 = I Cor 10:23-24.
64. *Decretum*, D. 1, c. 1 (especially Gratian's *dicta*) 3, and 5.
65. Cf. Mt 7:12, Lk 6:31.
66. I, 24. Compare this with the canonist Ivo of Chartres' (d. 1115) definition of dispensation: 'A dispensation is a temporary mitigation of the rigor of the law because of either momentary need or the Church's profit.' (PL 161:236).
67. RB 64.
68. I, 25.
69. I, 26.
70. II, 30.

A DIALOGUE BETWEEN A CLUNIAC AND A CISTERCIAN

Translated by Jeremiah F. O'Sullivan

AUTHOR'S PREFACE

TO THE LADY ABBESS K.[1] of the Lower Monastery [Niedermünster] which is at Regensburg;[2] who is respected by those worthy of respect. I, I[dung], a sinner monk wish you, in sincere and humble devotion, everlasting salvation in Christ.

Dear and praiseworthy Abbess, the foregoing greeting, proclaiming to everyone that you are to be counted as respected in the ranks of those worthy of respect, means that, through the godly and wise manner by which you rule your monastery, zealously caring for religious observance and good reputation, you have brought respect on yourself as an individual in the eyes of those individuals themselves worthy of respect. Indeed, your great generosity, which has consistently revealed you as a cheerful giver to the needy,* merits you the love of God—as the Apostle† says—and the acknowledgement of gratitude by all, but it also merits special thanks from me.

*2 Cor 9:7
†St Paul

Without requesting any special favor, you were always prepared, with your own particular brand of kindness, to relieve my wants. On this account, although I am unequal to your favors, I do nevertheless return thanks insofar as the heartfelt devotion of a sincere monk by praying daily for you can attempt to do so.

Thus, thinking as I do, I am afraid and, fearful as I am, I think that I have displeased your Prudence—just as I have displeased certain others, even those who were bound to me in brotherly love [in religion]—by deserting the house and Order of my first conversion and entering another order.

I have penned this *Dialogue* with the express purpose that, through the reasons and authoritative evidence collected in it, it may serve as my legal counsel and defense against those who accuse and censure me. And so, because, having had no scribe at my disposal—as you can see by the irregular formations of the letters—I wrote this book with my own hand, I beg that the generous condescension of your indulgence may make easily legible what I have written, and also because, with the exception of the authoritative sources cited, this is the product of my own meagre mental endowment, as the unpolished wording of its style and its lack of organization show.

The *Dialogue* has three parts which can be said to be (1) *eclogue* because of my use of countryish and everyday speech, (2) *satire* because it contains censure, and (3) *readings* because it contains many useful and shrewd opinions which one would find useful not only to know but also to reflect upon.

Thus, by desiring I ask and by asking I desire to see [the *Dialogue*] copied legibly and carefully corrected by some of your sisters trained for this kind of work.

NOTES TO THE AUTHOR'S PREFACE

1. Kunigunde, abbess of Niedermunster from 1136-77. Huygens (p. 375) remarks on the possibility of the initial being R in some manuscripts, but is sure that Kunigunde was meant. He refers to F. Janner, *Geschichte der Bischofe von Regensburg* (Regensburg, 1883) I:555; A. Schonberger, 'Die Rechtsstellung des Reichsstiftes Niedermunster zu Papst und Reich, Land und Reichsstadt Regensburg,' (dissertation, Wurzburg, 1953) p. 163.

2. There were three monasteries at Regensburg: (a) Obermunster (*superius*), a benedictine abbey founded in 1010, (b) Mittelmunster, a benedictine abbey founded in 974, and (c) Niedermunster (*inferius*) a benedictine monastery for nuns founded in 760 or thereabouts. See Cottineau, *Repertoire topo-bibliographique des Abbayes et Prieures* (Macon, 1930) 2: cols. 2408-2409.

PART ONE

[I, 1.] CLUNIAC. Of all the faults which dominate the weak, none more deserves abhorrence than instability. Men enmeshed in the net of this failing are looked upon as being beyond hope, even in the holy way of life in which they present themselves, by men who use their reasoning powers and insights into character. Nor should we be surprised that in no aspect of their lives are the unstable stable except in their very instability. I can say, by making additional use of the evidence which so militates against them, that in Holy Scripture the Holy Spirit put a brand on them, as it were, when he said: 'Better the iniquity of a man than a woman doing a good turn.'* Although these words of holy authority contain the genesis of a different meaning, they still portray aptly and descriptively men of little depth but great inconstancy of character, men who suffer, so to speak, from a woman's shortcoming. If inconstancy in men in the world is loathed by other worldlings, such monks are not only to be loathed but even to be held in abhorrence who, contrary to reason, contrary to their own profession, contrary to the precept of the Apostle who says 'Let every man abide in the same calling to which he was called,' are by some impulsive force torn from the ancient and judicious order of Cluny and, in their light-minded inconstancy, go off to the untried novelty of Cîteaux.

[I, 2.] CISTERCIAN. I have no doubt but that your verdict of condemnation,[1] scattered abroad for all to see and hear while I am standing here, has

*Si 42:14

*1 Co 7:20

particular reference to me. I say this because you know very well that I was a *conversus*[2] for ten years in the Cluniac order, or according to its customs, and yet I was a professed monk barely three days.[3] Hoping for God's mercy, I transferred from the Cluniac Order, or from its customs, to that of the Cistercians —not, as you falsely charge, to their injudicious novelties but to their ancient judgement and ordered truths—and this I did, not enraptured by any frivolousness or by inconstancy but after long deliberation. Because reason so dictated and the authority of the Lord so drove me, I followed my profession of him and obeyed that command of the Apostle which you have just used against me; driven by the impending danger of my own spiritual shipwreck and urged on by a clamorous voice, as if by a divine oracle, through a certain monk [of Reichersberg], I passed from one ship to another. Not without God's beckoning, therefore, did I abandon the customs of Cluny, which are for the most part unjustified accretions condemned by decrees and conciliar legislation and even opposed to the holy Rule [of St Benedict] itself.

[I, 3.] CLUNIAC. There is no end to my astonishment at the way you so shamelessly heap blame on the heads of members of our Order who were found pleasing to God. You reject the traditions of our holy fathers, you fasten on them the charge that they acted contrary to synodal and decretal enactments and to the holy Rule itself, you act as the personification of deputy[4] of the great intruder.[5] For this reason it is no surprise to me that you bend every effort to knock down and refute the truth of what I say, even though the truth is so evident that, as the poet says, it can be seen even by the half-blind and by barbers.*

*Horace, Satirae 1,7,3.

[I. 4.] CISTERCIAN. The nature of the monastic state demands that I listen gracefully and without anger to your harsh and unrestrained language. You say that I am a shameless and great intruder. You say that I should listen to you meekly and without any indignation, and that, without any feelings of vexation, I should realize that your outrageous charges are heaped upon me because it will do me good to hear the truth. If the truth scandalizes you, authority—which is my defense counsel[6]—will exculpate me. I mean the authority of St Gregory, who says: 'If you are scandalized by truth, then it is better that there be scandal than that the truth should be repressed.'*

*Hom.77 in Ezechiel; PL 76:842. Cf. Bernard, Apo; SBOp 3:94; CF 1:33-69.

Truth itself [Christ], as the Gospels testify, paid tribute which he did not owe lest he give scandal to his creditors.† Yet when the Scribes and Pharisees were scandalized because he said defilement comes to man not because of what enters his mouth,* he was completely unconcerned about causing them scandal because he spoke the truth, saying: 'Let them alone; they are blind and leaders of the blind.'* Listen! Although he said that blind leaders should be cast aside, he commanded that those who heard them should obey them when he said: 'The Scribes and Pharisees have sat on the chair of Moses; whatever they shall say therefore, do. Do not act according to their works.'*

†Mk 12:14, Lk 20:22.
*Mt 15:11.

*Mt 15:14

*Mt 23:2-3.

What is it that the Wisdom of the Supreme Father teaches us—but which at first sight seems a verbal inconsistency—if it is not that we must heed our superiors with complete obedience, even though they lead improper lives, so long as they rule over us and instruct us in accordance with the authority of divine law? If, however, they are so completely perverted towards moral ruin that they do not follow the authority of divine law in ruling over their subjects but follow instead their own willful impulses and fancies, then let us, as scandalized and displeased subjects heedful of the dictates of divine law, flee from them as we would from blind leaders, lest together with them we fall into the pit of eternal damnation.[7]

It does not surprise me that when you were insulting me you made use of the words of poets, because to you and to others of your Order, poetic imagery is so pleasing that you make a study of it, you pore over it and you even teach it during the times which St Benedict intended and decreed should be set aside for spiritual reading and for manual labor.⁸

[I, 5.] CLUNIAC. As a general rule we read secular books so that through reading them we can acquire a better understanding of Holy Scripture, because, in our Order, as you yourself know, spiritual reading and prayer follow upon each other. We pass from reading to prayer and return from prayer to reading.⁹ As yours is an active Order because you have chosen to do manual labor with Martha, so ours is a contemplative because we chose holy leisure with Mary. Because, as Christ bears witness, Mary chose the better part,* there is no doubt in my mind but that our Order is more worthy than yours.

*Lk 10:42

[I, 6.] CISTERCIAN. In the Gospel, Christ said to the Jews: 'You err, not knowing the Scriptures.'* Begging your pardon, but I can legitimately say to you—and I say it in the compulsion of charity: 'Brother, you err because you do not know the Scriptures.'

*Mt 22:29

[I, 7.] CLUNIAC. Charity, about which the Apostle was speaking, because it is long-suffering and because it is kind,* does not force you to the point where you taunt and insult me by reproaching me for being wrong and ignorant of the Scriptures. Rather, the passion in that soul of yours is actually indignation and it is really nothing but that counterfeit justice¹⁰ of which St Gregory says: 'True justice is compassionate, counterfeit justice is actually indignant anger.'¹¹

*1 Co 13:4

[I, 8.] CISTERCIAN. Charity, which is recorded as being long-suffering in bearing injury, is generous in conferring favors. As Dom Bernard, abbot of Clairvaux of happy memory, bears witness in one of his letters: 'charity vents its anger with tenderness, it sooths without resorting to guile, it is long-suffering in anger, humble when outraged.'*

*Ep 2:1. Cf. Apo 3-4; SBOp 3:84-9; CF 1:38-45.

[I, 9.] [missing from text]

[I, 10.] CLUNIAC. That abbot about whom you were just speaking, having by means of an exceptionally great gift from God surpassed bishops and abbots in holiness and in learned and eloquent wisdom, was the great ornament of your Order, its stoutest pillar of support. Although he was so outstanding a person that the Apostolic See leaned upon his prudence,* he still in no way cast aspersions on our Order. But rather he extolled and praised it by word of mouth and by writing in a special treatise in its praise.[12] By taking it under his protection he praised it and by praising it he took it under his protection, thereby bequeathing to you a good example of how to act. He dissuaded those who were desirous of transferring from our Order to yours by pointing out that it would be a useless and superfluous change of life in religion and habit. All who came without commendatory letters from our Order to his monastery and who sought to subject themselves to his regular jurisdiction he refused and sent back.*

*Cf. Csi 1-6; SBOp 3: 393-400.

*See Epp. 84, 86, 101, 293. Cf. RB 61:13.

[I, 11.] CISTERCIAN. Things are not as you say. Read his collected letters and you will find that the situation was far different.* Those who were eager to persevere he did receive; others, however, he sent back to their abbots. As a prudent and thoughtful man he got rid of those in whom he intuitively sensed some signs of instability in days to come. He received those who were eager to persevere and he himself tells us about one such monk whom he received against his abbot's wishes and whom he kept with him until the monk's death despite the abbot, who continued to complain of the injury done him. I claim that he makes plain his position in one of his letters sent to that very abbot after the monk died. These are his words:

*E.g. Epp. 65, 67.

In short, we did not purposely seek him out and beg him to come to us. We did not pester him to come to us and to leave you. The opposite is true. God knows that, despite his requests, his prayers, his insistence, we agreed to receive him only after we attempted to send him back to you. When he would not agree to it, we gave in grudgingly to his importunities.

*Ep 65:3

In another of his letters, a great portion of which I am reproducing for your and others' edification, he gave the following answer to monks who were complaining about a similar case:

My good brothers, it is up to you to be sensible and to realize that you must be content with our prior agreement about your complaint and henceforth give up inveighing against those who have done you no wrong. But because you have made your previous bad conduct worse and because you have sent us new and additional seeds further to foment the quarrel (God grant that they germinate no better among us than did their predecessors), we are answering you, lest by not answering we seem to admit a wrong which does not really exist. We are again giving a true answer to the charges you have so insolently made. Here is the sum total of our transgressions, sofar as I can make them out.

This great wrong which we committed against you consists in our having received a monk who was alone, a traveler, without resources, pitiable, fleeing in peril of his soul, anxiously seeking out a way of saving it. As a supplicant he came to us and we took him in. We do not cast out, without good reason, a monk whom we have received in this manner, because what we have built we do not set ourselves up to destroy again. It is for this reason that we are adjudged breakers of the Rule, of the decretals, and even of natural law!

In your allegations you ask us how we have the presumption to associate with a monk who was one of yours and whom you have excommunicated. We are not willing to tolerate this charge from anybody. What answer shall we make about the excommunication when you yourselves have already given satisfactory answer for us? You know full well that he was received by us before he was excommunicated by you. Because he had been received by us first, and in accordance with the Rule,* your sentence of excommunication was directed not against one of your own monks but against one of ours. You see to whether or not you had the

*RB 61:5, 13.

legal right to do this.

What remains to be known—and this is the main issue in our disagreement—is whether or not there were reasonable grounds for receiving him.[13] Because you cannot deny that a monk from an unknown monastery may be received in accordance with the Rule,* you are contending that yours was known to us. This we deny, yet you put no credence in our denial. But if you will not simply believe our denial, then believe us when we swear to it. On Truth itself—which is God—we say to you: we neither knew you nor do we know you. We received letters written by persons whom we did not know and we sent an answer to persons we did not know. We feel deeply your goads and reproaches, but even so we do not know our goaders and reproachers. You, however, in order to convict us of feigned ignorance, posit the irrefutable argument that we cannot not know when we have put the name of your monastery and its abbot on our letter—just as if the fact that we know the name of something means we know the thing itself!

How very nice it would be for me to know the names of Michael, Gabriel and Raphael, if just because I had heard them called by name, I would be blessed with the knowledge of these blessed spirits. I can say that it has profited me in no small way to learn the words 'paradise' and 'third heaven' from the Apostle,* but I have never been caught up with the Apostle nor by these words alone do I know nor have I heard the secret heavenly words which man may not pronounce. What a fool I am! I already know the name of my God, yet every day, for no reason at all, I give expression to my over-flowing anguish when I repeat after the prophet: 'Your face, O Lord, will I seek,'* 'When shall I come and appear before the face of the Lord?'* and 'Show us your face and we shall be saved.'*

What are we doing to you that we do not want done to us? You think that we would like one of our monks to leave his monastery and be received into another. I only wish you could save everyone under

*Cf. Ep 67 &
RB 61:13.

*2 Co 12; 2, 4.

*Ps 27:9
*Ps 42:2
*Ps 80:3

our charge without us! If one of ours should take flight to you in searching for greater perfection or desiring to lead a stricter life, not only would we not hurl accusations at you if you encouraged him, filled with much zeal, but we would rather emphatically beg you to do so. Far from complaining about being offended, we would manifest our willingness to help in the process.

*Ep 68:1-3.

You have here in his own words proof that [Dom Bernard] did not reject and return to your Order all who came from it to him.

[I. 12.] CLUNIAC. As far as I could gather from his words while you were reading them aloud, that abbot did not intend it to follow that because he knew the name of both the abbot and the monastery, he therefore knew the monastery itself. Tell me, if you know, because I am anxious to find out, what kind of knowledge he did want before he would not permit a monk who wanted to transfer from one monastery to another to be received without his own abbot's consent?

[I, 13.] CISTERCIAN. As I understand the matter, a question on this very subject was raised at a Chapter General of our Order.* Some said that monasteries located in one and the same diocese, because their monks had received Holy Orders from one and the same bishop, should be regarded as being known to each other. Others said that 'those monasteries were known to each other whose proximity bound both abbots and monks in familial friendship' and that a monk [from such a monastery] was not to be received without his own abbot's consent, in order that the bonds of familial friendship might not be sundered. The abbot of Clairvaux, however, brought about the final decision: *Neither proximity nor familiarity constitute the knowledge we are discussing, if the monks follow either their own fancies or man-made tradition and do not live in accordance with their profession of the Rule of St Benedict, the law which has been given to monks by God through the lawgiver, St Benedict, who acted as another Moses.*

*1134, XVII;
Statuta 1:16-17.

Christ, according to the Gospel, accused the Pharisees of breaking the Law: 'Why do you transgress the law [of God] for the traditions of men?'* he said. We must say, in company with the Apostle: 'We must obey God rather than man,'* or together with the Pharisees we must hear: 'Why do you transgress the law for the traditions of men?'¹⁴

*Mt 15:3.

*Ac 5:29

Here you have the answer to your question. You tell me in what treatise he [Bernard] praised your Order, which follows not the Rule but man-made traditions instead? I find it hard to believe that an abbot so cautious, so holy, and so judicious in his written works and spoken words could have contradicted himself so completely.

[I, 14.] CLUNIAC. In the treatise* which he wrote to the monks of our Order at Chartres,¹⁵ and in the long letter† which he wrote to William of St Thierry, also of our Order.¹⁶ Read them both and you will find in both outspoken praise of our Order.

*Pre, Praef., SBOp 3:243; CF 1:103.
†Apo; SBOp 3: 81-108; CF 1: 33-69.

[I, 14.] CISTERCIAN. I have read and re-read them both and have given them a great deal of thought. My impression was not unlike yours when I read them for the first time. That should not surprise anybody, because he uses in each that genre of speech which deceives the simple-witted and those who merely skim over what they read.

[I, 16.] CLUNIAC. What is this genre of speech which obscures the minds of its hearers when they hear it and the minds of the readers when they read it?

[I, 17.] CISTERCIAN. Rhetoricians call this 'veiled illusion';* it is to be used as part of the legal defense of a defendant whom the case examiners dislike so much that they have no desire whatever to listen to the defense counsel's pleas. At that stage, the defendant's advocate begins his statement of rebuttal of charges by calling the hostile witnesses to testify by accusing the accusors of the person whose release he intends ultimately to obtain. Then later on, by the marvelous artfulness of words, he sets about weakening what he has made strong, exculpating whom he has accused, thereby turning a lawsuit which was

*insinuatio

headed in one way in the opposite direction.[17]

Do not be one whit surprised if a man of learned holiness and eloquent wisdom used the method of veiled illusion practised by a meticulous orator in writing to you at the time when your monks hated our monks with intemperate hatred, calling them slanderers and manglers of the Order, and thinking them to be esteemed more lowly and contemptible in the eyes of the world [than themselves] because they seemed to be a singular and new kind of monk living in your midst. This is what Archbishop Hugh of Lyons[18] said when in one of his letters he used the very words which I have just quoted. That holy man wrote as a holy man should write, that is, as one whom St Jerome described in expounding the words of the book of the prophet Daniel: 'They who are learned shall shine as the brightness of the firmament, and they who instruct many to justice are as stars for all eternity.'* When explaining the differences between holy men, he says: 'You can see how great the difference is between learned holiness and holy crudeness. The difference is as great as that between one star and the whole firmament.'[19]

*Dn 12:3

[I, 18.] CLUNIAC. Though we have both this treatise and this letter in almost all our monasteries, and though in our Order there are many learned and liberally-educated men, not one of them has ever understood them as you do—as glorifying your Order and degrading ours. Furthermore, monks and abbots of your Order who have been our guests and whom we know quite well have never put the interpretation on these writings that you do, but they have agreed with ours. And if by any chance both Orders were ever mentioned, as it were in one and the same breath, all praised and paid respect to our Order and said that the transfer made by many from our to your Order was made without profit, without need, and that it was done more out of empty-headed inquisitiveness and instability than out of necessity and advantage.

[I, 19.] CISTERCIAN. Among his store of maxims the ordinary man usually has one to suit the occasion, such as: 'I must sing the song of the man whose bread I eat.'[20] Many of our monks, being less than perfect while they were your guests, heeded that same proverb even without uttering it. Although they are possessed of knowledge, they are not possessed of the fervent love of God. (Again, there are those who possess a fervent love of God but haven't much knowledge.) If there are those who possess both, that is zeal for God based on knowledge, they are sparing in the time they spend as guests. As Solomon says: 'All things have their season, a time for silence and a time to speak.'*   *Qo 3: 1, 7.

I am firmly convinced that they kept silent longer than they chatted about the customs of your Order. Nor do I believe that they are to be blamed for their silence during that time. Hence, as Augustine says in commenting on psalm five: 'Clearly one must not be blamed whenever it is clear that he is keeping silence about the truth.'*

*Enarr. in Ps 5, 7; CC 38:23.
Decret. C.22, q. 2, c. 14.

[I, 20.] CLUNIAC. According to Ambrose and according to the truth of the matter, it is much safer to be silent than to speak, because many sin when they speak, few do so by remaining silent.* Hence Jerome in his *Commentary on the Letter to the Ephesians* says: 'As often as we speak, be the time appropriate or not, be the place appropriate or not, and be what we are saying suitable for our listeners to hear or not, so often does evil speech proceed from our mouths to the ruination of those who hear us. We must pay close attention to what we say because at the day of judgement we shall have to render account for our every idle word. Even though we do no harm, we do not edify the listeners and we will have to pay the penalty for evil speech.* This opinion, promulgated widely by blessed Jerome, can strike terror to all who are quick and prone to speech, especially to monks whose profession demands that, in accordance with the precepts of the Rule, they should be zealous at all times in observing silence.[21]

*Decret. C.22, q.5, c.20.

*PL 26:546A.
Cf. Decret. C.22, q.5, c.21.

[I, 21.] CISTERCIAN. Truth, who produced human speech through the mouth of a donkey*—an   *Nb 22: 21-31.

irrational animal—has now wrenched from your mouth the great condemnation of your Order. Because you do not realize what you were saying, you are not unlike that donkey.

[I, 22.] CLUNIAC. Because I am very eager to hear what constitutes this condemnation [of my Order], I am meanwhile putting up patiently with being impudently called a jackass.

[I, 23.] CISTERCIAN. Not impudently, but in that manner of charity which, in accordance with the words of the wise man, 'is wont to vent its anger in tenderness,'* for the correction of the transgressor. It is for this reason that the Apostle called the Galatians 'senseless.'* I do not see how you can utter a harsher denunciation of your Order than by dragging front and centre that terrifying sentence of Jerome and that precept of the Rule about the zealous observance of silence at all times. If monks must at all times be zealous in observing silence— that means a forceful application of the mind to maintaining it because a *forceful application* of the mind to the maintenance of silence and to being *zealous about its maintenance* are equated, just as *decree* and the *matter decreed* are equated—then they should be zealous about keeping it then and after Chapter.[22] But at those times [after Chapter] they eagerly gossip and chatter back and forth by permission of the Order—if indeed it is of the order and not more of the disorder. They sit because the time is so drawn-out and extended that they cannot stand, and each chatters on about whatever he chooses with anybody he chooses.[23] To take a seat is itself the signal for such application. Rumors fly from the loftiest to the lowliest and contrariwise from the lowliest to the loftiest. And because each speaks with those sitting near him there arises a kind of confused din, with a sound akin to what one would hear in an inn or in a tavern full of sots where all the men are talking with their fellow souses and all the women drinkers talking with their drinking companions. Sometimes they reproach each other so bitterly and so harshly in conversation that they do

*Bernard. See I,8 above.

*Ga 3:1.

all their accusing there rather than in Chapter. From this permission to chatter idly arises the wherewithal for brawling. From the brawl come threats and acrimony, so much so that at times it is necessary to recall the Chapter by striking the wooden clappers [used for summoning Chapter].[24]

Is this that 'holy leisure' you were talking about a little while ago when you said: 'Our Order is contemplative because of its holy leisure and yours is active because of its prescribed measure of manual labor,'*—as if you were ignorant of what really constitutes the active and contemplative life? This is the reason I answered you as I did above: 'Brother, you err, because you do not know the Scriptures.'*

*Above I, 5.

*Above I, 6.

CLUNIAC. You have expressed yourself in sufficiently mordant strictures about our Order's dispensations [from the Rule].

[I, 24.] CISTERCIAN. Actually, I have not been talking about the Order's dispensation, but its dissipation.* Dispensation should not and cannot be given except for some great need, so that when the need has come to an end that also should end which was done for necessity's sake or for some compensatory good of great utility. Nor may he grant dispensations who lives under the very precept which is to be dispensed. A dispensation is nothing more than a permitted discontinuation of what has been ordered. And who can give himself permission to discontinue unless he does so with the most absurd presumption? According to the wise man's saying: 'It is not yours to dispense; it is yours to be dispensed.'*

*Cf. Csi III:4,18; SBOp 3:445; CF 37:102-3.

*Source unknown.

[I, 25.] CLUNIAC. Do you mean that abbots cannot dispense from precept of the Rule?

CISTERCIAN. They cannot, except as the Rule provides.[25] They too are subject to the Rule, which teaches that the abbot is to do everything in accordance with the Rule.* If I may put it more forcefully—with all due respect to abbots—it is more necessary for them to obey the teachings in the Rule than it is for their subjects who are only monks. Abbots, in fact, profess the Rule twice: the first

*RB 2, 3, 22.

time at their profession as a monk; the second at their installation as abbot. I ask you, what dispensation is necessary from those precepts which are remarkable for their discretion.

CLUNIAC. None that I know of, because if a dispensation is necessary the precepts are not remarkable for their discretion.

CISTERCIAN. You agree with me! What is our Rule but certain legal precepts regulating the monastic way of life and forming the conduct of monks?

[I, 26.] CLUNIAC. Nothing else. As St James demonstrates when he says in his Epistle: 'He who offends in one point'—here he has in mind the precept of the law—'is guilty of all'—here he has in mind the breaking of the law, because the law is nothing other than the sum of all its precepts and, conversely, all its precepts are nothing other than the law. The same St James said to this point: 'He who offends in one, offends in all.'* And he added a careful and proper gloss when he said: 'He who said "You shall not commit adultery," also said "You shall not kill." If you do not commit adultery but do kill, then are you become a transgressor of the law.'† Here you have what we mean by a transgressor of the law and what we understand by a culprit in all.

*Jas 2:10.

†Jas 2:11.

CISTERCIAN. I find that what you say pleases me, but what I am about to say will displease you.

[I, 27.] CLUNIAC. By and large, everything you have so far said has displeased me. Why wonder if what you are about to say will also be displeasing? But tell me what else there is, for I want to listen with an open mind to such things and I want to be wrought up by them.

CISTERCIAN. The confession of your own lips and the concession in your statement incontestably prove that the Customs of Cluny† are a deviation from the law given us by God, that is, from the Rule. And thereby they bring dishonor on the giver of the law, that is, on God, and on the expounder of that law, that is, on St Benedict.

†PL 149: 634-778.

CLUNIAC. Far be such a confession from my mouth and from my thoughts such a concession.

[I, 28.] CISTERCIAN. Pay heed in patience and think carefully and you will understand the truth of what I say. Your mouth did confess and your statement did concede that precepts of remarkable discretion in no way lend themselves readily to dispensation.

CLUNIAC. I don't deny it.

[I, 29.] CISTERCIAN. But the precepts of the Rule are remarkable for their discretion, as the Holy Spirit bears witness when, using blessed Gregory as his instrument, he said: 'Peter, I do not wish to conceal from you that that man of God, Benedict, was renowned in this world by reason of the miracles he performed and, in addition, he was equally famous for his teaching. He wrote a Rule for Monks *remarkable in its discretion* and rich in its clarity of expression.'† †Dialogue II:36; FCh 39:107.

You have heard one witness, and an extremely reliable one, Gregory, on the remarkable discretion of the Rule. Now listen to another, even to St Benedict himself and to his words in the Prologue [to the Rule]: 'Therefore we must establish a school for the Lord's service, in whose founding we hope to ordain nothing harsh or burdensome. But if for a good reason, for the amendment of evil habits or the preservation of charity, there is some strictness of discipline, do not be at once dismayed and run away from the way of salvation, the entrance to which must needs be narrow.'† †RB Prol. 45-48.

He himself implies that his Rule is a dispensation from other monastic rules when he says: 'We do, indeed, read that wine is no drink for monks. But since monks nowadays cannot be persuaded of this, let us agree at least upon this, to drink temperately and not to satiety.'† †RB 40:6.

[I, 30.] CLUNIAC. What are these Rules which are so harsh and rigid that our Rule dispenses them?

CISTERCIAN. The Rule of Augustine, which ordered that the flesh be beaten into submission 'by abstinence in eating and drinking insofar as one's state of health allows';* the Rule of St Pachomius,† written by an angel,[26] forbade monks the use of wine

*Ep 211:8.
†'regula Bachumii'

and fish sauce.²⁷ Gather from its own words the great austerity of the Rule of Macarius, which says: 'The wise man works with his hands, thereby obtaining his own daily food and increasing his prayers and fastings. If he should accept food from another, what good does it do him to pray and keep watch? Like the bad hired laborer, he went forth naked.'†

†Ep Macarii ad monachos; PL 103:452C.

CLUNIAC. This language is indeed harsh. Who can heed it?

[I, 31.] CISTERCIAN. The language is harsh and we monks are its hardened listeners, because it is of no matter to us. We are always ready to receive but never will we say 'That is enough,' because each one's greed is his own. Tell me if you ever heard of a monastery which had sufficient—and more than sufficient—revenues and whose monks would accept nothing from those who had made offerings to them?

CLUNIAC. Why put that question to me when you already know full well that even the rich monks had made for themselves a law to accept gifts from every giver, even from the wicked?

[I, 32.] CISTERCIAN. Nowhere is this found either in natural or in written law. As a matter of fact, Jerome says the contrary in expounding the words of the Psalmist, 'He who gives food to the hungry'.* He says to monks: 'Monk, pay attention, you who give food to the hungry and not to the regurgitating; you who are surfeited, take your food but do not take the bread of the hungry. Take what you can put into your stomach not what you can put in a bag. Take what you can put on your back, not what you can put into a chest.'²⁸ Prosper [of Aquitaine] in his Rule for Canons agrees with St Jerome when he says: 'To give something to those who already have is nothing other than to lose it.'²⁹ I hold with Prosper's opinion—but I do not hold with his exact words that alms should be given only to those poor who are so ill and weak in body that they are unable to make a living by working. When a poor man of sound body accepts alms, he is, so to say, stealing the portion of alms which should be allotted to the poor sick man.³⁰

*Ps 146:7

[I, 33.] CLUNIAC. It seems to me that this language is no less harsh than the language used by St Macarius. I do not see why we monks who are healthy in body and rich in revenues should accept alms.³¹

CISTERCIAN. Neither do I. Alms and mercy mean one and the same thing. The former is Greek in etymology, the latter is Latin. Mercy and misery mutually complement each other. Therefore, where there is no misery, there is no room for mercy, that is, for alms. If the donation of a wicked man is accepted by those who already have enough of their own [without it], the misdeed is twofold; if prayers are said for him after his death—and he had not repented—the misdeed is threefold.

[I, 34.] CLUNIAC. Because I do not completely understand, please give me a clearer explanation of what you have just been saying.

CISTERCIAN. You do not understand that the first misdeed lies in accepting the donation, the second in accepting it from a wicked man, the third in praying for this unrepentant donor after his death. Dom Rubert, abbot of Deutz and our contemporary, bears witness that a wicked man's donation is not to be accepted. He says: 'A donation accepted from a wicked man is not only of no profit to the donor, but it also makes a colluder of him who receives it, because the first sins obstinately and the second continues to eat the product of his sins.'³² It is for this reason that the apostle John bears witness that we should not pray for him who dies in his sins when he ordered: 'There is a sin unto death: I do not say that you should pray for him.'† Read, besides, Bede's *Life of Abbot Fursey*, and you will discover that monks accept donations from the wicked to their great peril.³³

†1 Jn 5:16

[I, 35.] CLUNIAC. What are you implying when you speak this way, when you call what the wicked man gives not alms but a donation?

CISTERCIAN. Alms not properly directed [toward their appointed end] are not alms, that is, mercy.

CLUNIAC. How should they be directed?

CISTERCIAN. The person who wishes to give alms must begin with himself. This means that he has first to have mercy on himself, that is, he must repent of his sins, because it is written: 'Have pity on your soul' et cetera.* Again: 'He who is evil to himself, to whom will he be good?'† According to the Gospel this is what Truth said to the Pharisees about the frequency with which they gave alms: 'You Pharisees make clean the outside of the cup, not the inside . . . . Give alms, however, of what remains and all will be clean with you,'* as much as to say: before anything else, give yourselves by believing in me, and give your goods afterwards.

*Qo 30:24
†Qo 14:5.

*Lk 11:39 & 41.

CLUNIAC. I like what you say.

[I, 36.] CISTERCIAN. Your Order, because it, unlike our Order, did not cut off at the roots the delights of the five senses, receives more because it wants more—not because it needs, but merely because it wants, more.

CLUNIAC. What are these [delights]?

CISTERCIAN. Beautiful paintings, beautiful bas-reliefs, carved [in ivory usually] and each embossed with gold, beautiful and costly cloaks, beautiful hanging tapestries painted in different colors, beautiful and costly [stained glass] windows, blue-colored sheet glass,[34] copes and chasubles with golden orphreys, chalices of gold and precious stones, books illuminated with gold leaf.[35] Necessity and utility do not require all these things, only the lust of the eyes does.*

*1 Jn 2:16.

[I, 37.] CLUNIAC. So that I may hold my tongue about the other items, I ask what more becoming thing can be done than to pay honor to the most holy sacrament of Christ by using the most precious metals?

*De officiis
2, 28, 137-8.
Cf. Decret.
C.12, q.2, c.70.

CISTERCIAN. In his treatise On the Duties [of the Clergy]* St Ambrose has Christ make a case against a bishop in these words: ' "Why do you allow my poor to perish of hunger?" The bishop answered: "I have given what I have to the poor." Christ said to him: "Do you have gold?" "Only in your chalice," replied the bishop. And Christ answered: "My sacraments do not require gold." '

St Jerome in his Letter to Nepotian says: 'Either we reject gold together with other superstitions of the Jews, or if the gold is pleasing, the Jews must also be pleasing.'[36] In that very letter in which you say he praised your Order, the abbot of Clairvaux casts aspersions on the same Order when he says with great irony: 'Ask the poor [monks], if they are poor, what gold is doing in their sanctuary.'† †*Apo XII, 28; SBOp 3:104; CF 1:64.*

[I, 38.] CLUNIAC. Yes, that's true. I have read it myself and I have marvelled why he [the abbot of Clairvaux] would so criticize outward expressions of our devotion to God as to rake up satirical censure on us.

CISTERCIAN. Did the founding fathers of your Order, who are unknown, think that at the Last Judgement Christ would say, among other things, to his elect: 'Come, you blessed of my Father,* *Mt 25:34. because you have fashioned for me a golden cup and a chasuble emblazoned in gold,' and that he would say the exact opposite to the wicked?

CLUNIAC. Why did you say the founding fathers 'who are unknown', when Saints Odilo and Maiëul drew up our Customary?[37]

[I, 39.] CISTERCIAN. Where did you read that? You do not find that in Cluny's Book of Customs, but you do discover that St Odilo instituted one rather strange custom, and that was that a monk who has fallen into the crime both base and vile [sodomy] is to be punished in secret if there is any way to keep it hidden. I heard, when I was a member of that Order seeking information [about this custom] from my seniors, that the Cluniacs had borrowed it from some insignificant monastery* which *Baume, dioc. later on they took under their jurisdiction. The Besancon. monks still argue about who authored this particular constitution and to this very day it is an unresolved legal argument among them. Who does not wonder, and in wondering does not become incensed, that the institutes of the Rule, whose author was filled with the spirit of all the just and who had the spirit of prophecy, are by you placed second to institutes whose authority is in doubt and which are contrary to all canons?

[I, 40.] CLUNIAC. Tell me, I pray, in what particulars are our customs contrary to the canons?

CISTERCIAN. In many.

CLUNIAC. Of the many, enumerate at least a few. But before you do, take up again and finish what you were saying about the [remaining] four delights of the senses in which, according to you, we take pleasure. You have already said enough about [the fifth sense] sight.

CISTERCIAN. Necessity and utility do not, but itching ears do, require many large bells of different tones and of such ponderous weight that two monks can barely ring one.[38] Some monks—as they themselves have told me—have worked so strenuously at pulling the ropes that the great weight caused them injury. This is the use to which is put the great expense and the great effort of manufacturing bells.

Those high-pitched and gelded voices to which you have given the name 'graciles'† and which are usually sharpened by a drink made from liquorice and choice electuaries—what are they but delights to the ear forbidden by the precepts of the Rule?[39]

† 'gracefully thin'

CLUNIAC. Where does the Rule forbid them?

CISTERCIAN. Where it orders that we read and chant 'with humility and dignity'†. St Ambrose in his book *On the Duties [of the Clergy]* also forbids them in the following words: 'Let the voice be full with manliness and not pitched like a woman's.'† Contrary to the respected canonical decrees, you make use of such voices in new and frolicsome songs on your new and unauthorized feast days.

†RB 47:4.

†De officiis ministrorum; PL 16:58-9.

CLUNIAC. What are these new and unauthorized feast days of ours?

[I, 42.] CISTERCIAN. The Feast of the Transfiguration and the Feast of the Holy Trinity which should have no special feast day since we praise and venerate the Holy Trinity in hymns, psalms, responsories and masses everyday when we say 'Glory be to the Father, Son and Holy Spirit'.

And since the opportunity has presented itself, I cannot keep quiet about one great and ridiculous incongruity of yours: you celebrate the solemn office of the Lord's circumcision and you sing the office hymn *Vultum tuum** of St Martina, Virgin and Martyr, but you make no commemoration of her. Nor should we overlook the fact that while your deacon is reading the Gospel he turns toward the East. In this custom of yours, you are acting contrary not only to holy authority but also to your own mother churches and to yourselves.

**Introit, Mass for Virgins.*

[I, 43.] CLUNIAC. According to what Solomon said, 'a man who keeps not a guard over what he says shall meet with evil,'† and I have no doubt that a man who has no guard over what he does shall also meet with evil. Our heed for ourselves would be of little or no avail if we acted contrary to our own interests. It could even be said that not only would we be heedless of our own future good, but that our actions would be wilfully illegal.*

†*Pr 13:3.*

**Cf. 2 Th 3:6.*

CISTERCIAN. In your private Masses, which way do you turn when you read the Gospel?

CLUNIAC. To the north.

[I, 44.] CISTERCIAN. As it should be. Augustine says so in one of his *Letters*:* 'The reader of the Gospel faces northward because the Lord said to the Prophet: "Proclaim these words to the north." '* In the book which bears the title *Sacramentary*[40] one reads: 'While the deacon is reading he is so positioned that he stands facing northward because the Gospel is being preached to those whose faith has become chilled.* But in Rome where the men stand facing south and the women toward the north, the deacon turns in the direction of the worthier sex.'† Here you are! Contrary to sacred authority, contrary to the roman way, contrary to your own way in private masses, you read the Gospel facing eastward when celebrating public masses. Tell me, I ask you, do you know of any reason for this strange custom of yours?

**Ep 140 to Honoratus; FCh 20:104.*
**Jr 3:12.*

**Sacr. 84; PL 172: 789C.*

†*Sacr. 31; PL 172: 763D-64A.*

CLUNIAC. I cannot tell you of one for the simple reason that I know of none, nor do our superiors give any other than the authority of our own Customary.

[I, 45.] CISTERCIAN. Usage which goes contrary to reason and sacred authority is ab-use rather than use. St Ambrose in his book *On the Duties [of the Clergy]* orders: 'Do nothing if you cannot give an unqualified reason and one that will withstand proof for what you do.'†

†De officiis I,47,229 & Decret. C.22, q.4, c.8.

CLUNIAC. Does St Ambrose want me to disobey my superiors?

CISTERCIAN. Most certainly he wants you to obey, but not in matters which are contrary to reason and sacred authority.

CLUNIAC. Our abbots do not agree with St Ambrose's opinion.

CISTERCIAN. 'Our abbots,' because they are human beings, can make mistakes. The Holy Spirit who speaks through Scripture cannot make a mistake because he is God. To whom do you owe greater obedience, God or man?

CLUNIAC. I answer in the words of the Apostle: 'We should obey God rather than man.'†

†Ac 5:29.

CISTERCIAN. St Basil in his *Rule for Monks* used the same evidence drawn from sacred Scripture. In this Rule he delineated the obedience due respectively to sacred Scripture and to man.

CLUNIAC. I should like to hear his conclusions. If you remember it, please quote it.

[I, 46.] CISTERCIAN. Basil says:* *In all our business transactions or conversations which are carried out among us, certain ones are governed by God's command and are to be transacted in accordance with Holy Scripture, but there are others about which Scripture says nothing. Of those which are dealt with in accordance with Scripture, no one is ever given permission to do what is forbidden or to leave undone what is commanded. Of those matters about which Scripture is silent, the Apostle gave us an obvious ruling: 'All things are lawful for me, but all do not edify. All things are lawful, but not all are expedient. Let no man seek his own but another's good.'†*

*Interr. 13; PL 103:506B & 12: 505BC.

†1 Co 10:23.

Here you have the way in which you should regard obedience to the precepts of the holy Rule.

CLUNIAC. I understand, but I wish I did not because that quotation from St Basil patently contradicts our Customary.

CISTERCIAN. Your Customary has many who contradict it on the basis of Holy Scripture.[41]

CLUNIAC. Who are they?

[I, 47.] CISTERCIAN. Ambrose, in his book *On the Duties [of the Clergy]*;* Jerome, in the *Rule for Monks* which he wrote and also commented on in his *Letters*;[42] Augustine, in his book *On the Work of Monks*,* questions—with the intention of destroying it—the idea of leisure as you have propounded it in your Customary; and Cassian, in almost every one of his treatises, especially in his treatise on depression and restlessness.* The interpreter of our own Rule contradicts your Customary because ours states that monasteries whose monks all wear breeches are not to be praised, because they do not have proper respect for the Rule.[43] In the expository chapter entitled 'On Daily Manual Labor,' he removes from you all claim to life in accordance with the Rule when he says: 'Wherever chapter [of faults] is not carefully observed, at that place you know for a certainty that there is no monastic observance.'[44]

**De officiis;*
PL 16:57.

**CSEL 41.*

**Inst. 10;*
NPNF 11:266-75.

Those who talk nonsense about us [Cistercians] either do not read those who contradict your Customs, or if they do read, then they do not understand, then in their anger's heat and in their single-minded hatred of the truth, they say: 'You, who in your instability have passed from the old and well-balanced Order of Cluny to the unbalanced novelties of the Cistercians, have thereby done violence to your primary pledge of faith and have not persevered in the calling to which you were called.' By talking this way, they really want to cloak over their own irregularity. Instead of cloaking it, they lay it bare, because our Order, by observing the Rule—if the Rule is old—is old; if the Rule is well-balanced, our Order is well-balanced. But their Customary, because it does not follow the Rule, is out of balance. And what could be more unbalanced than something contrary to reason and authority? These monks have done violence to their primary pledge of faith on the very first day of their profession, because they, lacking stability, neither follow nor have followed the true observance of the Rule which they professed. Furthermore, they have not persevered in that calling to which they were called, 'nor have they lived up to their sworn word; like their fathers, they turned aside like a crooked bow.'† †Ps 78:57.

About the first and greatest of the unstable ones, to wit, about the father of lies, it has been written: 'And he stood not in the truth.'† And because he chose to be unstable with regard to truth, he became unchangeably stable in falsehood, as Cicero corroborates in his book, *On Duties*: 'Men devised the word "faith" because what one promised is "finished" '.† They who on that very first day of their profession did not do what they promised lack stability, even if they have never gone outside the monastery, because they have not remained steadfast in their promised integrity[45] to the Rule and, accordingly, they have violated their primary pledge of faith, and they have not persevered in that calling to which they were called.

†Jn 8:44. Cf. Aug. Tract. in Joh. 42, 13; CC 36: 371, 2.

†Fides ... fiat. De officiis i, 7, 23.

The place to which a monk is called is one thing: the monastic calling is something quite different. The monk's calling consists in his very profession of the Rule in its integrity; if he keeps it whatever place he is, he is true to the calling to which he was called. If he does not keep it, even if he never leaves the monastery he first entered, he is (according to Augustine) outside it.[46] Much more telling are the words of the Apostle: 'Let every man abide in the same calling in which he was called.'† They accuse us of having violated our primary pledge of faith—we, who entered the Cistercian Order because our main purpose was to keep the Rule—even though both charges can be lodged against them, anyway you look at it, for they have turned aside from observing the Rule.

†1 Co 7:20.

We have followed the counsel of St Basil, who

says in his Rule: 'To live closely with those who have put away the Rule is extremely harmful.'† And as the saying of Solomon bears witness: 'Do not live with an angry man . . . lest you learn his ways and accept snares for your soul';* and again we are told: 'Go out from among them and be separate.'* Be sure to keep this in mind. The Apostle orders the same thing: 'And we charge you twice in the name of the Lord Jesus Christ that you withdraw yourself from every other brother who walks disorderly.'* He calls those disorderly who are unwilling to work with their hands as he had ordered.*

†Interr. 2; PL 103: 493B.

*Pr 22:24-25.
*2 Co 6:17, Is 52:11.

*2 Th 3:6. Cf. Inst. 10:9-25.
*2 Th 3:8.

[I, 48.] CLUNIAC. After giving full consideration to your manifold arguments, I have, in sum, adduced that the very weapon which we hurl at you, you hurl back at us in justifying yourself, forgetting the precept of the Lord: 'Revenge is mine; I will repay.'*

*Rm 12:19.

CISTERCIAN. I have done this not to justify myself but to correct you, because 'a reply must be made to a fool according to his folly, lest he be wise in his own conceit,'* that is, lest he thinks he has become wise.

*Pr 26:5.

CLUNIAC. Why did Solomon give a command which is contrary to this command, saying: 'Answer not a fool according to his folly'?*

*Pr 26:4 paraphrased

CISTERCIAN. It seems to me that he said this about the fool who is beyond hope of correction, whom he called a scorner when he said: 'Rebuke not a scorner, lest perchance he hate you.'* But let us return to our problems. All who love God and their neighbors love to see men pass from a life in religion which is irregular [not in accordance with the Rule] to one which is regular. Accordingly, St Gregory in his *Moralia* gives his opinion, which is well worth knowing and should be given particular attention by abbots. He said: 'Proud teachers who are lacking in charity do not want anyone to live by truth whom they cannot use for their own transient glory. The true mother, however, is content that her son at least lives, even if he lives with strangers, because true teachers are willing that other teachers should

*Pr 9:8.

take honor from their students, just as long as the students can maintain their integrity. For the true mother can be recognized by mother-love, just as the dignity of any teaching will be proven by the test of charity. And she alone deserves to receive the whole who has, in a sense, given it all away. For faithful masters not only are not envious when their students work to the glory of other men, but they even hope and pray that they will have even greater success. They will receive back their sons, alive and well, when at the Last Judgement they will attain to the joys they have merited as a reward for the lives they have led.'*

*Greg., Moralia XXI,10,7; PL 76:199BC-200A, In I Regum 14,4; CC 144:482.

Any vainglorious prelate who reads these words of St Gregory takes no notice of them even while he is reading them, because he loves this world's glory. He prefers that his subordinate be a man subject to his own prelature and administration rather than an angel subject to another's tutorial guardianship. Why is he this way? Most likely, so that he will be able to boast about his students, rejoicing more in the physical numbers of his students than in their regular [well-ordered] religious life.

[I, 49.] CLUNIAC. From the fullness of your heart, your mouth speaks.* Your heart is fully intent upon making the monks of our Order careless about breaking the vow of stability should they leave our monasteries and enter yours. In this way, many become imitators of you and partners with you in breaking their vow of stability.

*Lk 6:45; Mt 12:34.

CISTERCIAN. When a jackass hears the lyre being played, he becomes an authority on lyric music.⁴⁷ You are no jackass, but you feign a high degree of deafness. As if you did not understand the reasons and the authoritative evidence by which I showed that the monks who follow your Customary are unstable vow-breakers, you answered by saying that I was eager to have lots of company in breaking my vow of stability. Be that as it may. Up to this point it is as if nothing had been said and nothing proven. Now I am adducing more evidence of great authority which will close your mouth, which speaks lies.*

*Ps 62:12.

The redactor of our Rule, St Benedict himself, offers great freedom from concern on the subject of a change of place made for God's sake and the soul's profit when he said: 'Wherever he is, let him serve one God and fight for one king.'* St Gregory gives the same peace of mind in the Rule and in the same words because St Gregory's Rule is St Benedict's Rule.[48] Pope Alexander II bears witness to this when he says: 'The canons of St Benedict, which are also the canons of blessed Gregory our predecessor, forbid a man to be professed as a monk in less than one year.'[49]

*RB 61:10.

CLUNIAC. In our Order they become monks sometimes within a month [of their entry].[50]

[I, 50.] CISTERCIAN. This is your custom then, and it is contrary to the Rule and to the canons. But we will have more to say later about your violations of the canons. For the time being, let us pay attention to the more pressing question: whether the roman privileges which glory-seeking superiors have managed to obtain can be impediment to the leeway granted monks by blessed Gregory and St Benedict. Pope Zosimus unravelled the knot of this problem when he said: 'To grant, or to change, anything contrary to the statutes of the holy fathers is not within the authority even of the [papal] chair.[51]

CLUNIAC. You have come well prepared, for you back up your every charge with pre-planned evidence.

[I, 51.] CISTERCIAN. Nobody is allowed to say on his own authority what seems right to himself apart from the witness of Scripture, as Jesus Christ said when he was speaking of the Holy Spirit: 'For he shall not speak of himself, but what things so-ever he shall hear, he shall speak;'† or again: 'For I have not spoken of myself, but the Father who sent me has given commandment what I should say and what I should speak.'† St Basil, who used a method of question and answer, replied to his monks as follows: 'Who is it who can reach that point in rashness where he is bold enough of himself to speak anything or even to think it? First and foremost, we

†Jn 16:13.

†Jn 12:49.

must admit we all need the Holy Spirit to guide us on our journey, that he may lead us into the way of truth in thought, word and deed.'† St Ambrose concurs with these opinions when he says: 'How can we usurp as ours something which we do not have from Holy Scripture?'†

†Interr. 12; PL 103:505AB.

†De officiis 1, 23, 102; PL 16:58-9.

Your Customary appropriates illegally a great deal which is not only without basis in Scripture, but is even contrary to Scripture. We should at least realize that work done for God can please him only when it is done in accordance with his will. But where are you to search for his will if not in the Holy Scriptures to which he committed it? Every godfearing man seeks it there because his searching after God's will in Holy Scripture indicates his [holy] fear. Augustine testified to this in saying: 'The godfearing man diligently searches out His will in Holy Scripture.'† This passage from Wisdom regards it so: 'He who fears God neglects nothing.'* Gregory VII ridiculed the usurpatious customs of singular opinions in these words: 'They set their customs against us. Now, Christ said: "I am the truth";* he did not say: "I am custom", but—to available ourselves of the language of blessed Cyprian—any custom, however widespread, must absolutely be esteemed less highly than the truth; and its usage, when contrary to truth, must be abolished.'† Your Customary is imprudent therefore; in fact, more than imprudent, because it legislates not only without authority, but even contrary to authority.

†De doctrina christiana II, 9, 4; CC 32:40.
*Qo 7:19.

*Jn 14:6.

†Decret., D.8, c.5; Cf. Ivo, Decretum 4, 213, Panormia 2, 166.

CLUNIAC. Is your Order not bound to keep canons along with keeping the Rule?

CISTERCIAN. As yours does neither, so ours does both, because it is faithful to the footsteps of the Rule in ecclesiastical as well as in other observances.

[I, 52.] CLUNIAC. For my own edification, I would gladly listen to the *Exordium*[52] of your Order and to a brief summary of its history. And because it is not the monk's place to contend but to confer, let our discussion not be a contention but a conference.

CISTERCIAN. The Apostle commanded us when he said: 'Let all your actions be done in charity.'† Charity turns stern and immoderate words, provided they are spoken in charity, into kind and temperate words.

†1 Co 16:14.

The founders of our Order wrote an account of their activities.[53] These same activities, which I found in the original documents themselves, I am about to relate to you in an abbreviated form.

Robert, the abbot of Molesme of your Order,[54] together with some of his brethren, *through the inspiration of God's grace spoke often among themselves*[55] *about how the Rule of St Benedict, the Father of monks,* was being sinned against. They lamented; they were saddened as they saw that they themselves and the other monks who had solemnly professed to observe the Rule actually kept it so very little. They knew they were thereby knowingly committing the crime of perjury.*[56] *On this account and on the authority of the apostolic see, they came to this waste-land in order to comply with their profession by observing the Holy Rule. Being not unmindful of their solemn promise, they unanimously decided by voted agreement*[57] *that they would establish and observe the Rule of St Benedict in that place [Cîteaux], casting aside whatever gainsaid the Rule—such as frocci*[58] *, pelisses,*[59] *finely-woven woollen shirts, cowls, and underwear, combs,*[60] *blankets, straw mattresses, divers courses of food in the refectory,*[61] *even animal fat,*[62] *in addition to anything whatever that would militate against observing the Rule in all its purity.*

*Dial. II, 36.

Thus taking the straightness of the Rule as their standard of conduct for everything in their life, they were faithful and resolute in following the Rule's footsteps in matters ecclesiastical as well as in all other observances. Putting away the old man they were glad to put on the new.* And because neither in the Rule itself nor in the Life of St Benedict *did they find that learned men ever possessed churches,*[63] *altar dues,*[64] *free-will offerings, burial fees, or tithes*[65] *from any other men, or bread-ovens, mills, farms,*

*Col 3:9-10.

serfs, or that women ever entered his monastery, or that the dead were buried therein—with the exception of [St Benedict's] sister*, they accordingly renounced all the foregoing, saying: 'Where holy father Benedict teaches that a monk should become a stranger to the things done in the world, did he not clearly state that such things should never abide either in the acts or in the hearts of the monks who, by the very fact that they have fled from the world, should live in accordance with the etymology of their name?' Our holy founders, who were agents of the Holy Spirit, also recommended a quadripartite division of their tithes: one part each for the bishop, the priest, guests, and maintenance of the fabric of the church. And to transgress their statutes is to commit sacrilege.

*Dial. II, 34.

Here you have in answer to your request a brief but nonetheless true account of the activities [of our founders].

CLUNIAC. Your concluding remarks about tithes horrify me no end because our monks' revenues are derived more readily from tithes than from any other form of property.

[I, 53.] CISTERCIAN. After such a lengthy digression I must now return to our original discussion—justification for breaking a vow. I am not doing this for my own sake, but for those fainthearted monks who would be willing to pass over to things better and more akin to their salvation if they were not afraid that they would be charged with breaking their vow. In his *Sentences*, Master Anselm of Laon[66] proves the legality of passing from one monastery to another, more strict, on the authority of St Augustine, who said: 'He who passes from one monastery to another more strict does not break his vow; instead he fulfills it to the full.'[67] The same Master advised a monk who wanted to pass to another monastery to seek his superior's permission: 'Ask your superior for permission. If he does not want to give it, know full well that there is no charity in him, and go your own way with God's permission.'[68]

To the words of this Master I add that the superior's acts are not only against charity but also contrary to precept.

[I, 54.] CLUNIAC. Where is it specified that abbots are to permit their monks, who wish to do so, to change their monasteries?

CISTERCIAN. In the Rules of the Holy Fathers, Serapion, Macarius, Paphnutius and the other Macarius.[69]

CLUNIAC. What do their Rules have to do with us?

CISTERCIAN. A great deal to do with us, because anything St Benedict was silent about in our Rule, he ordered us to search for in other books and especially in the *Institutes* of the Holy Fathers.* The title of the last chapter of our Rule teaches us that 'the full observance of justice is not established in this Rule,'† which means that not everything which monks should by right observe is found in the Rule. Yet no chapter of the Rule should be observed in monasteries more strictly and to better purpose than this one, the observance of which assures lasting peace between monasteries.

**The* Institutes *of Cassian.*

†*RB 73.*

CLUNIAC. You could not have spoken a truer word. But the fact that [this chapter] is not observed can be laid to whose door other than to that of the enemy of peace, our ancient foe?* Tell me this—because I would like to hear.

*Satan.

[I, 55.] CISTERCIAN. Macarius said: *Seeing that truth has declared publicly: 'On the word of two or three witnesses every charge shall stand,'† we must not be silent about the manner in which a lasting peace may be maintained between monasteries. We do not permit a monk from one monastery to be accepted by another without the consent of his superior. And not only [is he to be] not accepted, but there is not even to be the appearance of acceptance. As the Apostle says: 'Anyone who invalidates his first pledge has rejected the faith and is worse than an infidel.'† If however he begs his superior to be allowed to go to another monastery, let his superior recommend him to the superior of*

†*Dt 17:6, 2 Co 13:1. Cf. Aug., Ep. 211.*

†*1 Tm 5:8.*

the monastery he desires to enter and let him be received there. He must be reconciled to the fact that there will be as many who outrank him as there are brothers in the monastery. No one should wait to find out his mettle; rather his mettle should be tested at the outset.[70]

CLUNIAC. Indeed, reason itself teaches that the observance of this chapter is of incomparable value to monasteries as a practical method of maintaining peace and charity between abbots and monks.

[I, 56.] CISTERCIAN. But when the chapter says: 'He must be recommended by his immediate superior to the superior of the monastery which he now desires to enter', this must be correctly understood to mean [entrance into] a monastery equal in observance to his present monastery or a monastery where observance is more strict, but not a monastery less strict in observance, because that would be to apostatize.[71] One may pass to a stricter monastery even without permission; to a monastery of equal observance only with permission, but never to a monastery of slacker observance, even with permission.

Actually God's calls are twofold: there is one by precept, another by counsel. Precept calls us from an imperfect to a good life; counsel calls us from the good to a better life, and to one more propitious to salvation. We should shun, as we would an evil father, anyone who impedes us from following the precepts, and we should shun as an evil father anyone who impedes our following the counsels, if he is filled with boastful vanity. Yet if he is not vainglorious but is fond of his son—in a physical way—and does not want to be deprived of his [son's] presence, although we should not shun him not as a evil father we should instead give preference over him to the immortal Father. The last precept of our Rule, which St Benedict very appropriately placed at the very end, implies this when it says: 'Love your abbot with a sincere and humble affection, but prefer nothing whatever to Christ.'†

†RB 72:10-11.

[I, 57.] CLUNIAC. Because obedience, when practised either in an ordinary way or in the highest way possible makes perfect the cenobitic monk, no knowledge is more necessary to us than to know how to obey. Some say that the only perfect obedience is obedience without delay* and without discussion of whys and wherefores.

CISTERCIAN. According to Augustine, we owe this kind of obedience to God alone. He says: 'We must obey, not argue, when God thunders his command.'†

CLUNIAC. Why is this kind of obedience not owed to superiors, of whom Christ said, 'He who hears you, hears me; he who despises you, despises me.'†

CISTERCIAN. It is not owed to superiors because they are only men, and it is written: 'Many are the roads which seem straight to men, but they merge at the end in the depths of hell.'⁷² On this account St Benedict ordered us to follow the Master, the Rule,* in all things, because (since we are men) there are times when we deceive and are deceived. Following the precepts of the Rule, because they are god-given—inasmuch as the Holy Spirit instituted them through St Benedict and recommended them through St Gregory [the Great]—we do not deceive nor are we deceived.

Christ's words, 'he who hears you hears me,'† must be understood in the following sense: He who hears my agents hears me, because when they issue an order which is not to be obeyed, then they are not agents but adversaries. In his Rule St Basil rendered by distinction a firm and judicial decision on the measure of obedience due to men. You who are eager to know how to obey—which is assuredly something one should be eager to know—ought to read what he wrote. And you will be taught a valuable lesson.

[I, 58.] CLUNIAC. Tell me about this judicial settlement, because hearing someone explain it by word of mouth is more effective than reading it.

CISTERCIAN. Basil wrote: On being given an order, *we must remember the Apostle's precept: 'Do not despise prophesies, but prove all things. Hold fast*

*RB 5:1.

†De civ. dei 16:32;
CSEL 40/2:182;
CC 48:536.
Cf. Ps 18:14.

†Lk 10:16. Cf.
Pre 17; SBOp
3:265; CF 1:
117-18.

*RB 3:7.

†Lk 10:16.

to that which is good and refrain from all appearances of evil'.† If an order conforms to God's command and is good for your soul, and someone orders you to do it, you accept the command promptly as the will of God. And we ought to accept and to fulfill what was written 'supporting one another in the charity of Christ.'†

†1 Th 5:20.

†Ep 4:2, Col 3:13.

If someone orders us to do something which in our view is contrary to God's command, or to do something which would subvert the command's integrity or defile it, however, it is time to say 'we must obey God rather than man'.† We must also keep in mind the saying of the holy Apostle who, to safeguard us, dared not spare even an angel, but said: 'Even if an angel from heaven preaches a gospel to you besides the one which we have preached to you, let him be anathema.'† From this we learn that even if there is someone who is very dear to us, even if he is very distinguished and holds a very important position, yet he inhibits us doing what God has commanded or, on the other hand, orders us to do something which God has prohibited, he must be abhorrant to anyone who loves God.†

†Ac 5:29.

†Ga 1:8.

†Interr. 13; PL 103:506AC.

[I, 59.] CLUNIAC. I do not know how many times I have read this chapter, but never have I understood it as well as I do now. But when he said, 'even if he holds a very important position,' I think I understand what he means, but my understanding may seem childish to you.

CISTERCIAN. What is your understanding?

CLUNIAC. Since the word *pope* is derived from *papa*—which is a word expressing an admirer's emotions—perhaps by these words* [Basil] means the Pope, because *papa* is construed as *highly placed*.†

*in admiratione positus.
†admirabilis.

CISTERCIAN. Even if he was referring to the Pope, would he not be in error, for St Benedict ordered 'that nothing whatever is to be preferred to Christ'.†

†RB 72:11.

[I, 60.] CLUNIAC. You want our Order to be [regarded as] inferior to yours in monastic life.

CISTERCIAN. This is precisely what the Abbot of Clairvaux wants, and you yourself say that he praises your Order. He maintains, even while he praises, that a monk is permitted to pass from your Order into ours, but not to go the other way because that would be to apostatize.

[I, 61.] CLUNIAC. In the Gospel, Christ prohibited apostasy in describing it and in forbidding it he described it, saying: 'No man, putting his hand to the plough and looking back, is fit for the kingdom of God.'† Tell me, I pray: if the Pope were to order you to return to our Order, would you be willing to obey him in an apostasy of this nature?

†Lk 5:62.

CISTERCIAN. I will not answer your question today. Today's answers should be enough for you. Tomorrow, perhaps, after having given additional thought to your questions, I will give you better considered answers.

END OF PART ONE

PART TWO

[II, 1.] CLUNIAC. Here I come, ready to listen to the answer you promised me.

CISTERCIAN.[1] Your question does not deserve my answer because it is two-pronged, and a secret snare lurks for me in each prong. But the sophism which he conceals usually catches the man who puts sophistical questions to another and he falls into the trap of his own cross-examination,* just as did the Pharisees to whom Christ answered: 'Render to Caesar the things that are Caesar's and to God the things that are God's'.† **Ps 35:8.*
†*Mt 22:21.*

CLUNIAC. Tell me, what are these snares in which you are so afraid of becoming enmeshed?

CISTERCIAN. I would have to answer either *yes* or *no* [to your question on obedience]. On the one hand, were I to say that I would obey [a papal order to return to Cluny], most likely you would heap scorn on me and say, 'Shame on the teacher when his own guilt makes a liar of him'.† You who preach [strict] observance of the Rule in all things, how do you keep this precept of the Rule: 'You will prefer nothing whatever to Christ'*, if you put the Pope, Christ's vicar, ahead of Christ by obeying him up to the point of an apostasy which Christ himself forbade in saying: 'No man putting his hand to the plough and looking backward is fit for the kingdom of heaven'?* How do you interpret Saint Basil's sentence in his Rule: 'He who orders what Christ forbids, even if he occupies a high position, must be looked upon with abhorrence by anyone

†Dist. Catonis *I*, 30, 2.

**RB 72:11.*

**Lk 9:62.*

who loves God'?*

On the other hand, were I to say that I would not obey [the pope], you would tell all and sundry that I held the Apostolic See in contempt.

[II, 2.] CLUNIAC. Suspicion has fabricated these things in your mind. How can you be in the right if you harbor a suspicion? To pass judgement on things hidden and inexplicable is contrary to the following precept of Christ: 'Judge not that you be not judged.'* And, says the Apostle: 'Who are you to judge your brother?'*

CISTERCIAN. I know that suspicion is a vice, but carelessness about one's interior [spiritual] life makes this vice so common among monks that some of them think they are not sinning by being suspicious.

CLUNIAC. You would prefer, if I am not mistaken, not to obey rather than to obey, but it would be safer to obey. No abbot would presume to harbor you in his community in defiance of our apostolic Lord [Pope]. 'Prudence metes the outcome of things.'* Accordingly, I consider prudent a certain abbot in your [Cistercian] Order who for well-nigh thirty years has lived as the father of his monastery, learned, disciplined, and held by all in high esteem; a man who years before came to religious life in our [Cluniac] Order. This man, as I have learned from a reliable source, admits that he would undoubtedly return to our Order if the Pope ordered it. What seems right to you in this case, since the very last precept of our Rule orders that 'nothing be preferred to Christ', and St Basil says, 'Even if the person who orders what God forbids holds very high position, he should be abhorrent to anyone who loves God'?

CISTERCIAN. I will answer you by quoting the words of St Augustine: 'The man who fears God carefully searches out his will in Holy Scriptures'.* Tell me how you like having this apostasy grafted on to praise for your Order?

[II, 3.] CLUNIAC. He did indeed praise our Order but he was not praising it in that one aspect.

*Interr. 13;
PL 103:506.

*Mt 7:1.
*Cf. Rm 14:4.

*Boethius,
The Consolation
of Philosophy 2.
Pr 1, 15.

*De doctrina
christiana; CC 32,
p. 40 para. 13.

He should have said that it would be apostasy to pass from our Order into yours, because our office of Prime alone, together with the litany and its various adjuncts, takes longer than all the offices which you offer God all day long in the oratory, with the exception of Mass and Vespers.[2]

[II, 4.] CISTERCIAN. With remarkable discretion, St Benedict ordered that our office be recited in the oratory.* In discarding this discretion, you have incurred a remarkable indiscretion. But above all else, by doing as you have done—contrary to the precept of the Rule and to the precept of the Apostle*—you have stolen the time for manual labor.[3] Listen to St Augustine as he questions this custom of yours:

*RB 11:13, 24:4.

*RB 48. Cf. 2 Th 3:10.

I would like to know what monks do who do not want to work physically when they have nothing to occupy their time. Give ourselves to prayer, they say, to psalms, reading and the Word of God. Plainly a holy life, praiseworthy and pleasing to Christ. But if we are not to be called away from these [pursuits] then we are not going to eat and food is not going to be prepared every day to be set before us and consumed. But if the dictates of bodily weakness compel the servants of God to take leisure at specified intervals of time for attending to these matters, why do we not also reserve other intervals of time for observing apostolic precepts? One prayer by an obedient man receives quicker audience than a thousand by a scornful man. Men working with their hands can also, easily, sing hymns to God, and have their work lightened, as it were, by the divine coxswain. Do we not all know of skilled workmen who give their hearts and tongues to the vanities and occasionally even to the degradations of theatrical productions, while their hands never stop working? What is there then to prevent God's servant from working with his hands and at the same time meditating on God's law and singing the praises of the Most High?

And on the same subject: *Would to God that they who want to keep their hands quiet would also want to keep their tongues absolutely still.*

Again on this subject: *Do those who assert that they need leisure time to read not find in that reading what the Apostle has commanded? What, then, is more perverse than to be unwilling to comply with what is read while still wanting leisure time to read?*

Again he says: *What is more iniquitous, to the apostle, I say, not to us, than to be willing to obey in little things and to be unwilling to obey in the greater things?*[4]

Have you noted the righteous zeal with which St Augustine inveighs against, and by the fact that he does inveigh proceeds against, that inactivity of yours which you say you chose with Mary? Would to heaven it were with Mary!

[II, 5.] CLUNIAC. In what treatise and against whom did he say all that?

CISTERCIAN. In the book, *The Work of the Monks,* and against monks. There lived at that time in Carthage some monks who did not have a proper understanding of Christ's words when he said: 'Mary has chosen the best part which will not be taken from her'.* Like you, these monks did not want to perform manual labor but to spend their leisure time only in reading and prayer. This was extremely displeasing to St Aurelius, archbishop of Carthage, and he asked St Augustine to write a treatise against them and to put an end to their errors.[5]

*Lk 10:42.

[II, 6.] CLUNIAC. Why did you say: 'Would to heaven it were with Mary'?

CISTERCIAN. Because you don't want to imitate Mary.

CLUNIAC. How should we imitate her?

CISTERCIAN. Mary, at the moment when she heard the word of God from the mouth of the Word of God, directed her whole attention to what she was hearing, she kept quiet and ceased from all activity. At other times, like other women, she spun, she sewed and perhaps she wove, though not gold brocades. So also you, when you hear the word of God from the mouths of your superiors, must pay very close attention[6] and cease from all activity. During the hours designated in the Rule for manual labor, you should obey the Apostle and your Rule.

[II, 7.] CLUNIAC. As I understand it, St Augustine, using the simile of the skilled artisans' desire to work, exhorts us to sing outside the oratory, while doing manual labor, those prayers which we add on to the regular Hours in the oratory, namely *preces*,[7] suffrages,[8] psalms, the Long Litanies[9] and the Office of the Virgin Mary. In that case, what would then become of the prolonged prostration of the whole body, which cannot very well be made at manual labor, and by means of which we, humbled beneath God's powerful hand, supplicate him through Litanies? It is in this [humble prostration] that we think there is embodied the near perfection of our holy religion and of our religious holiness.

[II, 8.] CISTERCIAN. Anything which takes liberties against reason and the regulations of our saintly Fathers can never rightly be called religious holiness or holy religion. Accordingly, prolonged prostrations of the whole body, taken on without warrant and contrary to the decrees of the holy Fathers, and the celebration of Lauds and Prime together at unsanctioned hours contrary to the ordering of the Rule, will bear less spiritual fruit than the hymns which should be said at these same hours; thus they cry out against you and, so to say, accuse you of presumption.

So as to say nothing for a while about the precept of the Rule, let us concentrate on what Cassian shows were the saintly Fathers' decrees on the above when he said:

While we are willing to exceed the limits long ago laid down by our elders, we hurry to reach the end [of the service] by trimming the number of remaining psalms, thinking—and seeking opportunities— rather to rest the sagging body than to use the time for benefit and profit from prayer.

That is not the way with our Fathers of Egypt; before they kneel they spend a little while in prayer, and they spend the great part of their time standing in supplication. Next, for the briefest of moments they prostrate themselves on the ground as if in adoration of God's mercy. They arise as quickly as possible and stand straight with arms outstretched; they pray standing in the same way as before and so continue, intent on their prayers.[10] *They say that to lie on the ground for too long exposes one not only to distractions of all kinds but, more serious, even to drowsiness. We know that this is true and would that we did not know it by experience and daily habit, for we oftentimes hope to prolong our prostration on the earth a little longer, not on the pretext of prayer so much as for relaxation.**

*Inst. 2:7.
Cf. 3:5.

[II, 9.] CLUNIAC. Cassian confessed and did not deny [this], because he too was a human being. Is it any wonder that some of our monks doze during a prolonged prostration of the whole body, some drift off, some even snore, for, as the moral pagan* says, 'Is sleep allowed to creep in stealthily when work is long?'†

*ethnicus ethicus

†Horace,
Ars poetica,
354.

CISTERCIAN. Would that nothing worse happened than dozing, falling asleep, or snoring!

CLUNIAC. What could be worse?

CISTERCIAN. Can they not, while asleep, through the sneakiness of our ancient enemy fall prey to disgustingly vivid imaginings and illusions? The founders of our Order, having these in mind and buttressed by the Rule's remarkable discretion, put aside that very ill-considered devotion in your Customary. And because it is written that 'obedience is better than sacrifices',* they preferred to obey the holy Rule, the master, than to offer sacrifices to your Customary. For, on the contrary, they would be guilty of the crime of soothsaying if they would not bow to so discreet a master, the holy Rule, and in doing so they would dishonor God himself who gave the law, St Benedict who proposed the law, and St Gregory who commended the law. They were also completely aware that God demands the humiliation and prostration of man's inner self, as the Prophet bears witness, saying: 'A humble heart God does not despise.'* Truth himself also testifies in the gospel that the prayers of the publican were heard even though he was standing.†

*1 S 15:22.

*Ps 51:17.
Cf. II,30 below.
See Decret. C.25,
q. 7, c. 5.
†Lk 18:10-14

[II, 10.] CLUNIAC. By these fairly-well thought out reasons and authoritative sources you praise your Order and denigrate ours.

CISTERCIAN. Contrary to the precepts of the Rule, you snatch that sweet early morning sleep denied to monks. You are not unaware of how presumptuous it is of you to do this. You sleep when you should be at vigils and you keep vigil when you should be sleeping; and by turning the order of things upside down like this, you do not observe the proper [liturgical] Hours.

[II, 11.] CLUNIAC. What is the proper time for singing morning Lauds and what is the proper time for the celebration of Prime?

CISTERCIAN. Dawn is the proper hour for singing morning Lauds, as the words of the hymn 'Dawn begins its course'* intimate; sunrise is the proper time for Prime, as the hymn for that Hour indicates with the words, 'Now that the daylight fills the sky'. The sky-filling daylight is the sun. Listen to what Cassian felt about those who sleep during these [liturgical] Hours.

*Aurora cursus provehat

*Nam lucis orto sydere

Several [monks] in this province, not knowing the reason for the institution and introduction of Prime, the first Office of the day, go back to sleep after singing the Matins hymn. They fall into the very practice which our predecessors were trying to check when they instituted this Office. They are in a hurry to finish it at that hour so that an opportunity for going back to sleep is afforded the indifferent and careless.

By no means whatever should this be done, (as we have already explained more fully in the little book* which we wrote describing the synaxis *of the Fathers of Egypt) for fear that our purification, acquired through suppliant confession, be contaminated either by the surges of our natural passions and pre-dawn prayers, or polluted by some dream fomented by the enemy to stain us, or even that our spiritual fervour be interrupted by the rest which accompanies a pure and natural sleep, making us lazy and sluggish all day long with the torpor brought on by sleep.*

*Inst. 2:13.

*Inst. 3:5.

*prime=first hour.

*Rm 12:1.

*Ga 5:16.

*Conf. 4, 11.

So that this will not happen, the Egyptian Fathers, since they usually rise at stated times even before cockcrow, prolong their night watch until daylight after the morning Office has been celebrated; [the purpose is] that the advancing light of morning may discover them firmly set in fervor of spirit and, in addition, may keep them fervent and careful throughout the day, sustaining them in the conflict and fortifying them for their daily combat with the devil through the keeping of night watches and strengthening them in spiritual meditation.

[II, 12.] CLUNIAC. I know and I am quite certain that Cassian could convince us by none of his unproved assertions to go without the morning sleep with which the saintly Fathers, the founders of our Order, indulged us.

CISTERCIAN. Roused by the ringing of the bell, you arise during the summer after sunrise,[11] and before you sing Prime, you generally complete your tasks, be they business or busyness, deferring the celebration of Prime until almost the *second* full hour of the day.* Both the beginning and the end of this service refute this custom of yours, for it has been so designed to precede and not to follow your daily duties.

The first verse of the hymn for Prime witnesses to this: 'Now that the daylight fills the sky / we lift our hearts to God on high / that he in every duty done / would save us from the evil one.' And the final prayer of the Office has the same theme: 'Lord God, who has brought us safely to the beginning of this day, defend us by your strength, and grant that this day we fall into no sin, but let all our words come forth and our thoughts and actions be directed toward the accomplishment of your righteousness.'

Where then is 'your spiritual service'* which the Apostle commanded? He also said: 'Walk in the Spirit, and you shall not fulfill the lusts of the flesh.'* According to Cassian, 'to walk in the spirit' means that you follow the rational endowment of the mind,* or according to Augustine, [it means] that you follow Holy Scripture which was written through the Holy Spirit, and you do not fulfill the lusts of the flesh;* this means you are not to do things according to your own fancies. *Source unknown.

[II, 13.] CLUNIAC. We do not follow our own fancy because that is not permitted to monks, but we do follow our Customary.

CISTERCIAN. On what grounds, unless it is that you are well-disposed toward your Customary but ill-disposed toward your law, that is, the Rule? These were not the kind of men who followed Mattathias into battle; of them it is written: 'And they followed him in the law, each one by his own choice.'* And the psalm says of the blessed man: 'But he chooses the law of the Lord, and in this law he meditates both day and night.'* You do not keep the sanctified sevenfold number which the Rule prescribes for holding divine praise in the course of the day.*

*1 M 2:42.

*Ps 1:2.

*RB 16:1-2.
Cf. Ps 119:164.

[II, 14.] CLUNIAC. What's this you're telling me? Why do you destroy your own soul by lying this way?

CISTERCIAN. You do not have morning Lauds because all year long you celebrate it not in the morning but at night, so that in the morning, when Christ rose, you can go on sleeping; and so at your houses [Lauds] are not morning but nighttime Lauds. For, as Priscian[12] says, *matutinae* [morning] is pronounced *manuninae*, which means it comes from *mane*, [morning] which is the first part of the day, (in which the householder in the Gospel went forth to conduct affairs in his vineyard).

CLUNIAC. We do not sleep-in in the morning all year long.

CISTERCIAN. I know for a fact that you sleep mornings every day from Easter until All Saints,* but that from All Saints until Easter you sleep mornings during the twelve lessons which you often have [at the Office]. And when you sing Prime before daybreak in winter-time the following verse does not apply to you: 'Seven times a day I have given praise to you, O Lord.'* Rather, it is 'Five times a day in winter and six times in summer have I praised you, O Lord.'

*1 November.

*Ps 119:164,
RB 16:2.

CLUNIAC. We ourselves do not look upon these things so shrewdly and subtly, but we walk simply and, accordingly, confidently.* *Pr 10:9.*

CISTERCIAN. Simplicity without common sense is simplemindedness rather than simplicity.¹³

CLUNIAC. Then why did Christ say: 'If your eye is simple, your whole body shall be full of light'?* *Mt 6:22.*

CISTERCIAN. By 'the eye' Christ meant common sense, to which he joined simplicity, as he did in this instance: 'Be therefore sensible as serpents and simple as doves.'* *Mt 10:16.*

[II, 16.] CLUNIAC. Some of the statements you made have not yet escaped my memory. What did you have in mind to explain to me by them? You stated at the beginning of your conversation, 'I was a late vocation* in the Order of Cluny for ten years and a monk barely three days'.† **a conversus. See note 2. †I,2.*

CISTERCIAN. I mean those three days at the time I read my letter of monastic profession because I was silent for the next three days after that and I slept in my habit. This is why I said that I was a monk of barely three days. Now, in fact, I am saying that I was not even a three-day monk, because only a legitimate profession makes a monk. There is no legitimate profession, however, unless it is preceded by a legitimate novitiate and that time of testing cannot be of less duration than one year.* Accordingly, St Benedict states in his Rule that the complete Rule is to be read to the novice three times by the end of the year; if, on that day which marks the end of the year, he promises that he will observe every part of the Rule which he had heard read and was told he had to observe, then 'from that day forward he may not leave the monastery nor withdraw his neck from the yoke of the Rule which he was free to refuse or accept over a long period of deliberation'.* I never reached that day. **RB 58:9-13. *RB 58:15-16.*

Accordingly my profession was made in violation of the law. The authority of the Apostolic See says: 'Whatever is presumed to be contrary to the law, deserves to be absolved by the law.'¹⁴ I want to by-pass in silence the conclusion which can be drawn from the foregoing because it is enough only to say that just as the installation of an abbot is illegal if he was not elected in accordance with the Rule* so, in like manner, a monk's profession is not valid if he has not spent a year in the novitiate as the Rule demands. Probation as demanded by the Rule is what puts the monk under obligation to the obedience and stability which the Rule demands.* Just as fools promise to give away what they do not possess so they also think they have the capability of doing what they cannot do until they have tested themselves, and a whole year is scarcely enough time in which to be tested. Credence cannot be given the imprudent promises of those who act rashly and impulsively, any more than Christ believed Peter when he promised what he could not fulfill: 'Yes, even though I should have to die with you, I will not deny you'.*

*RB 64.

*RB 58:17: 'he shall promise stability, conversion of life, and obedience.'

*Mt 26:35.

CLUNIAC. Your opinions seem to be reasonable even though they are contrary to our Customs.

[II, 17.] CISTERCIAN. If you would not be too irked at hearing about my own conversion, I would like to tell you how ill-advised, ill-considered, irrational and irregular the whole affair was in my case.

CLUNIAC. I would love to hear about the state of your mind which, as your words reveal, preceded as the efficient cause [of your action].

CISTERCIAN. Through God who punishes and is merciful, I fell so gravely ill that a skilled and wise doctor despaired of my life. A certain monk, who later became an abbot, came to visit me. When he saw me he said: 'Man, you are dying! Why don't you have yourself carried to the monastery?[15] I wanted to answer but I could not until he had moistened my lips with water, so totally exhausted was my whole body. After I had pulled together the few remnant morsels of my strength, being barely able to answer, I said: 'I am lying here about to die, but I have no monastic status and I have not been made acceptable to God.' 'Do not despair,' he answered, 'I promise you in good faith[16] that I will go surety to

God on your behalf, provided you do what I ask.' When I had heard this promise I began to pin my hopes on it and I said: 'Give me your surety by shaking hands.'[17] So the bargain was made.

I was taken into the monastery. The monks who stood around my bed in the infirmary said: 'You ought to ask the Lord Abbot to make you a monk.' I asked him. The letter enclosing the monk's profession was written for me. Then I, who could not turn from one side to the other, barely able to read the letter, promised—without any conditions attached—to perform the great works done by the strong, that is, conversion, obedience, and stability in accordance with the Rule of St Benedict, of which I was almost wholly ignorant.[18]

[II, 18.] CLUNIAC. Why do you use the words, 'without any conditions attached'?

CISTERCIAN. I said, 'without any conditions attached,' because if the words, 'provided I return to health from my illness' had been added to my promise, my profession would have been less foolish and more consonant with reason. Later, when through God's mercy I had recovered from my illness, they led me from the infirmary and stood me in front of the altar and had me read my letter of profession for the second time. Thus, inside of four months they made me a monk twice, but according to the Rule and the canons, I could not become a monk even once in less than a year.

CLUNIAC. By acting as they did, they were not following the Customs of Cluny but their own judgment.

[II, 19.] CISTERCIAN. After the Rule had been read to me and I had listened to it, I discovered something quite different, and I was surprised when I had a talk with my abbot about it. Though he did not listen altogether willingly he did answer that he preferred to dispense with my novitiate rather than to receive me according to the Rule. From his answer I understood that he was not overly concerned about his own law,* that is about the Rule. Though I would have liked to have heard

*1 M 2:42.

the chapters of the Rule being read and explained in Chapter[19] —a thing they neither did nor had they any desire to do—I came to the conclusion in my own mind that these words about reading and interpretation were nothing but the idle words which the Rule condemns with a perpetual ban.* [I also concluded that] they were not only the most idle of words but also the material from which scandals are fashioned.

*RB 6:8.

It so happened that on that I had a conversation about these matters with G[eoffrey], Lord Abbot of Admont, a man learned in holiness and great in integrity.* His answer was: 'In Chapter, I explain the chapters of the Rule with a feeling of shame, for the simple reason that my monks do not behave that way nor do they want to do. They consider them worthless.'

*Geoffrey of Admont, 1138-65.

When I counterposed to him these words of holy authority: 'He who turns away his ears from hearing the law, his prayer shall be an abomination,'* he expressed his own mind to me with the very wise and succinct response: 'I do not turn away, but rather I am turned away.'

*Pr 28:9.

CLUNIAC. That abbot, so kind and affable, had a reputation for great generosity and great goodheartedness.

[II, 20.] CISTERCIAN. I cannot help but wonder how the abbots of your Order, who should do so much but who do almost nothing about the observance of the Rule, can so shamelessly want those whom they received contrary to the Rule to observe the Rule by not abandoning the monastery for their souls' profit when, [to abandon such a monastery for this purpose] is not contrary to but in accordance with the Rule. By their everyday example, the abbots teach violation of the Rule because they have their table in the refectory with the brethren, whereas according to the precepts of the Rule* abbots should always eat in the guest house with the guests and travelers.[20]

*RB 56:1.

CLUNIAC. We consider it a mark of great monastic demeanor for the abbot to dine in refectory with the brethren.

CISTERCIAN. God forbid that this should be monastic demeanor, particularly since it is a transgression of natural and written law, and it means that you are not only sitting in judgment on the law[21] but you are also making it look foolish.

[II, 21.] CLUNIAC. What you say is wonderful, if you can prove it. [From what you are saying,] the logical conclusion is that we and our abbots are committing rather serious faults.

CISTERCIAN. Natural law says: 'Do not do to another what you do not want done to yourself.'* *RB 4:9, 61:14. Mt 7:12, Lk 6:31.

CLUNIAC. That's the way it is.

CISTERCIAN. Abbots themselves are reluctant to be deprived of the respect[22] which the Rule demands should be accorded them.* *RB 53:1-2,12 & 63:13-14.

CLUNIAC. That's right.

CISTERCIAN. The abbots themselves deprive the guest of the respect which the Rule specifically orders to be accorded him,* that is, they do not pour water on his hands, nor refresh him with spiritual food, nor do they honor him by dining with him—all of which is ordered by the Rule.[23] By taking away the respect due the guest they do to another what they would not want done to themselves; to deprive a man of his dignity is a greater robbery than to steal his shirt.[24] Against whom is this violence perpetrated if not against Christ? He is the One who will say at the Last Judgment: 'I was a guest in your house but you robbed me of my dignity.' *RB 3, 31, 53.

Since they are of the opinion that it is suitable for the abbot to eat with his brethren in their refectory, it follows that they consider the precept of the Rule forbidding it unsuitable.[25] In this way, they sit in judgment on the Rule.

[The Abbots] are also of the opinion that they are acting wisely in wanting to have their table in refectory with the monks. It follows that they think the Rule legislates unwisely: and so they make it look foolish.

Solomon's parable suits them: 'The sluggard is wiser in his own conceit than seven men who pronounce sentences.'* The Holy Spirit is septemviral *Pr 26:16.

through his seven gifts; he pronounces sentences in the Holy Rule which you and your abbots esteem less than your own sentences and, in particular, than your own errors. The rules of SS. Paphnutius, Serapion and of both the Macarii bear witness to the fact that you have gone astray for they say: 'For his own edification, a traveling brother is not allowed to eat with the monks but with the superior.'† In the *Conferences* we read: 'It is unreasonable and completely absurd to ready a table for a guest, as if for Christ, and not to go near him during the meal.'* Who does not see the dispensation of remarkable discretion allowed by the Rule, '[Let the abbot eat with the guests] but when there are no guests, the abbot has the power of inviting those of the brethren whom he chooses.'*

†*PL 103:438C = RM 97-99.*

*Conf. 2:26.

*RB 56:2.

What is the reason for this if it is not to afford the invited monks a little recreation, with better food than that generally served in refectory? Therefore reason advocates and authority commands that abbots have their own table and that it be not in the refectory with the monks but in the guest house with the travelers and guests, as much for the edification of the travelers and guests as for the recreation afforded brothers invited to the abbot's table.

'But', said an abbot of your Order who wanted to defend this uncanonical custom of theirs to me, in the presence of my abbot, 'we do not want to have our table with the guests and travelers but in the refectory with the monks because if we were to have our table in the guest house we would not be able to get rid of silly-headed women.'[26] Such an excuse is groundless and foolish, as our Order has proved. We exclude from the monastic enclosure not only silly-headed women but any kind of woman.[27]

There are reasons—and this is nearer the truth—for eating with the monks: the expenditure is less and [the monks] eat better. They have forgotten that wisdom is not found in the land of good living.* Because God, through St Benedict as through another Moses to his people fleeing out of Egypt,

*Jb 28:12-13.

that is, to monks leaving the darkness of this world behind them, willed to give a law and to this end He endowed him so much more than all others with the spirit of the just,[28] that he saw by the spirit of prophecy the actions of monks away from the monastery, he heard the thoughts of monks in his presence, he foretold the future and he performed wonderously astonishing miracles.*

*Dial. 2:8-11, 12-21, 3:23.

Why all this? To the end that nobody might express doubts about the law given by him and no one dare sit in judgment on it.

[II, 22.] CLUNIAC. Please desist from such a violent denunciation of our abbots, because if you continue with this viciously censorious checklist you will not have me for an audience. Tell me what you meant by what you said about Mary: 'that she spun, she sewed, and perhaps wove, but not gold brocade.'*

*II,6.

CISTERCIAN. I meant that it is not becoming for nuns and women who are dedicated to God to take pains on this kind of work; besides, gold threads do not cover nakedness or keep out the cold; they feed the curiosity of the eyes and that alone, and therefore women doing this kind of work can be called not so much workers as delighters of the eyes. This is why Jerome in his *Letter to Laeta* about her daughter's education wrote: 'She should spurn silken fabrics, costly Chinese fleeces and gold brocades, and putting gold in threads.'* But the monks of your Order, who should discourage such handiwork, encourage them and pay high prices for them, all the while robbing the poor.[29]

*Ep 107,10; CSEL 55:300-301

[II, 23.] CLUNIAC. God forbid that we 'rob the poor'; the monk in charge of the poor-house exercises very careful supervision over the property donated to them.[30]

CISTERCIAN. Whatever you spend unnecessarily and use superfluously is robbery of the poor. Just by way of example, albs and maniples are worn on feast days[31] by the highest and lowliest, by your *conversi* as well as by monks, even by murderers.* What is that but robbery of the poor?

*See III, 46.

CLUNIAC. We do not use them superfluously because they have a sacred symbolism.

CISTERCIAN. Your celebrants at the altar are a good example of that symbolism. By this rationale you can use every day rich red cowls of a kind of cloth which in our language is called *scarlat*.[32] You say: 'We use red cowls every day because we must be ready and willing every day to shed our blood for Christ; by the same token we use costly material because 'costly in the sight of the Lord is the death of his saints'.* Superfluous symbolism is really no excuse for superfluous habits.

*Ps 116:15.

[II, 24.] CLUNIAC. Why do bishops and their clergy use elaborate vestments like these in their cathedral churches?

CISTERCIAN. I am not obligated to answer that question since the Abbot of Clairvaux answered it adequately in that book which you claim praises your Order, when, in reality what he says condemns more strongly because it insinuates [its criticism]. He plants his objective in the reader's mind in a few words when he says: *'The lips of the priest shall keep knowledge and they shall seek the law at his mouth, because he is the angel of the Lord of Hosts.'* What law? [We are seeking not] that law which any kind of an original written document recommends or which the ordinary reasoning process proves, because in the law we should neither look for a master teacher nor heed anyone who forbids its fulfillment.** Our Rule is our Law, which both the ordinary reasoning process proves, and an original written document, that is the *Dialogues of St Gregory*, recommends. In the execution of the law's precepts therefore, we are not to look for a master teacher nor are we to give ear to him who forbids its fulfillment.

*Mal 2:7.

*Pre IX, 21;
SBOp 3:268-9
(freely quoted, probably from memory);
CF 1:122.

[II, 25.] CLUNIAC. You have rather diligently made observations and stored away in your bosom censures[33] by which you intend to build up your Order and ruin ours.

CISTERCIAN. While you were reading his insinuations, they entered, whether or not you wanted it, into the marrow of your mind, particularly that part where he spoke against detractors when he said:

'How,' you ask, 'do they keep the Rule who wear pelisses, and who have three or four different dishes of food served in refectory, who perform no manual labor—something ordered by the Rule—and who keep those parts of the Rule they like and discard those they don't like?' I am right. These charges cannot be denied. What happens if someone who does not observe these externals is humble, although you who observe them are not humble? Which of you is better? Is it not he who is the more humble? Humility wrapped in pelts is preferrable to liveried pride. We are duty-bound to practise the one [humility] and not to slight the others [external observances], because Scripture says, 'Take a psalm and bring hither the timbrel.'*

*Ps 81:2. Apo VI, 12; SBOp 3:91-2; CF 1:46-9.

[II, 26.] CLUNIAC. I acknowledge that when I read this passage I did not take it to heart because it was not to my liking. You, on the contrary, took it to heart because it was to your liking since it furnished you with ammunition against us. Did you put into the recesses of your mind something more from the same treatise with which to attack us?

CISTERCIAN. Where [Bernard] speaks about the obedience owed by a monk to his abbot according to the Rule, he expresses himself so:[34] 'The monk can be legally driven neither farther from nor closer to, much less contrary to, the vow which his lips pronounced at his profession.'† Here you have the limits of obedience posited by the Rule because a monk professes nothing other than the Rule.

†Pre, V, 11; SBOp 3:261; CF 1:113.

[II, 27.] CLUNIAC. Why did he himself deny this by saying: 'Nobody promises the Rule, but [one promises] to live in accordance with the Rule.'*

*Cf. Pre IV, 10; SBOp 3:260; CF 1:112.

CISTERCIAN. I have no idea why, unless it was by such blandishments insinuatingly to tickle the ears of those who are looking for a pretext to forsake the Rule. The Apostle himself, on the same subject, however, chose to observe the law and to live according to the law, saying: 'For not the hearers of the law are justified [before God] but the doers of the law.'*

*Rm 2:13.

And St James the Apostle said: 'Be doers of the word and not hearers only, deceiving yourselves';* and Christ said to the Jews: 'Did not Moses give you the law and yet not one of you keeps the law?'*

*Jm 1:22.

*Jn 7:19.

It is the same thing to *profess* the Rule, and to *promise* the Rule; and to *proceed strictly according* to the Rule and to *live according* to the Rule are the same, *because the Rule is law*.³⁵

Contrary to these two pieces of authoritative evidence taken from two Apostles, your only wish is to be hearers and not doers of your law, thereby so deceiving yourselves that you cannot excuse yourselves on the grounds of ignorance.

[II, 28.] CLUNIAC. No matter how you understand the abbot's other words in the same treatise, in the [series of] balanced similes which he draws from the Gospel and applies to the Rule,³⁶ you can take no other meaning than that he was defending our Customs. He even says: *Just as all good-living Christians do not observe all the Gospel, so it is that not all good-living monks observe all the contents of the Rule and yet they all live in accordance with the Rule. Now some people are married, some are continent and virgin, some have their own property, some there are in this world who, for the sake of Christ, have no property at all; and yet they all obey the Gospel. Thus, the Cistercians act in their way, the Cluniacs in theirs, and yet both obey the Rule.**

*Pre XVI, 48; SBOp 3:286; CF 1:141 in part. See Huygens, p. 420.

[II, 29.] CISTERCIAN. Because mercy is the component necessary to bring the erring back to the path—even though I know you take pleasure in your straying—I will, however, make you understand his balanced similes properly. In the simile above, where the conclusion is fitted to its antecedent, two interpretations are possible—one of which is true, the other false. The false defends your breaches while the true attacks them. For when you say: 'not all good-living monks observe all the contents of the Rule and yet they live in accordance with it,' if by 'good-living monks' you mean well-disciplined monasteries, your statement is false and that falsehood is your lot.

If by 'good-living monks' you mean the superiors[37] of this one and same well-ordered monastery of monks, what you say is true but that truth is not in you. In one and the same monastery, after all, everyone lives according to the Rule, yet not everyone observes everything contained in the Rule. The gatekeeper does not attend the cellarer's chapter nor the cellarer the gatekeeper's. In like manner, the weekly reader does not attend the weekly cooks' chapter nor the cook the reader's—and yet they all live in accordance with the Rule. The abbot himself [Bernard] seems without too much thought to have stretched the similes applied from the Gospel to apply to the Rule because, of the contents of the Gospel, some are counsels and some are precepts. All of the precepts contained in the Rule, that is, in the *Institutes of St Benedict,* are counsels for novices, but all are precepts for monks.

CLUNIAC. With your trained mind and the artful words which you learned long ago in the schools, you are trying to muddle my uneducated wits.

[II, 30.] CISTERCIAN. I feel that you are the personification of that poet's verse: 'He who saves a man who does not want to be saved does the same thing as killing him.'* You are forcing me, accordingly, to repeat earlier arguments to see whether in this way I can correct your errors.

CLUNIAC. Which arguments are those?

CISTERCIAN. You have grudgingly admitted to me that precepts remarkable for their discretion are not open to dispensation.

CLUNIAC. I can't deny that.

CISTERCIAN. And I have posited: 'But the precepts of the Rule are remarkable for their discretion', and I have proven this proposition by logic and authority. The conclusion which I did not draw then, I draw now. Once the dispensation which was the only possible cover for your breaches is removed, all that remains is transgression of the Rule, dishonor of God and of St Benedict and, according to Pope Damasus,

*Horace,
Ars poetica 467

blasphemy against the Holy Spirit.*

CLUNIAC. As long as you want to debate for the purpose of giving my mind some exercise, I will be polite and listen to you. But never will I admit the dreadful conclusions you draw from your arguments.

[II, 31.] CISTERCIAN. What an astonishing and dangerous distortion it is that at the time which rightly belongs to manual labor, I mean after Chapter, the whole community sits down to take its leisure and to gossip. Is that what this verse taught you when it was read in Chapter to the full community: 'Look upon your servants, O Lord, and direct the works of our hands upon us; yes, direct the work of our hands'?* For ten years I sought and searched, and I was never able to find out what it meant that everybody, as the *Book of Customs* commands, holds in his lap a closed book while he is enjoying his leisure and gossiping.[38] I was never able to find the rationale for this particular custom. This is nothing but [scrupulous] religiosity which has been described as follows: 'scrupulous religiosity is superfluously manufactured observance'.* This kind of observance is quite contrary to authority.

CLUNIAC. To whose authority?

CISTERCIAN. Augustine's.

CLUNIAC. Where does Augustine forbid it?

CISTERCIAN. In the Rule he wrote for monks and nuns, he says: 'Anyone who demands a book outside the regular time for asking, should not be given it.'[39]

[II, 32.] CLUNIAC. Augustine wrote a Rule for Canons Regular but not for monks.[40] And Canons Regular like nothing less than being called monks.

CISTERCIAN. Whether they like it or not everyone who has professed that Rule is a monk. Either they are monks or they do not belong to an order.[41]

CLUNIAC. Brother, tell me—if you really are still our brother and not our antagonist—why do you make yourself obnoxious to three Orders: to wit, the Black Monks, the surpliced Canons Regular,

*Decret. C. 25, q. 1, c. 5.

*Ps 90:17.

*Isidore of Seville, Etym. 8,3.6.

and the habited Norbertines?[42] Stop your foolish arrogance lest you be branded with the slanderer's brand.*

[II, 33.] CISTERCIAN. There is a hackneyed proverb: 'Truth begets hatred'.* I say it not only begets hatred, it also begets martyrdom, as Truth bears witness when he says in the Gospel: 'And you shall be hated by all men for my name's sake.'* Christ's name is Truth as he himself bears witness, saying: 'I am the way, the truth and the life.'* For the sake of the Truth, martyrs are put to death, and hatred precedes and leads [to martyrdom], because the Truth begets hatred and hatred begets martyrdom. In the Old Testament the holy prophets became martyrs for the Truth, and therefore for Christ. In the New Testament infants and suckling babies fell the first martyrs for Truth, that is, they were killed for Christ.*

[II, 34.] CLUNIAC. I don't see how the words of the Prophet which the Church sings on their feast day [Holy Innocents] have any pertinence to them.

CISTERCIAN. What words?

CLUNIAC. 'Out of the mouths of infants and sucklings you have perfected praise'*. They could not praise Christ with their mouths because they were infants and sucklings, unless it be that 'mouth' is used as a substitute for 'death'; for by dying they gave praise to Christ. But I never heard that the word 'mouth' could be substituted for the word 'death'. I never read it and thus it seems to me is outrageously absurd.

CISTERCIAN. Holy Scripture does not particularly care about observing the fine points of etymology. An outcry can only come from the mouth or from the heart. The outcry emitted through the mouth is audible to men, but the outcry that comes from the heart is heard by God alone, because God spoke to Moses crying out not through his mouth but through his heart, and asked: 'Why do you cry to me?'* Abel's blood, poured out on the earth, had neither mouth nor heart, yet God said to Cain: 'Behold, your brother's blood cries to me from

*Cf. Pr 24:9.

*Terence, Andria 68 (1,1,41).

*Mt 10:22.

*Jn 14:6.

*Holy Innocents, Mt 2:16.

*Ps 8:2; Mt 21:16. Introit for Holy Innocents (28 December).

*Ex 14:15.

the earth.'* *Gn 4:10.

You are a simple-minded theologian if you do not know that inanimate creatures, devoid of sense and life, speak to God and praise God. What else is the meaning for us of the Hymn of the Three Children* and the very last praises in the psalms* where all creatures are invited to praise God?[43] What does the divine oracle tell me to discuss now? I must return to the business at hand which you interjecting that obscure passage from the Prophet ['Out of the mouths of infants.']. *Dn 3:57-90.
*Pss 148-150.

CLUNIAC. What is your business?

[II, 35.] CISTERCIAN. What I must demonstrate by reason and authority is that I do not deserve the righteous hatred of all three Orders, nor, as your threats have alerted me, should the mark of the slanderer be burned on my forehead by the branding iron of evil gossip.[44]

CLUNIAC. Is there such a thing as righteous hatred? You were speaking just now 'of the righteous hatred of the three Orders'.

CISTERCIAN. Not only is there a righteous hatred, there is even a perfect hatred. Hence the Psalmist says: 'I have hated them with perfect hatred: and they become enemies to me.'* There is also, and this may be more of a surprise to you, holy pride. *Ps 139:22.

[II, 36.] CLUNIAC. Holy pride? Whoever said such a thing?

CISTERCIAN. In Jerome's *Letter* to the virgin, Eustochium, he exhorts her to have holy pride.* What will surprise you more, in his *Commentary* on Jonah the Prophet, he asserts that a virgin can lawfully kill herself if she cannot otherwise escape from a violater of her flesh,* although, according to blessed Lucy and according to the truth of the situation, violation of the flesh without the consent of the mind in no way diminishes the worth of her virginity.[45]

*Ep 22:16.

*In Ionam *I.12;*
CC 76:390 &
SC 43:72-3;
Decret.,
C. 23, q. 5, c. 11.

CLUNIAC. Jerome said strange things, very different from what many other orthodox Fathers have said, yet not counter to them. I do not think that there is anything in his assertions contrary to the teachings of other Holy Fathers.

CISTERCIAN. Once again you have made me digress again from pleading my case.[46]

CLUNIAC. Such digressions have their uses. Go on, get to your point, always keeping in mind this funny proverb: 'He who is in a hurry to say what he wants will hear things he does not want to hear.'*

*Terence, Andria 920 (5, 4, 17).

[II, 37.] CISTERCIAN. To tell the truth is not to detract provided one tells it for Truth's sake, not for maligning the good reputations of those about whom one talks, but for correcting them and profiting those who hear it. What is detraction except taking away something respectable from another; it means to snatch away someone's reputation by a verbal theft and to tag on to him, verbally, something less honorable?

Were I to take away the title *Canon* from a Norbertine and substitute for it the title *monk*, would I be taking from him an honorable title and conferring on him one less honorable? The title *monk* is as sweet and as worthy of respect as *monas*, or unity, is sweet and worthy of respect;[47] *monas* is derived from *monade*, i.e., from unity, whose mother is charity, which makes of many hearts one heart and of many souls one soul.

CLUNIAC. Who were the first monks in the Church?

CISTERCIAN. The early Church itself,[48] that is, those of whom it is written: 'They were all of one heart and of one soul*. Their unanimity made them monks and all monks are their imitators. Hence it is that an expounder of the psalms, in commenting on that verse in which occur the words: 'He who makes them live in unanimity in the house,' substituted *monks* for *in unanimity* and said: 'He who makes monks live in the house.'* That everyone living the common life [in community] and everyone imitating those of whom it was written: 'They were all of one heart and one soul' are called monks, is verified by [Cassian's] *Conference* on the different kinds of monks.* And St Augustine in his exposition of the

*Ac 4:32.

*Aug. Enar. in Ps 132. 1-2-3; CSEL 40:1926-27 & CC 40: 1926.

*Conf. 18:5.

Psalm, 'How good and how pleasant it is for brothers to dwell in unity'* agrees with him, saying: 'These words of the Psalter, this sweet sound, this soothing melody gives birth to monasteries as much by song as by understanding. In the terms of this psalm they are monks.'* In the opinion of St Augustine, nothing else constitutes coenobitic monks than being brothers living together in unity. Thus the Norbertines and all who lead a common life are monks. I have read about many holy monks but never about one single holy canon.

*Ps 133:1.

*Enarr. in ps 132; CC 40:1927.

[II, 39.] CLUNIAC. What's this you're saying? Surely blessed Augustine, who is a saint, was himself a canon!

CISTERCIAN. Where did you read that? Nowhere does he give evidence of such a thing, nor does any authenticated writing. Moreover, he himself made it clear that he was a monk.

CLUNIAC. In what treatise did he do that?

CISTERCIAN. In one of the sermons he preached to the congregation. In speaking about himself and about his clergy, who together with him led a common life in the episcopal residence, he stated: 'This is how we live. In our community nobody is allowed to have anything of his own; instead, we have all things in common.'[49] Because he and his clergy were brothers dwelling in unity, they were on that account monks, for what is being coenobitic monks except being brothers living in unity? And although [some] Norbertines, in their senseless bragging, deny that they are monks because they want to be called preachers and parish priests, the Prophet rebukes them by saying: 'Blush, O Sidon, says the sea.'*

*Is 23:4.

[II, 40.] CLUNIAC. What pertinence does that prophetic rebuke have to them [the Norbertines]?

CISTERCIAN. It is pertinent to them symbolically because the learned man and the legal expert are symbolized by Sidon; the laymen of the world who are ignorant both of letters and the law [are symbolized] by the sea. So when, by using reason as their only guide, laymen see that [the Norbertines] are monks in the true meaning, they call them monks. They [the Norbertines] are not the least bit ashamed to deny this self-evident truth even though they are learned and expert in canon law.

CLUNIAC. Now look, you've offended them by both designations.

CISTERCIAN. By which ones?

CLUNIAC. You called them Norbertines and you called them monks. Just as they do not want to be called monks, neither do they want to be called Norbertines.

CISTERCIAN. A while ago did you yourself not call them Norbertines and habited Canons Regular?

CLUNIAC. It just crossed my mind for the first time that their unwillingness [to be called either] is not something to be praised.

CISTERCIAN. You are right in saying that their unwillingness should not be praised. Do you happen to know why they do not want to be called by either name?

CLUNIAC. It would seem that, to them, both these titles are marked with disgrace.[50] That is the way they see it, not the way I do. I conclude when I see their habits shortened, however, that they want to be preachers and parish priests[51]—offices not permitted to monks, as blessed Jerome the monk says about monks: 'The role of the monk is not to teach but to lament; he should weep for himself and the world about him.'*

*Contra Vigilantium 15; PL 23: 367A. See II, 49.

Perhaps they do not want to be called Norbertines because hearsay has it that their founder, Dom Norbert, defected and went from being a barefoot donkey rider to being a well-heeled and well-dressed rider of caparisoned horses, from being a hermit he became a courtier in the court of the Emperor Lothair, from black bread and lowly pottage he went on to royal and sumptuous banquets, from greatly despising the world to greatly manipulating worldly affairs.[52]

[II, 42.] CISTERCIAN. The very name by which they are called, Canons Regular, is incongruous, because *canon* and *rule* have one and the same meaning.[53] Hence *canonicus* and *regularis* are absolutely identical in meaning and so to say canon regular is nothing other than saying regular regular.[54] Calling them Canons Regular is misleading and incongruous, because they are not and never were canons. They do not make profession of the *Rule for Canons* which is a collection of excerpts from canonical legislation—those who do make profession of that Rule are rightly called Canons, that is, they are clerics installed in their mother church who may legitimately possess individual private property. So it is that a chapter of that Rule begins with the words, 'Although canons legitimately have their own houses, etc.'[55]

This order had not yet come into the Church at the time of Ambrose, Jerome, Augustine, Gregory and Isidore [of Seville]. Hence, in all their writings, these holy men made no mention of canons because this order first began under the Emperor Louis the Pious.* He convoked a synod of bishops at which, as the work of the Emperor himself, the *Rule for Canons* was redacted.[56] The writer of the same Rule implies this several chapters by saying: 'The holy gathering has decreed', etc.

*814-840.

CLUNIAC. I have listened with pleasure to the subjects you have been discussing because I was ignorant of them; what I never heard about, I also never read about.

CISTERCIAN. Would that the freewill offerings of my mouth* would benefit you because then they could begin to bear fruit in your soul.

*Ps 119:8.

[II, 43.] CLUNIAC. Tell me, I beg you, in as much you have shown that the Norbertines are not canons, in what order do they belong, for they do not want to be monks.

CISTERCIAN. In none, to their way of thinking. However, when positing two descriptions of monks, at the beginning of his Rule, St Augustine bears witness that they are monks when he says: 'This is what we command to be observed: that they who dwell in the monastery observe two main precepts—love of God and love of neighbor; primarily because you are gathered together into a unity, let the chain of charity and unanimity be maintained in the house, and may you be of one heart and one soul.'⁵⁷

To dwell in a monastery and to be monks are the same thing, as [Cassian's] *Conference* on the types of monks bears witness: 'The word *monastery* is nothing more than a physical place, that is, it means a dwelling place for monks. *Coenobium,* however, describes the kind of life and discipline followed there as well. The name *monastery* can even be given a place where one monk dwells, but *coenobium* can only be applied to one united community of several monks living there together.'*

*Conf. 18:10.

[II, 44.] CLUNIAC. It crossed my mind that I read something in Isidore's [of Seville] *Etymologies* which proves they are monks. When treating all the orders in the Church, Isidore made no mention of canons. When treating of monks, however, he said: 'There are two kinds of monks: one is eremitic and the other coenobitic. Hermits imitate Elijah and John the Baptist, but the cenobites imitate the Apostles.'* Therefore, according to Isidore, the Apostles were coenobitic monks.

*Etymol. *VII, 13;*
PL 83:293.

CISTERCIAN. Look, if you don't believe me, believe the *Conferences* of the Fathers, believe the holy Doctors of the Church, Augustine and Isidore.

[II, 45.] CLUNIAC. How did the Norbertines fall into the error of denying that they are monks?

CISTERCIAN. Either ignorance or pride, or both, caused their error. They pride themselves on being preachers and learned men, and say: 'The monk does not have the role of teaching, we do'—never understanding correctly the meaning attached by St Jerome to these words and never paying attention to what the Apostle said: 'How are they to preach unless they are sent?'* Thus, being sent by itself makes the preacher. And they say: 'we [Norbertines], because we are clerics, have the duty of preaching by the very fact of our clerical status.' We answer them: 'Therefore, monks who also hold Holy Orders, because they are clerics, have the duty of preaching the very fact of their clerical status.' They give us a somewhat ignorant answer and say: 'Monks are granted clerical

*Rm 10:15. Cf.
Codex Juris
Canonici,
cns. 1337-1339.

status as a favor, we receive it as our due.' They are wrong in both respects—when they say, 'it is our due' and when they say, '[it is] yours is by favor.'

[II, 46.] CLUNIAC. I wonder why you say they err in this respect because Master Hugh* in his book *On the Sacraments* said the same thing, that monks are given clerical status as a favor.[58]

*of St Victor.

CISTERCIAN. 'There are times when the good Homer momentarily nods in sleep.'* This well-aired proverb, which is known and repeated by people who never read its author, Horace, seems to fit Master Hugh and two Roman pontiffs, Gregory VII and Urban II, and some of the bishops who met at the Council of Autun.* They all thought that the Norbertines were not monks, but rather, should be called Canons Regular. Accordingly, the bishops left in their wake written ordinances about them containing decisions which are not very sensible.[59]

*Horace, Ars poetica 359.

*Council of Autun (1094); Mansi 20: 801-802.

[II, 47.] CLUNIAC. I hear strange things. You are brash enough to lay the hand of censure on the popes themselves. But, by censuring them you have mitigated your censure of us. Many times have I heard that the roman pontiffs, the successors of Peter, never err and that Christ ordered this on their behalf as a favor to Peter. Christ did indeed promise it when he said: 'I have prayed for you, Peter, that your faith may not fail.'*

*Lk 22:32.

[II, 48.] CISTERCIAN. Far be it from me, mere man that I am, to be so brash as to say that the apostolic prelates deviated from the faith! Nevertheless, since [popes] are human beings, they can on occasion be deceived by other human beings—for example, through the insidious influence of their own staff members, who are close to them and perhaps corrupted by bribery; or perhaps they order that something be done without seeking advice about it, or they grant favors without giving the matter due thought—as the little book, *Advice to a Pope*, by Dom Bernard, Abbot of Clairvaux, bears witness.*

In the book which he sent to the Archbishop of Sens† he speaks as follows:

The Romans do not care much about the final

*Csi IV: I, 1; SBOp 3:448-65; Cf. 37:109 ff. †'Henry the Bloody,' 1122-42.

results of such things [intrigues]; but because they dearly love presents they follow up pay-offs. I speak the naked truth; I am not uncovering anything awesome but am describing awful practices. Would to God that what is being done were done in secret! Would to God that no one would believe those who talk about these things! Would to God that they would at least leave us modern-day-Noahs the wherewithal to cover our nakedness just a little! Shall we alone remain silent now that the whole world sees the scandal? My head is pounding and my blood boiling, and should I think of covering my head? Whatever I put over it will shortly be covered with blood; all the greater will be my confusion for being willing to conceal what cannot be concealed.*

    Gn 9:23.

    Mor 7.

Read the *Letter* he sent to the young man whom its Grand Prior had coaxed back to Cluny. In it he chided the decision of the Roman pontiffs very severely saying:

They who were the real authors of the wrong were made to look right, were justified; those who initiated the suit lost it; the guilty party was absolved without being compelled to make compensation. Furthermore, this lenient verdict of absolution was ratified by a harsh ordinance. The content of the Letter, *the sum of the judgment, the real meaning of the suit was none other than that they could keep what they had taken and those who lost were bound over to silence.*

*Lord Jesus, I appeal to You as my judge; I bow down before the decision in your court, where a good conscience has greater value than a full purse.**

    Ep 1, tr. James, p. 13.

CLUNIAC. Very harsh and extremely bitter is his invective against the Apostolic See, and hard to believe.

CISTERCIAN. If you do not believe what I say, believe your own eyes. Here, read it!

[II, 49.] CLUNIAC. Before I read it I want to hear your interpretation of these words of St Jerome: 'The role of the monk is not to teach but to weep', and your reason for saying that Master Hugh got drowsy.

CISTERCIAN. Blessed Jerome wrote a treatise, against a certain Vigilantius, who was criticizing hermits. He said: 'If everyone becomes a recluse and goes into solitude, who then will celebrate [the Offices] in the churches?' [St Jerome] defended [the monks] by saying: 'The role of the monk is not to teach, but to weep.'* The word *monachus* [monk] has the same etymological meaning as *solitarius* [solitary]. Jerome did not say this about a coenobite but about the solitary whom Jeremiah described in this way: 'He will sit solitary and hold his peace because he has taken it upon himself.'*

*Contra Vig. *15;* PL *23:367A.*

*Lm *3:28.*

The obligation to teach is incumbent upon every man who has the intelligence, which means the talent that the good-for-nothing servant buried in the earth*—provided he is not a solitary, providing his dwelling-place is with men—because by teaching he has to bring back to the path of rectitude his brother whom he saw straying from the road of truth and good habits. This is why blessed Gregory says: 'Every man endowed with intelligence should be quite sure that he does not remain silent lest the Lord come and say: "You good-for-nothing servant, why did you not put my money in a bank and I on my return would receive it back with interest?" '[60]

*Lk *19:23,* Mt *25:27.*

Only they who are sent, that is, bishops and priests in their churches and abbots in their monasteries—those to whom the cure of souls is entrusted—have an obligation to preach, that is, to teach in public.

[II, 50.] CLUNIAC. How does anyone take it upon himself to rise above himself?

CISTERCIAN. Abbot John the Hermit shows us. He was perfectly at home in both kinds of life; which means in the eremitical, or contemplative life, and in the coenobitic, or according to Cassian, the 'active', but according to St Benedict the 'mixed' life.* He tells about his upliftings and says:

*RB *1.* Cassian, Conf. *19, 4.*

If anyone, delighted with the recesses of the desert, would put away all human companionship and say with Jeremiah, 'You know I have not desired the day of man.'* I confess that by the blessing of God's grace, I also secured or tried to secure this.

*Jer *17:16.*

And thus by the kind gift of the Lord I remember that I was often caught up into such an ecstasy as to forget that I was enveloped in the burden of bodily frailty and my mind suddenly forgot all exterior sensual stimuli and completely severed itself from all things material, so that neither my eyes nor my ears performed their normal functions. My soul was so filled with meditations on God and contemplation of his Spirit that quite often at eventide I did not know whether I had eaten any food; the next day I was unsure whether I had broken my fast the day before. For this very reason, a seven day ration of food, I mean seven sets of biscuits, were put to one side in a hand-basket on Saturdays to take away all doubt whether supper had or had not been eaten. By this habit another mistake arising from forgetfulness was avoided, namely that when that number of biscuits was gone, the course of the week was finished too, the weekly services had made full turn, and the feastdays and solemnities of the Congregation could not escape the solitary's notice. If the ecstasy we spoke of earlier were to have interfered with this arrangement, the mistake would be checked all the same by means of the days' work which would indicate the number of days.*

*Conf. 19:4.

Here, you can see from the way this narrative ends that even the most perfect contemplatives did manual labor every day. Thus you, you who think you are contemplatives, are wrong because you do not do manual labor. If you remember I said to you: 'Brother, you are wrong: you do not know Scripture.'* No one is said to be a contemplative because he refrains from works of mercy on account of his great longing for contemplation. Manual labor is a furtherance rather than a hindrance to contemplatives. Hence, as Cassian states:

*I, 6.

Paul, the most experienced of the Fathers, while living in the vast desert which is called Porphyry had no cares because of the date palms and a small garden and plenty of food and means of support. He could not find other work to do for his upkeep because his dwelling place was removed from towns and inhabited places by a journey of seven days or more through the desert, and more would be demanded for the transportation of goods than the work would be worth. He gathered palm leaves every day and demanded of himself that he perform this task every day just as if it were his means of support. When his cave had been filled with the year's work, he would year after year set fire to what he had worked so hard at and so carefully, thereby proving that without manual labor a monk cannot persevere in his place nor attain the heights of perfection. Though the need of food did not require him to do this, yet he did it to purify his heart and integrate his thoughts; by remaining in one place, his cell, he gained a victory over accedie and banished it.* *Inst. 10:24. Among the Egyptians this saying was considered inviolable by the Fathers of old: 'The monk who works is attacked only by one devil, but the idle monk is tormented by many.'* *Inst. 10:23.

[II, 51.] CLUNIAC. Though we do not work in the garden or in the fields, yet, on the whole, we are not idle. Some read and some work with their hands.

CISTERCIAN. I know well these idle works of yours.

CLUNIAC. Why do you call them idle works?

CISTERCIAN. Just as words which do not edify are idle, so works which are not pertinent to necessary employment are rightfully called idle. Let me, meanwhile, keep silent about all the other things; what is grinding gold into dust[61] and illuminating huge capital letters with that golddust, if it isn't useless and idle work? Even those works of yours which are necessary are contrary to the precepts of the Rule because you pay no attention to the time assigned to them in the Rule. But it seems to me that it is a greater infraction of the Rule not to observe either the time or the manner specified in the Rule for the Work of God.

[II, 52.] CLUNIAC. When belittling the kind of manual works we perform, you say they are idle and useless, implying that the kind you do are real hardships and very useful.

CISTERCIAN. We put great effort into farming which God created and instituted. We all work in common, we [choir monks], our laybrothers and our hired hands, each according to his own capability, and we all make our living in common by our labor.

[II, 53.] CLUNIAC. We have it on hearsay, even from your own [monks], that not one person could live on the work done by thirty of your monks,[62] because your farming is not labor but recreation and a frittering-away of the passing day. Accordingly, we believe that it is more profitable to our souls, while we sit in the cloister, to attend to psalmody or to spiritual reading out of compunction of heart, thereby fulfilling the saying of the Psalmist: 'Be still and see that the Lord is sweet'.*

*Cf. Ps 46:10 & 99:4.

[II, 54.] CISTERCIAN. Monks who defect from our Order and go to yours usually say such things. They libel us viciously, but you are under no obligation to believe those who lie to God. I will, however, tell you this—that although the Prior carefully takes precautions that, in accordance with the Rule's precepts, 'everything be done in due proportion for the sake of the fainthearted',* yet many are the times when we eat our bread in the sweat of our brow upon returning from work [in the fields].

*RB 48:9.

While at work, those who love and fear God not only sing the whole Psalter, through the mercy of God, but suffer heartfelt remorse and frequently shed tears.[63] The same men, if they were sitting in the cloister, contrary to the Rule's precept, might perhaps doze off or let their minds wander into useless fancies.

[II, 55.] CLUNIAC. You have talked enough about manual labor. It remains for you to tell me why you said Master Hugh dozed off.

CISTERCIAN. Here is one of Master Hugh's catnaps: though he had professed a monastic Rule, specifically, that Rule which gives precepts to those dwelling in a monastery, he did not look upon himself as a monk.[64] Another catnap: he said that the clerical status which we have on the basis of our law, that is, by our Rule's ordinance, is ours as a favor. Our Rule orders that worthy persons be chosen for the priesthood and diaconate, and that those who are priests and deacons and persevere in asking admission, be received [into the monastery].

But their [Augustinian] Rule makes no mention of either priesthood or the slit tunicle,[65] or even the name, *canon*; for it was written for nuns.[66] We have sufficient evidence to support our clerical status because the authority of Isidore [of Seville] and the *Conferences of the Fathers* say we are imitators of the Apostles.[67]

[II, 56.] CLUNIAC. What is your authority for saying that their Rule was written for women?

CISTERCIAN. It says so in the Rule's prologue.

CLUNIAC. Their Rule does not have a prologue.

CISTERCIAN. Because they deleted it and changed feminine nouns to masculine.

CLUNIAC. According to these reasons we hold clerical status because that is our due, but they hold it by way of favor. But what priest exercises cure of all their souls and to whom does that Rule order they give more and more respect?

CISTERCIAN. Every priest receives from his bishop the cure of those souls who live within his parish. And because the priest within whose parish a monastery of nuns was located had to celebrate Masses for them, give them Holy Communion, and hear their confessions, this seems to me the reason St Augustine ordered the nuns to give more and more respect to the priest.

CLUNIAC. What you say may very well be true.

[II, 57.] CISTERCIAN. We said above that the clerical state was held as a favor but anyone who wants to investigate further what the clerical status is will find something quite different.

CLUNIAC. And what is clerical status?

CISTERCIAN. It is to officiate at the altar, which does not make for a holy life but which does require not only a holy life today, but a blameless life in the past, that is, the husband of one wife,* and many other qualifications enumerated by the

*1 Tim 3:2.

Apostles and canon law. So it is that St Augustine[68] says: 'People say, "A bad monk makes a good cleric." But I say that it is difficult for a good monk to be a cleric.'* It is like saying, so great is the dignity, so lofty the service of the altar, that even those who are holier than other human beings—that is, good monks—are scarcely worthy of exercising that office. This is what John Chrysostom testified, saying: 'The soul of the priest should be more resplendent than the rays of the sun so that he is never forsaken by the Holy Spirit but can say, "I live; no, not I, but Christ lives in me!" 'Ⴕ That good monks are holier than other human beings, Augustine has shown in one of his letters: 'Just as it is hard to find better men than those who live virtuously in monasteries, so I have not found worse than those in monasteries who have lapsed into sin.'*

*Ep 60,1; CSEL 34:221= Decret. C. 16, q.1,c,36, Yvo, Decretum 7,7; Panormia, 3,180.

Ⴕ Chrysostom, De sacerdotio libri sex; PG 48: 679. Gal 2:20.

*Ep 78:9; CSEL 34:344; Decret. D. 47, q. 9.

In olden times even holy monks were so afraid of accepting clerical status that some fled, others who had been forcefully ordained priests suspended themselves from officiating at the altar,[69] others cut off their ears, in order in this way to evade Holy Orders.[70]

[II, 58.] CLUNIAC. Several chapters are to be found in the *Lives of the Fathers* about men fleeing the clerical status, but there is not one found about anyone seeking the clerical status. What is the rationale, then, that yearnings for priesthood so tickle modern monks that they all want to be ordained to the priesthood whether they are worthy of it or not?

CISTERCIAN. Perhaps it lies in the fact that they take pleasure in the honor attached to the higher status, never giving a thought to its burdens and dangers. The higher status, even if it is held with propriety, is sought after with impropriety. The monk who is worthy of ordination becomes a priest only when coerced, but the unworthy one does not have to be coerced. He ascends to such high status by not only transgressing the Rule and canon law but also by the false testimony of those who present him to the bishop for ordination.

[II, 59.] CLUNIAC. Having collected all the

foregoing reasons and the examples of the Holy Fathers into a unit, we are quite correct in saying that clerical status is not bestowed upon a monk as a favor, but rather, as a favor is denied him. If that most holy office of the altar [priesthood] does not make a man good and holy, what will make him good and holy?

CISTERCIAN. Nothing but faith! That faith which operates through love and in accordance with knowledge.* But those abbots who say that nobody is worthy [of ordination] and yet when the opportunity presents itself have almost all their monks—without discrimination and without election—ordained priests, do not know what they are saying because they sit in judgment on the Rule and canon law; and not only do they sit in judgment on them, they make them look silly. Although our Order nearly agrees with your Customary in the matter of ordaining priests, it still guards more faithfully in other aspects the hallowed decrees of the canons.

*Cf. Gal 5:6, Rm 10:2.

[II, 60.] CLUNIAC. In what other aspects?

CISTERCIAN. In the following: Our priests never celebrate a private Mass with only one person to hear it. Your Customary does not observe this at all because ordinarily [your priests] celebrate private Masses with one person listening, thereby disobeying the Rule and contradicting reason. Pope Sother both gave a precept and appended the reason to the precept when he said: 'As it has been decreed we decree that no priest is to presume to celebrate Mass unless he has at least two others to whom he can say at the proper places, "The Lord be with you." '†

†Decret. D.1, c.61, de consecratione.

CLUNIAC. In our language we address in the plural a single person whom we want to honor.

CISTERCIAN. It would be the height of absurdity for a priest to honor the one listener by greeting him in the plural and saying: 'The Lord be with you—all'; and the other, in answering, would show disrespect for the priest by saying in the singular: 'And with thy spirit'.

[II, 61.] CLUNIAC. Some maintain that the priest's greeting refers to the Church in general.

CISTERCIAN. They don't know what they're

talking about, because if [the priest] were greeting the holy Church [universal], he would never turn to his audience since it has been decreed [that he is to look straight] ahead of him to the East, to the opposite direction for the West, to his right for the South and to his left for the North.

While [we are] on the same subject, your Customary is quite wrong when, contrary to canon law, you have untonsured monks wear albs;[71] in our Order they do not even touch albs.

[II, 62.] CLUNIAC. It is for this purpose that some of our monasteries have unblessed albs to be worn by untonsured monks.

CISTERCIAN. You should not have the vestment unless it is blessed because that is the rule. The vestment is procured therefore by robbing the poor. What unbearable rashness it is that your untonsured monks, when they are serving as attendants for priests celebrating private Masses, at the Offertory offer the celebrating priests the chalice, together with the bread and wine, whereas in our Order they dare not ascend the sanctuary step except to receive Communion: they dare not even touch the wine cruets in which the [communion] wine is kept; nor do they dare touch the cincture of the blessed vestments.

I do not know what to say beyond what I have already said. The usurpation of authority by your Customary has gone beyond all bounds because it does whatever it wants and it puts to one side whatever it does [not] want. The present opportunity compels me to enumerate the things you do which you should not do, and the things you omit which you should not omit. Because of their great number I cannot [give a complete list] since, weary of speaking, I am aiming to end this conversation. I cannot pass over in silence that custom of yours which at times moves me to laughter, that the weekly cooks do not go into the kitchen, nor do they wash the brothers' feet as the Rule commands.* Instead they touch the insteps with three moistened fingers in the

*RB 35:9.

briefest of contacts and draw away their hands immediately.

[II, 63.] CLUNIAC. Washing feet is not necessary these days because each monk washes his own feet beforehand.

CISTERCIAN. If there is no need to wash them, the need to touch them is far less. Now our cooks, obedient to the Rule, wash our feet so that another washing is not necessary.

CLUNIAC. I am waiting for you to talk about the delights of the three remaining senses, seeing that you have already spoken about two.

[II, 64.] CISTERCIAN. You are asking about a way of life of which you have had personal experience, for you yourself know that meat pies, cheesecakes, pancakes, food seasoned with pepper, and pastries, are nothing but delights to the taste and ticklers of the taste buds; they are delicacies, not food for monks, and thus rejected by our Order.[72]

CLUNIAC. What foods are the monks' proper fare?

CISTERCIAN. I am not going to hurry to give you my opinion about monks' fare, but you should consult the Rules of the holy Fathers about what the foods should be and how they should be prepared. When I have finished my investigation of the above sources I will give you an answer when time and place afford opportunity. Our conversation for today is ready to be brought to a close; let us finish here, lest we overstep the bounds of propriety.

END OF PART TWO

PART THREE

[III, 1.] CLUNIAC. Since we have met at a place and time convenient to both of us, lest the opportunity slip by fruitlessly, let us talk about such subjects as will exercise our minds, increase our knowledge and strengthen our way of life. By discussing such matters in this fashion we will not glide into gossip and into the 'idle words' which the Rule forbids 'with a perpetual ban'.* *RB 6:8.

[III, 2.] CISTERCIAN. You give sound advice because if we do not avoid idle words with the utmost care but speak in such a way that our conversation is remembered on the coming Day of Judgment, idle wagging tongue and wandering mind will all too quickly inject themselves into our business, with evil spirits feeding such words to the mind.

Since two men met for serious conversation can just barely exercise such protection over the tongue, whenever several men, old men, young men, and teenagers, all talk at the same time, they cannot possibly keep from idle words. Such a gab-fest among monks contravenes the Gospel, the Apostle and the Rule. [To hold such an informal gab-fest] in the time allotted for leisure contravenes the Rule in particular and the Apostle. [To spend that time] in idle chatter is contrary to the Rule and the Gospel. [Such conversations] are held not by permission but by your own unlawful preference, not by dispensation but by dissipation. Wherefore, the monk whom zeal for his Rule consumes says in his heart: 'It is time to act, O Lord; they have violated your law.'* *Ps 119:126.

The monks of your Order consider it quite legitimate for book scribes, monks who write within the monastery, who absent themselves from the regular Hours, that is, from the work of God, to join in a conversation if they want to, contravening their own law, that is, the Rule, on two counts: by conversing and by writing while the work of God is being performed in choir.

[III, 3.] CLUNIAC. Scribes do not transgress the Rule by not attending the Divine Office because they are obeying the abbot's command.

CISTERCIAN. Both things contravene the Rule: the monks obedience and the abbot's command.

CLUNIAC. What did you say just now? What you said is contrary to what the Rule states, that the abbot must be obeyed even if he orders the impossible.* Thus, both persons believe that both acts are within the law—the abbots if they issue such an order and the monks if they obey the abbots.

*RB 68:1.

CISTERCIAN. [Spiritual] blindness has laid hold on both abbot and monks when they go looking for ways to sin. What else is there to say that Truth has not already said in the Gospel: 'If the blind lead the blind, both will fall into a ditch.'*

*Mt 15:14; Lk 6:39.

[III, 4.] CLUNIAC. If you do not furnish proofs based on reason and authority to uphold what seems to me a silly opinion of yours, it is my judgment and the judgment of others that you advertize your own blindness and errors.

CISTERCIAN. It is mental blindness not to understand these very patent words of the Rule: 'Let nothing be put before the work of God.'* To disdain them once they are understood is pride of mind. The abbots fail in their duty more by issuing such orders than the monks do in obeying them.

*RB 43:3.

CLUNIAC. You are one of those people who have sharp eyes for focusing on other peoples' derelictions, but are bleary-eyed when you look at your own.

[III, 5.] CISTERCIAN. Because you say that my opinion is silly—actually it is not mine at all but the consensus of keenly discerning persons—let us heed the Abbot of Clairvaux as he establishes the limits beyond both abbatical commands and monastic obedience:

*The will of the superior is restrained further, in that while the professing monk promises obedience, it is not absolute obedience; the dominant element is the Rule, none other than the Rule of St Benedict. The superior is not to slacken the reins of his own will on his subjects; rather, he must bear in mind the limits fixed on this matter by the Rule. One last factor he must always have in mind—his right to modify his authority gravitates around this one essential point: that what he does is right. And not haphazardly, but right only as the aforesaid Father instituted, or that it is of a certainty in accordance with what he instituted.** *Pre IV, 10; SBOp 3:260; CF 1:112.

[III, 6.] CLUNIAC. This distinction—that 'what the Holy Father Benedict instituted' or what is 'in accordance with what he instituted'—describes each of our Orders. Your Order holds to what he instituted, which means physical [literal] observances, but our Order holds not to what he instituted but to what is 'in accordance with what he instituted', that is, good usages which, according to him and according to the truth of the matter, are not out of harmony with the Rule. That same man [Bernard] has said: *When a monk is being professed he does not pledge himself solemnly to the Rule. His promise is limited by, 'in accordance with the Rule'.**[1] *However, the same verbal promise is made everywhere [throughout the Order], but since the focusing of the mind on the same objective is not identical in all, doubtless each promises nothing more than what seems to be the holy life of those with whom he has chosen and arranged to live.** He also said: *As long as physical [literal] observances which saint Benedict instituted are on the side of charity, they are immutably fixed and not even the superiors themselves can change them without infraction. If, contrariwise, they are seen to be opposed to charity, is it not manifest justice that something founded for charity's sake be, for charity's sake—where it seems expedient—either left out, or passed over, or changed to something* *Pre XV, 47; SBOp 3:285; CF 1:140.

*Pre XV, 48; SBOp 3:286; CF 1:141.

more profitable at least by those who have been given the insight and entrusted with this duty?*

In all his opinions he defended our Order.

[III, 7.] CISTERCIAN. He said these things either by way of insinuation or else by way of drowziness because 'there were times when even the good Homer nodded momentarily in sleep.'* We can gather by reasonings, direct as well as indirect, that these sentences taken in their literal sense are not in harmony with either reason or authority. The first statement reads as follows: 'When a monk is being professed, he does not pledge himself solemnly to the Rule.' Tell me, what is the Rule?

CLUNIAC. As everyone's common consensus attests, the Rule is nothing other than those precepts by which St Benedict ruled and ordered the lives of his monks, commanding what was to be done and forbidding what was not to be done.

[III, 8.] CISTERCIAN. Your definition can stand because it is open to modification in this way: The Rule is all those precepts and all those precepts bound up together are the Rule. St Benedict says of these precepts: Let him be received [into the community] to whom the Rule, that is those precepts, has been read in its entirety three times, 'then if he promises to observe all things and obey all the commands given him, let him be received.'* This means that he is not to be received unless he promises to observe all the Rule and obey all commands, that is, the precepts of the Customary.

These are Customary precepts properly so-called; they regulate such observances as are not mentioned in the Rule. It seems to me these are pointed out in the eighth degree of humility as, 'the example of superiors'.* The monk is to do nothing innovative, but only that which the Rule or the Customary stipulates, that is, the usage of his superiors, which means of those whom he finds in the monastery [when he arrives], because bad usages, that is, those which contravene reason and authority, are abuse rather than use, for example, idleness and gossiping at the time specified in the Rule for manual labor—

a period during which monks are not allowed to devote themselves even to sacred reading.

The precept relative to manual labor cannot be dispensed other than in the way St Benedict fixed when he said: 'Let things be done in moderation because of the faint-hearted',* or 'The sick or delicate brethren should be assigned a task or craft of such a kind that, on the one hand, they may not be idle and, on the other, not to be overborne by excessive toil so that they will flee [the monastery].*

*RB 48:9.

*RB 48:24.

You have heard the will of our Law-giver, the kind of solemn pledge he wants made at profession. Now hear this: 'Let everyone follow the master, the Rule, in all things.'* But if it is to be followed in all things by all, then it must be solemnly pledged in its entirety at profession. More yet. At the end of the Rule he gives us this precept: 'First of all, fulfill this minimal Rules for beginners.'* This means, Do it all because, as the Apostle says: 'It is not the hearers but the doers of the law who shall be blessed',* 'He who breaks [the law] in one point, is guilty of [breaking it] all,'* which means he is the transgressor of the law.

*RB 3:7.

*RB 73:8.

*Rm 2:13.

*Jm 2:10.

[III, 9.] CLUNIAC. Then all Cistercians are transgressors of their own law because there is not one of them who does not offend in something.

CISTERCIAN. Though one may transgress, he does not therefore despise the law, because he atones for his transgression by making satisfaction as the Rule prescribes. Because there is one of them who can say truthfully: 'I have hated evil and I have loved Your law, O Lord',* he has fulfilled even those precepts of the law which he is not able to fulfill, for what he wants to do but cannot do God counts as done.

*Ps 119:113.

But you Cluniacs, who neither carry out nor wish to carry out the precept of that law which God gave, Saint Benedict proposed, St Gregory recommends, and all the roman popes commend and ratify, and you who hold that law in the lowest esteem, you indeed establish your own system of law and are not even subject to God's justice, for God's will alone and that of St Benedict, which are identical, are those which should be observed in our way of life. Are you aware, even now, of what St Benedict wanted to have solemnly pledged at profession? The whole Rule, half of it or just some part of it?

[III, 10.] CLUNIAC. Nobody is so thick-witted as to doubt what he wanted, if only he gives some thought to his words, quoted earlier. They make it perfectly clear that in profession he wanted the whole Rule pledged and in action he wanted the whole Rule observed, calling it a minimal Rule for beginners.* But when our abbots and our other commentators explain these words they assert that he spoke as he did not because of the actuality of the situation but for the sake of humility. They say that so sublime and perfect is the Rule that no monk in his manner of life lives up to its perfect observance.

*RB 73:8.

[III, 11.] CISTERCIAN. Those who talk like this are not quite aware that perfection is one thing in loving disposition and another in execution.[2] Charity, which casts out fear,* produces that loving disposition and it is simple, which means it lacks constituent parts; because it is a virtue,[3] the habitual state of a well-disciplined mind, it is hard to move.

*1 Jn 4:18.

Those which exists in execution, that is, in the monk's manner of living, are so multiplied that St Benedict scarcely included half of them in his Rule. The other parts are contained in a book which is called *Ordo* or Customary,[4] which St Benedict ordered us to search out in authoritative books so that the Customary would not arrogate to itself something contrary either to reason or to authority.

Because the founders of your Order did not preserve this precept, they have thereby bequeathed to their successors traditions at variance with authority. Thus, not disclaiming humbly but proclaiming truthfully, he said: 'this is a minimal Rule for beginners', and so forth.

[III, 12.] CLUNIAC. Bring into the open some elements of the perfection which exists in execution so that what you've been saying may become clearer.

CISTERCIAN. Our Rule appears to forbid us to have lunch on Sundays in winter-time, but because both the Egyptian Fathers and the Canons of the Church excepted Sundays from the fast we do take an authorized lunch on Sundays. St Benedict passed over in silence the question of whether or not abbots were allowed to take women's monasteries under their direction. But because St Basil in his Rule* issued certain precepts to abbots about directing them and because the examples the Holy Fathers encourage such direction, abbots may, if they wish, act as spiritual guides to nuns.

*Interr. 197-201; PL 103:551-2; ET, Clark, 198-200.

[III, 13.] CLUNIAC. Why has the Cistercian Order forbidden its abbots such direction of nuns, by which [direction] a not insignificant spiritual profit can be produced?[5]

CISTERCIAN. For the very reason that not insignificant spiritual injury may also be produced by such direction. Abbots dread the backsliding of many and those all too frequent chats which take place in the nun's parlor[6] even with scrupulous abbots, contrary to the example of St Benedict, who conversed with his sister only once a year, and always on spiritual matters.*

*Dial. 2.23; Moricca, p. 125.

CLUNIAC. They remember neither St Benedict's example nor St Basil's Rule, which states: 'Insofar as it is in our power to do so, such conversations should be rare and speedily terminated.'*

*Interr. 198; PL 103:551D; Clark, 271.

[III, 14.] CISTERCIAN. Lest the abbot's opinions get you too inextricably tied up in your own error—if he really advanced the opinions which insinuatingly tickle your ears, if I'm not mistaken— let us return to the matters we should be discussing. 'Nobody, when being professed, solemnly pledges the Rule but to live according to the Rule'. By these words 'according to,' [Dom Bernard] wants us to understand not only those observances which St Benedict instituted but all the others which are not at variance with them, insofar as they are good and he calls them 'good customs'. This meaning of the words 'according to' would never harmonize with Blessed Mary's faith in replying to the angel: 'Be it unto me according to your word'.* She looked for no particular benefit beyond what the angel had announced to her.

*Lk 1:38.

The Master says to his pupil either 'Follow my orders', or 'Act according to my orders' and both mean exactly the same thing. And if the pupil does not want to do what the Master ordered but instead what he himself pleases, is the pupil obeying his Master? Not at all. In like manner, if we do not want to perform manual labor at the times specified by our master, the Rule, but we spend our time in sacred reading, are we obeying our master, the Holy Rule? Not at all. The manner in which St Benedict is to be obeyed, and through him God who by means of the Rule enjoined on us the cenobitic obligation, was settled by St Basil in his Rule; after a careful examination of the question, he said:

It is impossible otherwise for our work to be done with precision unless the will of him who enjoined it be remembered, so that in doing his will and diligently discharging our work, we will, as long as we are mindful of him who enjoined the work, be joined to God. For example, just as a blacksmith in forging an axe is mindful of the man whose work he is doing and keeps him always in his thoughts in calculating size, quality, and shape, and conforms his work to the wishes and will of him who commissioned it. If he forgets what or how it was ordered, he will probably make something altogether different from what was ordered.

*So, too, in his actions the Christian should bend all his efforts and all his energy to directing his work according to the will of God who enjoined it and to the end that his actions may be well-pleasing and that he may fulfil his will who gave the order. But if he turns aside from the Rule and spoils the observance of the order, one may from this conclude that he is heedless of God.**

*Interr. 2; PL 492D-93B.

[III, 15.] CLUNIAC. Because you Cistercians judaize in your attitude toward the Rule, you follow the letter that kills.* You make careful note of the authorities who cling to the unsullied letter so that

*2 Co 3:6.
Cf. Gal 2:14.

you can by them support your judaizing.

CISTERCIAN. Take a look at the hissing serpent, who deceived Eve! Through jewish forms of speech, hateful to Christians, he tempts us to turn aside from the truth in our Rule. Why do you judaize by following the letter that kills when it comes to abstaining from meat? Eat meat, lest you judaize; and abstain from the desires of the flesh which wage war against the soul!* What insanity, to ask for allegories in monastic Rules! In order momentarily to meet your obligations, the Abbot of Clairvaux strayed a little distance from the literal meaning and, tickling your ears by insinuation, he posited the antecedents of absurdities rather than [his] opinions.

*1 P 2:11.

[III, 16.] CLUNIAC. What are these absurdities and what are their antecedents?

CISTERCIAN. *Doubtless each monk promises nothing more than what seems to be the devout life of those with whom he has arranged and chosen to life.** Again: *The verbal promise is the same everywhere, but since the heart's intentions are not everywhere identical, the same observance of works cannot everywhere be followed without detriment to salvation and without harm to profession surely.**

*Pre XV, 48; SBOp 3:286.

*Pre XV, 48; SBOp 3:286.

[III, 17.] CLUNIAC. These opinions rest upon reason and are sanctioned by experts.

CISTERCIAN. How does what is based on reason posit what is highly absurd and highly irrelevant? If a monk did not promise at his profession what the words of profession actually mean, but promised rather 'what seems to be the devout life of those with whom he wants to live', then the words of our profession would suit the Norbertines equally as well as ourselves, because their life is devout. Furthermore, if a monk at profession does not promise what the profession actually mean but promises 'what seems to be the devout life of those with whom he has arranged to live', then Horace's verse, 'the mountains gave birth and brought forth a silly mouse',* pronounced at the profession would have just as much value as the words which are ordinarily written

*Ars poetica 139.

and pronounced.

And moreover, if he promises one thing with his mouth but another with his heart, what is his promise but a mockery of him to whom it is made? For example, if someone were to promise you a gold coin but to give a silver one instead, and then were to say: 'I promised of a gold coin with my mouth, but a silver one with my heart', would you not conclude that you were being laughed at? What you do not wish done to yourself, do not do to your neighbor, much less to God who is our neighbor, our Father, our Lord, our Creator and our Redeemer.

Irrational service is not acceptable to God, as the Apostle tells us in commanding 'reasonable service'.* What is more unreasonable, in fact more detestable, than deceitfully to vow something to him of whom the Prophet said: 'deceit was not found in his mouth'.* Deceit is the mouth saying one thing and the heart something different.

[III, 18.] CLUNIAC. Anticipating, as it were in a spirit of prophecy, this counter-argument to his opinions, he [Bernard] ended by saying: *If anyone is agitated and cannot believe this is so, but believing more in, and falling prey to, the stirrings of conscience leaves [the monastery] and seeks a place to fulfill the vows which is his own place and by his own judgement he made but did not discharge, just as I did not praise his departure so do I advise his return.*

[III, 19.] CISTERCIAN. He calls agitated the person who always has his guard up and is anxious about his salvation, paying less attention to the fact that he has, by a promise of heart and mouth, promised the Rule which means the observance of the Rule. Think this over with me and we will find that it is true.

The Rule of St Benedict is very well known among seculars, both lay and clerical, and its reputation extends far and wide. Accordingly, those who come from the world to conversion [to monastic life], enter monasteries with the intention of living as St Benedict taught and of learning, among other

*Rm 12:1.

*1 P 2:22, Isa 53:9.

*Pre XVI, 49; SBOp 3:286-7; CF 1:142.

things, the Rule. They believe that monks live this way, but they are unaware that monks deviate from the Rule, and when, at profession, they hear or read the name of St Benedict, they do not conceive in their minds of any other kind of life than that which St Benedict ordained.

There are not therefore two promises—one of the heart and another of the mouth. Instead, only one and the same pledge, of mouth and of heart, is made of the Rule, and that pledge is of a life regulated by the Rule and not by the Customs of Cluny.

Later on, however, when they hear the interpretation of Rule in Chapter and, analyze their own conversion of life, they are amazed at how different it is from that [Rule] instituted by St Benedict. They are led astray at this stumbling-block of a Rule created by interpretation—and it is nothing less than that—because at the Last Judgment they will not be able to excuse themselves for ignorance of the Rule. Because you have cast off the yoke of the Rule from around your necks, it has no authority at all among you.

[III, 20.] CLUNIAC. You are wrapped up in making accusations at us and have forgotten the answer you put off [earlier]: that is, what are the foods which are suitable for monks?* *I, 64.

CISTERCIAN. Let the Rules of the monks, the Institutes of the Fathers, and St Jerome give an answer to your question. St Basil in his Rule says: *When we speak of temperance, we do not mean that one must completely abstain from food (for this would mean ending life violently). What we do mean is that which provides to life its necessities but not its superfluities; when we flee from what is pleasant and use only those things which bodily necessity demands.** St Columbanus in his Rule says: *Let the monks' food be poor and eaten in the evening; let it avoid satiety and their drink avoid intoxication, so that the food may sustain and not harm life—vegetables and beans, flour and water paste with a small wheat cake—lest the stomach be burdened and*

*Interr. 8; PL 103:500A.

the mind stifled. For, indeed, those who desire eternal rewards should only consider usefulness and use.[7] Cassian says: *We should choose for our food then not only what dampens the heat of lust and arouses it least, but also what is easily prepared and cheaply bought and is suitable to the life of the monks and to their common use.** Jerome says: *Let the food be of poor quality and eaten in the evening. Let it be beans and vegetables, and serve little fishes now and then as a great delicacy. He who seeks Christ eats that Bread and does not spend much effort on things which will change from delicate tidbits into excrement.**

*Inst. 5,23.

*Ep 58, 6, ad Paulinum; CSEL, 54:535.

[III, 21.] CLUNIAC. These rules of the holy Fathers are not well suited to the modern monks' lack of stamina; they have more delicate bodies than our holy Fathers the monks had in the good old days.

CISTERCIAN. Even though men's nature is weaker now, it can still be satisfied by two dishes at one meal.*

*Cf. RB 39:1-3.

CLUNIAC. Nothing is truer than that.

CISTERCIAN. Why then do you have three or four dishes contrary to the Rule's command?

CLUNIAC. Perish the thought! We have only the regulation two dishes, because what is set out in charity between every two monks is not to be reckoned as a dish.[8]

[III, 22.] CISTERCIAN. What you are saying amounts to nothing because according to you clerics and layfolk, who ordinarily eat two to a plate, never eat a dish. For that very dish, which you do not bless because you take it without regard to the Rule, a blessing would be all the more necessary. Our order banishes from our dining room confections concocted of expensive and aromatic spices which delight our taste and smell. They are entirely unsuitable for monks, except, perhaps, for those who are ill in the infirmary.

You have three little bells in your dining room; we have only one and it suffices. Two of yours—one to announce that the second regulation dish is about to be served and another to announce the wine—are superfluous, but as the poet puts it: 'Over-abundance makes allowances for silliness'.*

Horace, Ep 1, 18, 29.

CLUNIAC. Many things seem superfluous to you now which seemed necessary when you were in our Order.

[III, 23.] CISTERCIAN. By reason alone in those days, nowadays by reason and experience I see these excesses. Aromatic smoke [incense] which is used all too frequently in expensive thuribles to delight the nostrils seemed to me then to be partly, but now to be wholly, superfluous, because our Order, except at the sacrament of the altar and on feast days only, never uses it and we suffer thereby no harm either to our body or to our soul. The expense which is superfluously laid out for frankincense and myrrh is taken from what supplies the poor in their need. Those bows all around the choir, those processions through the middle of the choir with your back all bowed over are rejected by our Order as excessively pious and unbecoming.[9]

It remains now for us to finish our conference by talking about the delights of touch. Contrary to the Rule's command, you dress in soft, warm fur garments, delightful to the touch, and pay no attention to Christ's words. 'These who dress in soft garments are in kings houses.'*

Mt 11:8. Cf. RB 55:4-7.

[III, 24.] CLUNIAC. Holy Scripture attests to this when it says: 'And the Lord made for them tunics of skin.* Since tunics of skin are still tunics, we use them not contrary to, but according to, the precept of the Rule.

CISTERCIAN. God made for them 'tunics-of-skin', but he did not make tunics for them, because a tunic-of-skins is not a [simple] tunic—which I could prove by Aristotlelian rule, but because I am a monk, I must avoid a show of arrogance.[10]

CLUNIAC. Perhaps you are speaking of this rule: whatsoever items are predicated conjunctively, those same items are disjunctively predicable, unless (a) there is an opposition in the adjunct, or (b) it is a case of accidental predication. Here there is neither opposition in the adjunct nor [is] predication accidental.

[III, 25.] CISTERCIAN. What, in accord with general usage—the norm of speaking—does this noun 'tunic' signify? Is it not a garment woven from woolen yarn? And what is one 'of skin' except a garment sewn together from pelts? Thus, these two are opposed to each other in such a way that if 'of skin(s)' is affirmed of anything at all, 'tunic' is thereby removed, that is, denied of that same subject. In this predication, therefore, by which it is stated: 'God made from them tunics of skins', there is an opposition [to the subject] in the adjunct. 'Tunic' can be taken for a 'garment' too, namely, as a special class (a 'species') [is taken] in place of a general class (a 'genus') and thus, that turn of speech will be 'accidental', that is, 'figurative'.[11]

Since therefore in the general usage of Latins and Germans the word 'tunic' means a garment woven from woolen yarn, it is clear that you do not have tunics-of-skins on the Rule's authorization; the expounder of the Rule attests to this also.

*I, n. 58.

In like manner, you do not have *frocci** and linsey-woolsey garments by authorization of the Rule. That article of clothing you call a cowl is neither a cowl nor a scapular. It is not a cowl because, although it lacks sleeves, it does not contain six yards[12] [of cloth] as required by Pope Boniface.* It is not a scapular because it is so wide that it covers not only the shoulder but also the whole arm. It is not, therefore, a regulation garment.[13]

*Council of Rome (610); Mansi 10: 505; PL 80: 105-106.

Why should I be surprised that you do not observe the chapter relative to clothing when you observe none, or very few, of the Rule's chapters? If you do not observe the precepts of the Rule because you do not want to, you are proud, as the Abbot of Clairvaux claimed in that very treatise which you say praises your Order. In this same deposition he says that if you do not observe the Rule because you are unable to do so, you are blameless. God will attest to what you are capable of by his own witnesses whom he raised up against you in order to convict you on the grounds of your capabilities.

[III, 26.] CLUNIAC. Who are these witnesses?

CISTERCIAN. Not only monks of our Order, but also delicate women who observe the Rule as it really is and imitate [the monks of] our Order.[14]

CLUNIAC. I wonder how highborn ladies, much pampered in the world, can endure such a harsh life.

CISTERCIAN. Holy love conquers all. I in my turn wonder how the Cluniacs can hate the Rule as it really is and yet profess, study, read, and interpret it.

CLUNIAC. Heaven forbid that we hate the Rule.

CISTERCIAN. There is no doubt whatsoever that if you loved the Rule as it really is, you would never rank it after the traditions of men. A master's honor is one key to wisdom. How can you honor your master, the Rule, when you outrank even its reasonable precepts by your absurd Customary? What would you do to your pupil if he did not obey your commands and heeded others more than you?

CLUNIAC. I would punish him for being arrogant and insolent.

[III, 27.] mCISTERCIAN. You yourself have pronounced the verdict of damnation on yourself. In order to avoid it, my advice to you is to enter some monastery in which you can, among other things, validate your first pledge of fidelity, which up to now you have rendered invalid. Henceforth do your duty and pay the Lord your God the vows spoken through your lips.*

CLUNIAC. Are you urging me to forsake my first love and abandon a fellowship of mutual love?

CISTERCIAN. You should never abandon love. True love is not confined to one place because it is not changed by a change of place.

Love itself for very good reasons sometimes separates bodies but not hearts. For example, I, who for the sake of observing the Rule left my brothers in body though not in soul, entreat God every day in my prayers on their behalf, with a special prayer for them.

[III, 28.] CLUNIAC. Please recite that special prayer. Perhaps it will edify me.

*1 Tm 5, 12; Ps 66: 13-14. Cf. Bernard, Ep I. 9.

CISTERCIAN. All right. 'O Lord, have mercy, have mercy on your servants N. and, guide them to the path of eternal salvation, so that with you as the Giver they may seek what is pleasing to you and with all their strength bring it to perfection. Grant, O Lord, that they may love you and their neighbor as much as you have commanded, and grant them an enlightened zeal for you.'

CLUNIAC. Your way of thinking doesn't deceive me. From your little prayer here I understand that you think your former brothers in religion have gone astray and do not have an enlightened zeal for God.

CISTERCIAN. What is going astray except leaving the straight path which the Rule, by its very name [regula—a straight measuring rod] teaches, and walking instead along the crooked road of Custom? Does your [Cluniac] zeal for God operate in accordance with knowledge, does your zeal which is aflame in the service of the traditions of men but lukewarm in the service of the law of God which is the Rule? If we strive to the death for the Rule, as we are obliged, we will be crowned with befitting martyrdom.*

*Cf. 2 Tm 2:5.

[III, 29.] CLUNIAC. I would stir up my brothers to more than a little excitement, inciting controversy and contention if, following your advice, I were to leave my brothers and enter one of your Order's monasteries.

CISTERCIAN. From that you can realize that they do not love you in the right way. If, as says blessed Gregory, they did love you with true charity, they would most assuredly rejoice to see you pass on to better things, things more approaching salvation.* Do not become agitated where there is nothing to fear.* Accept that feeling of assurance given to you by the abbot of Clairvaux who said:

*Source unknown.
*Ps 14:5 & 53:5.

> Listen to your heart, examine your intentions, as to why you left your Order, your brothers, your home. If you left in order to lead a stricter, a more direct, a more perfect life, have no fear, because you have not looked back; rather you can glory with the Apostle as he says: 'Forgetting what I have left

behind, reaching out to what lies ahead, I press on to the palm of victory.'*

*Ph 3:13-14.
Bernard, Ep. 1,9.

CLUNIAC. The abbot's words are in harmony with your advice.

[III, 30.] CISTERCIAN. Urban II sent a letter to the brethren of Rottenbuch concerning the monk Eppo. In this letter he detailed the limits of his privilege to them, declaring that it was lawful to go to a place where the monastic observance was greater and the purpose of the vow more exalted; to return [to the first monastery] was unlawful because that would be to apostatize.[15] Gratian, the legislator for canons, says the same thing when he says: 'A monk is free to pass to a stricter monastery for his soul's profit'.[16] Both [Cassian's] conference on definitions and the expositor of the Rule agree on this.[17]

CLUNIAC. What an abundance of authorities you do have! After listening to the first ones, I was under the impression you didn't have any more.

[III, 31.] CISTERCIAN. We have been listening to testimonies of authorities. It remains for us to hear what answer rational reflection will give in this business of ours.

All our monasteries are, so to say, a single body, because they are ruled by one head, together with advice communicated annually at our General Chapter. This gives the religious observance of our Order continuity.[18] But because your abbots are without a head, as it were headless,[19] having no master above themselves, each does as he pleases in his own monastery, each puts to one side what he pleases. For this reason, religious observance in your monasteries has no continuity.

The appointment and deposition of abbots of your Order are treated along with various troublesome cases by bishops as if they were in the public domain, which is unbefitting the monastic way of life.[20] But among ourselves these matters are kept to ourselves, done by ourselves in secret, in a way befitting the Order.

Because you collect tithes from other men, revenues from mills and farms, taxes from peasants (even the peasants you own)[21], from this multiplicity of possessions usually arise the disturbances which upset the monks' holy sabbaths.[22] Because our Order renounces all of these things, it enjoys monastic peace and quiet with its legitimate possessions. And because your monasteries are located not just in towns but even in cities and in places contiguous to cities,[23] while very few of ours are, we can on that account be called solitaries and contemplatives in comparison to you, although you said: 'Our Order is contemplative and yours is active'.

Furthermore, because women go freely in and out of your monasteries, while they are excluded completely from ours, and because monks of your Order speak freely with each other while monks of our Order speak with nobody except the abbot and prior, therefore the death which enters the soul through the windows of the body has easier access in your monasteries than in ours. Because of the better observance, therefore, Christ prefers to have his betrothed, that is, the faithful soul, dwell in our monasteries rather than in yours. It is no wonder, since a king of this earth prefers to have not only his betrothed but a golden vessel which he dearly likes kept in a well-guarded chamber rather than in a less well-guarded one. There is no golden vessel dearer, however, to Christ than that living vessel which he himself redeemed with his blood.

On this account Christ is more than a little offended when, for a golden chalice—the product of theft—Masses, litanies, community and private prayers are said; but for a brother seduced, pulled down, and pushed back into the world by the first and greatest of all thieves—the devil—there are no Masses, no litanies, no community or private prayers.

Are these not clear indications that gold is loved more than the soul of a brother for whom Christ died? Why are you so quiet? Why are you not full of talk as you ordinarily are?

[III, 32.] CLUNIAC. I do not know what to say, except this—truth can be tied up temporarily but it cannot be conquered.

CISTERCIAN. In my judgment I have explained to you—not too eloquently but sufficiently—how the inner man in me feels about both Orders. From here on, let the Abbot of Clairvaux speak to us in his letter, and in his own expressive words describe both Orders. Pay close attention to his words and signs and wonders:

B[ERNARD], ABBOT OF CLAIRVAUX
TO R[OBERT], A YOUNG MAN:

If anyone wonders how a shy, simple, and timid boy dared desert both his vows and his monastery contrary to the will of his brothers, the authority of his master, and the Rule's command, he should also wonder how David was cheated of his holiness, Solomon deceived of his wisdom, and Samson deprived of his great strength. What, after all, is there to be wondered about if he who expelled the first man from his happy homeland by cunning was able to snatch by cajolery a young man in a dreadful and vast, empty place? Moreover, outward appearances did not deceive him as they did the old men of Babylon, nor the love of money as Geizi, nor hunger for glory as Julian the Apostate; instead, holiness victimized him, religion seduced him, the authority of his elders debauched him. How, you ask?

To begin with, a certain Grand Prior was dispatched; outwardly, he appeared in sheep's clothing, but inwardly he was a ravening wolf. Having deceived the shepherds into thinking he was a sheep, alas, he was set loose in single combat, a wolf on a little lamb. Nor did the single little lamb take flight from the wolf, whom he also took to be a sheep. What happened next?

He set about attracting, alluring, and flattering [the young sheep]; the preacher of a new gospel recommended gluttony and condemned thrift; he called voluntary poverty wretchedness and labelled fasts, vigils, silence, and manual labor folly. On the other hand, he did not censure lazy 'contemplation'; he classified overeating, talkativeness, inquisitiveness, and finally intemperance as discretion. He posed the questions 'When is God pleased with our sufferings? Where do the Scriptures order anyone to kill himself? What kind of religion is it to dig the soil, to clear woods, to cart manure? Is the Saviour's opinion not: 'I desire mercy and not sacrifice'*, and 'I do not wish the death of the sinner but that he may turn from his sin and live'*, and 'Blessed are the merciful because they shall obtain mercy.'* Why did God create food if he does not let us eat it? Why did he give us bodies if he forbade us to keep up their strength? Lastly, to whom is that man valuable who looks upon himself as worthless? What man, knowing himself healthy, hates his own flesh?

*Mt 9:13, 12:7, Hos 6:6.
*Ez 33:11.
*Mt 5:17.

Tricked by such allegations, the trusting boy is led astray, he follows his seducer; he is led to Cluny, given a haircut, shaved, bathed. He is stripped of his countryish, soiled, well-worn habit and dressed in a new and elegant one, and like this is received into the cloister.

But with what sort of honor, with what triumph and what deference do you reckon [they received him]? He was shown more deference than anyone in his age group. A sinner, because of what he desired in his soul, he was honored as if he were a conquering hero returning from the wars. He was raised on high, settled in a better than middling rank so that this teen-ager took precedence over many of his seniors.[24] Favors were heaped upon him and so was flattery. The community as a whole congratulated him. Everyone rejoiced like victors sharing the spoils, the captured booty.

Good Jesus, what a lot of things were done for the ruination of one little soul! Whose heart is so hard it does not melt at all this? Whose inner eye, no matter how spiritual, is not upset by them? Who would possibly examine his own conscience in the midst of all this? Who, finally, surrounded by so much pomp, would have the strength to recognize reality or to acquire humility?

While all this was going on a delegation was dispatched to Rome on his behalf. Pressure was put upon the apostolic authority, and so that the Pope would not refuse his assent, they conveyed to him the notion that [the young man] had been offered [as an oblate] to the monastery by his parents while he was still a child. There was nobody on hand to refute this—no one even waited for a witness to contradict it. The case was decided in favor of the plaintiff while those who were being judged [the defendants] were not present.

Those who had committed wrong were vindicated; those who had suffered lost the lawsuit while the culprit was set free without making amends. The foolish verdict of absolution was ratified by a harsh exemption, news of which confirmed the indecisive boy's ill-advised stability and the waverer's security. The tenor of the [papal] letters, the essence of the verdict, the decision of this whole lawsuit is this: they who stole may keep and those who have lost may remain silent.

Meanwhile, a soul for whom Christ died must perish, just because the Cluniacs want it so. He makes profession after profession; he vows something he will not keep; he promises something he is not going to observe. And because the first contract was nullified his transgression is doubled by the second.

He will come, he who re-judges wrong judgements, he who will refute what has been unlawfully sworn, who will render verdicts favorable to those enduring injury, who will judge the poor justly and will inflict censure, he will come in righteousness, on behalf of the meek of the earth. He who threatened us through the Prophet when he said in the psalm: 'When I shall have fixed a time, I will judge in accordance with justice'*—he will most certainly come. What will he do about wrongful verdicts, this one who shall judge justice itself? He will come, I say, the Day of Judgment will come; pure hearts will avail more than wily words and a good conscience more than a full purse, for that judge will not be wheedled by words or persuaded by gifts.

*Ps 75:2.

Lord Jesus, I appeal to your court; I wait in anticipation of your verdict; Lord God of Sabaoth,

*Cf. Ps 7:9.

I commit my case to you, who judge justly and try the reins and hearts;* whose eyes, as they will not deceive, cannot be deceived. You behold your own, you behold them because they seek your own.

You are well aware of the gnawing compassion by which I attended him in all his temptations. You are aware of the number of groans with which I hammered on your gracious ears, how I was burned up, tormented and prostrated by each of his aberrations, emotional upheavals, and discontentments. Even now I am afraid that it was all for nothing. For I think, insofar as I can tell by my own experience, that for a young man already seething and becoming arrogant by himself, emotional upheavals of this kind did his body no good and these enticements to all kinds of honor did his soul no good. And so, Lord Jesus, my judge, O Lord, let my sentence come forth from your countenance, let your eyes look upon the righteous.

May they see and judge which has more legal validity—the vow of a father on behalf of his son or [the vow] of a son on his own behalf, especially when the son vowed the better thing.

Let your servant and our legislator, Benedict, also decide which was more in accord with the Rule—[the vow] made for a very young child, who knew absolutely nothing about it, or one which he knowingly made for himself later on, when he had come of age and could answer for himself; though, in fact, there is no doubt that he was promised [to Cluny]—not given. Nor was the petition, which the Rule prescribes, drawn up on his behalf by his parents, nor was his hand together with a petition wrapped with the altar-cloth, that he was in this way offered to God in the presence of witnesses.

The Cluniacs point to a piece of land which they say was donated with him and for him. But if they received him together with the land, how is it they did not keep him together with the land? Is it perhaps that they decided that they wanted the offering more than the offspring and valued the land more than the soul? Furthermore, what was the oblate of a monastery doing in the world outside? Why was God's ward exposed to the devil? Why was one of God's lambs discovered exposed to the teeth of the wolf?

Robert, you are your own witness that you came to Cîteaux not from Cluny but from the world. You begged, you petitioned, you knocked, but, much against your wishes, you were put off for two years because you were too young. When the time had gone by patiently and without any bad reports, at long last, in the midst of prayers and, if you remember, tears, you succeeded in gaining the mercy so-long awaited and you gained the entrance you had longed for so much.

You were tested over the ensuing year in all patience as the Rule stipulates, you behaved with perseverance and without complaint. At the end of the year you were professed of your own free will. Having then for the first time cast off your secular garments, you received the habit of religion.

You scatter-brained boy! What has bedazzled you into disregarding the vows which adorned your lips? Will you not either justify yourself by your own mouth or by your own mouth condemn yourself? Why are you so worried about your parent's but heedless of your own, when you have to be judged by your mouth not by his, you will have to live up to your vows not his?

Why does someone flatter you about an apostolic absolution to no avail, you whose conscience divine wisdom holds bound. 'Nobody,' he says, 'putting his hand to the plough and looking back is fit for the kingdom of God.* Will they who convinced you not to look back be the ones who say to you, 'Bravo! Bravo!'?   *Lk 9:62.

My dear son, if sinners cajole you, do not give in to them? Do not believe every spirit.* You need   *Cf. 1 Jn 4:1. many people, but let only one in a thousand be your [spiritual] adviser. Seize opportunities, spit back blandishments, shut your ears to sycophants, ask yourself about yourself, because you know yourself better than anyone else does. Pay attention to your heart, determine your purpose [in life], consider the truth.

Let your conscience answer you why you went away, why you forsook your Order, your brothers, your home, and me who am not only akin to you by blood but still closer akin in spirit. If you left in order to live a more difficult, a more upright, a more perfect life, put your mind at rest, for you have not looked back except to boast with the Apostle, who said: 'Forgetting what is behind me, I strain forward to what is before me. I press on towards the finish, for the prize [of God's heavenly call].* However, if the situation is otherwise, be not high-minded but afraid,* because, if I may mention your little lapse, to the degree that you pamper yourself in excessive food and clothing, in idle words, in unrestrained travel for curiosity's sake beyond what you in fact promised—beyond what you promised, and observed, when you were with us—there is no doubt you are looking back, you are avoiding the issue, you are apostatizing.

My son, I say this not in order to disquiet you further, but in order to warn you as I would a well-beloved son, because even though you have a great many school-masters in Christ, you do not have many fathers. If you do not mind me saying so, through my word and example I gave you life in religion. I fed you with milk which at that time was the only kind of food you could digest.* I would have given you bread as well, had you stayed until you were grown. But alas! You were weaned much too hastily and out of season, and I am afraid that everything I nurtured by coaxing, strengthened by reproof or encouragement, made whole by prayer is even now fading away, sickening and dying. And I weep, unhappy not so much at the hurt of lost labor as the unhappy loss of a hurt child. Does it please you that someone who expended no labor whatever on you is now gloating over you? My plight is not unlike that of the prostitute before Solomon, that is, she whose little boy was taken from her in stealth by another who had killed her own offspring when she

*Ph 3:13-14.

*Cf. Rm 11:20, 12:3, 15:5.

*Cf. 1 Co 3:2.

smothered it during the night.* You too were cut away from my bosom, from my womb. I weep for you, borne away; you, violently uprooted, I ask back. I cannot forget my vital organs, for when more than a small part of them has been removed, the part that remains surely cannot do otherwise than be wrenched with pain. *1 K 3:16-28.

For what particular advantage to you, for what dire reason did they set themselves against us, our enemies, whose hands are covered with blood, whose sword has pierced my soul,* whose teeth are instruments of war and arrows, whose tongue is a sharpened sword? If I have ever in any way offended them they have repaid me in full. I have received more than equitable punishment. If ever I did any such thing at their expense, I have now received exactly the same from them. To tell the truth, they did not take from me bone of my bones or flesh or my flesh; rather, they took from me the joy of my heart, the fruit of my spirit, the crown of my hope and, as I seem to myself to feel, the half of my soul. And for what reason? *Cf. Lk 2:35.

Perhaps they pitied you and, offended that a blind man was leading the blind, they took your guidance upon themselves lest you perish in my train. What a hurtful love, what a harsh necessity. They so loved your salvation that they struck at mine. My destruction is a prerequisite for your salvation! I pray God that they save you, independent of me! Would that you live even if I die! But how?

Does salvation, then, consist more in elegant clothes and in sumptuous food than in frugal fare and modest dress? If soft and warm furs, if finely woven and expensive cloth, if long sleeves and a full hood, if fur bedspreads and soft woolen shirts make a saint, why am I wasting time here and not following you? But, these are remedies for the sick, not the weapons of fighting men. 'Behold, they who dress in soft garments are in kings' houses.'* Wine and white bread, honeyed wine, and rich foods cater to the body, not to the soul. The body but not the soul is fattened from frying pans. Many fathers in Egypt *Mt 11:8.

served God over long stretches without [even] fish. Pepper, ginger, cumin, sage and a thousand other such spices delight the palate but they inflame the passions. Will you place my safety on such things, will you spend your teenage years safely in their midst?

Salt with hunger is spice enough for the wise and sober man intent upon the spiritual life. It is necessary to compound, out of I do not know what exotic flavors, more and more conglomerations which will refresh the palate, tickle the gullets and stimulate the appetites, only if one does not have to wait for meals.

You ask, 'What will he do who cannot do otherwise?' Fine! I realize that you are delicate and also that, accustomed to these ways, you are not now capable of more austere things. But, suppose you were to do the best you could? You ask, 'How'?

Listen! Stand up, put on your belt, banish idleness, show your strength, exercise your arms, unclasp your folded hands, do a little work, and right away you will realize that you hanker only for the food which relieves your hunger and not for that which tickles your palate. Physical labor restores to food the flavor of which inactivity deprives it. Many things you reject when idle, you eat heartily after hard work. Just as idleness begets excessive delicacy, hard work begets hunger. Strangely enough, hunger renders sweet foods which fastidiousness renders unsavory. Greens, beans, pottage, and any kind of bread fit to eat, with water, are not satisfying foods for the fastidious eater, but to the hard worker they seem choice treats.

By now, perhaps, unaccustomed to our tunics, you doubtlessly dread them because they are cold in winter and hot in summer. But, have you read that, 'He who fears the hoary frost, the snow shall fall upon him'?*

*Jb 6:16.

You dread vigils, fasts, and manual labor, but these things are very small indeed to someone who meditates on everlasting flames. Finally, calling outer darkness to mind makes one stop dreading solitude. If you ponder the account one day owed for every idle word, silence will be far from displeasing; when *everlasting wailing and gnashing of teeth are kept in the mind's eye, a straw mattress and a feather bed are one and the same thing. And lastly, if, as the Rule commands, we watch faithfully throughout the night, singing God's praise in psalms, the bed will be very hard indeed on which you do not sleep peacefully. If you work with your hands as much every day as you vowed you would, the food you refuse to eat cheerfully will be wretched indeed.*

Arise, soldier of Christ, arise. Brush off the dust, return to the battle from which you fled. You will fight much more valiantly after your flight and you will triumph all the more gloriously.* *Ep 1, 3-13; SBOp 7:3-10.

[III, 32.] CLUNIAC. You asked me to pay close attention to the words [of Dom Bernard], to mark well his inner meanings. I did pay attention, I did mark well. What I attended and marked insinuate to me that, in the opinion of the composer of the letter, the Abbot [of Clairvaux], the Grand Prior [of Cluny], seducer of the young man and preacher of a new gospel, by praising our Order censured it and by censuring yours, he was praising it.

CISTERCIAN. Your understanding holds to the straight road, as the Abbot himself attests when he says: 'If, therefore, salvation consists more in elegant clothes and rich food than in frugal fare and in modest clothing, why am I wasting time here and why do I not follow you.'* And so on. Rich fare is altogether contrary to the precept which St Augustine formulates in his Rule. *Ep 1, 10.

[III, 34.] CLUNIAC. What is that?

CISTERCIAN. Exercise dominion over your flesh by fasting and abstaining from food and drink as much as your health permits.[25]

CLUNIAC. Those who have professed this Rule [the Norbertines] do not observe this penitential precept.

CISTERCIAN. If they do not observe it they are violating their profession, and because they want to be preachers, as their shortened habits indicate, they are obligated to observe the Rule which that famous preacher observed and proposed that preachers observe: 'I chastise my body' and so on.* If the chosen vessel chastised his body by abstinence and brought it under subjection by manual labor,[26] lest in preaching to others he would himself become disqualified, what are we to think should be done with those preachers who know they are among the many called and do not know whether they are among the few chosen?*

*1 Co 9:27.

*Ac 9:15.

[III, 35.] CLUNIAC. I am of the opinion that for cleric-preachers and those who have charge of churches—because they live in the world and endure more temptations than monks—abstention from meat, wine and the richer foods is more necessary than it is for monks, though they say that they are allowed such foods while the monks very seldom are.

CISTERCIAN. Your thinking is correct. The falling away of teachers is the ruination of those who should be taught and the straying of guides is the downfall of those who should be guided.

CLUNIAC. The life of the preacher-cleric, therefore, is a roadway fraught with danger, and the life of the monk is, so to say, a highway without roadblocks.

CISTERCIAN. Because of this only the [spiritually] advanced should preach and direct the people of God, because in the world's slippery and dangerous road they do not easily totter.

[III, 36.] CLUNIAC. Who is properly said to be [spiritually] advanced?

CISTERCIAN. Those who follow the counsel of Christ who said; 'If you wish to be perfect, go and sell,' and so on.*

*Mt 19:21.

CLUNIAC. Good monks, then, who have given up themselves and all they possess for the sake of Christ, are the [spiritually] advanced.

CISTERCIAN. Just so. Because 'monk' is a term for [spiritual] advancement and 'cleric' is the term for an office which only the advanced should hold, for that reason the clerical state rightly belongs to monks. On the evidence of Isidore [of Seville] and the *Conferences of the Fathers*, monks are imitators of the Apostles, who were the first clerics in the church and to whom the Lord said: 'You who have left all and followed me,' and so on.* So it is that, when they become monks, they are signed with the tonsure,[27] the clerical sign of advancement.* For then they enter in God's portion and become heirs of God. Possessing the very God by whom they are possessed, they hold no earthly property and yet they possess all things in company with those—the Apostles —whose imitators they are.*

*Mt 19:27.

*Conf. 18,5 (Abbot Piamun)

*Cf. 2 Co 6:10.

[III, 37.] CLUNIAC. What you say is vastly different from the general opinion which even Master Hugh [of St Victor]* confirms. Almost everyone says that the monks' way of life is penitential, that their habit is penitential, and that the tonsure for them is not a clerical but a penitential mark.

*De sacramentis 3, 4; PL 176: 422D-23A.

CISTERCIAN. I, on the contrary, say that I am quite prepared to confirm on the basis of reason and authority that the monks' life is apostolic, that their habit is angelic, and that the tonsure they have is a clerical mark and also a mark of spiritual advancement. General opinion has deceived Master Hugh, as has perhaps the black habit of the Cluniac order which, because of its blackness gives the appearance of being penitential. St Jerome, in writing to a monk and cleric gives the opposite advice on the color of both the Cluniac and Norbertine habits when he said: 'Keep both your habits and your life white.'[28]

[III, 38.] CLUNIAC. Here you go again, praising your Order even for the color [of its habit], when it is neither white nor black, but grey. Perhaps you are looking for an opportunity to by-pass the proof you promised.

CISTERCIAN. Never. I have at hand both reason and authority, by which I shall prove all three.

You do not doubt that the life led by cenobitic monks is apostolic, because you have already agreed to this on the authority of Isidore who said: 'There are two kinds of monks; one is cenobitic, the other eremitic; eremites imitates Elijah and John the Baptist, cenobites imitate the apostles.'*

*Etymol.; PL 82: 293.

If this authority is not enough for you, listen to Cassian who gives a more lengthy explanation in the following narrative: *The coenobites' discipline had its beginning in the days when the Apostles preached. For so great was the multitude of people who believed in Jerusalem that it is described in the Acts of the Apostles this way: 'The multitude of believers was of one heart and of one soul, nor did any of them say that any of his possessions was his own, for all things were in common among them.** They sold their possessions and property and divided them all according to need'.* And again: 'For neither was there anything among them that they lacked, for as many as possessed lands and houses sold them and brought the money for the things they sold and laid it before the feet of the Apostles.'**

*Ac 4:32.

*Ac 2:45.

*Ac 4:34-35.

The whole Church, I say, was then like those few who are now, with difficulty, to be found in cenobitic monasteries. But with the death of the Apostles, the great number of believers began to grow cold, especially those had come to the faith of Christ from among strange and foreign peoples. Because of the rudimentary state of their faith and their inveterate pagan habits, the Apostles asked of them nothing more than that they should abstain from things sacrificed to idols, from fornication, from things strangled, and from blood.* So it was that a permissiveness conceded to the Gentiles because of the infirmity of first faith began by degrees to contaminate the perfection of the Church which existed in Jerusalem; and the fervor of that first faith cooled down as the numbers of natives and foreigners daily increased. Not only those who flocked to belief in Christ but even those who were leaders in the Church began to relax their strictness.

*Ac 15:29.

Some, thinking that what they saw conceded to the Gentiles because of their weakness was also promised themselves, believed they would lose nothing if they followed the faith and confessed Christ with all their possessions and belongings. There were those, however, in whom apostolic fervor continued, those who kept in their minds that original perfection, who departed from their cities and from communication with those who believed they could neglect a more disciplined life for themselves and for the Church of God. They began to live together in suburban and more remote places, and those things which they remembered the Apostles having instituted throughout the whole body of the Church, they began to practise privately and uniquely. Thus began the discipline of those disciples of whom we have spoken, who separated themselves from the spreading infection. As time slowly passed, these men, separated from the crowd of believers because they abstained from marriage and severed communication with their families and the life-style of this world, were called MONAXOI or solitaries from their strict way of lone and solitary life.* *Conf. 18.5.

[III, 39.] CLUNIAC. Another reason for the name monk, a reason by which you proved that all who profess the Rule of St Augustine are monks, is given by the author of that very Rule, who says: 'How good and pleasant it is for brothers to dwell as one!'* From this word in the psalm, they are called monks.*

*Ps 133:1.
*Aug., Enarr in ps. 132; CC40:1927.

CISTERCIAN. By both reasons they are rightly called monks because, dwelling in their monasteries, they are separated from those who live in the world and, dwelling as a unit, they are brothers. Here you have it that the monks' life is apostolic: they live the life which the apostles led with those they converted by preaching and of whom it is written: 'They were all of one heart and one soul and they had all things in common'.* Because monks have left all things for God and, accordingly, are of God's portion and have God for their portion, they are, on this account as it were, clerics in fact, although before receiving the mark of the cleric they lack the name and office.[29] Clerics are so called because they are of the Lord's portion or because they have God as their portion, as St Jerome bears witness, saying: *The Greek* cleros *is called* sors [portion] *in Latin. For this reason* clergy *is the term used because they are in the Lord's portion, or because the Lord himself is the clerics' portion or part. He who is the Lord's portion or has the Lord as his portion must show himself to be such*

*Ac 4:32.

a person that he may both possess God and be possessed by God. He who possesses the Lord and says with the Prophet: 'The Lord is my portion'* can hold on to nothing other than the Lord. If he holds to something other than the Lord, the Lord will not be his portion. For instance, if he holds on to gold or silver or possessions or household furniture, with portions such as these the Lord will not deign to be his portion.*

*Lam 3:24;
Ps 119:57.
Cf. Ps 73:26.

*Ep 52,2;
CSEL 56:421.
Cf. Decret.
C. XII, q. I.
cc. 5, 7.

[III, 40.] CLUNIAC. It seems to me that monks become clerics before they become monks, because before making their monastic profession they receive the clerical mark, that is, the tonsure, through [they receive] the same priestly blessing in the same manner as do all other clerics.

CISTERCIAN. Your surmise is correct. But you should know that the orthodox have used this word, cleric, with a wide, a narrow, and a mediate meaning.

It has a wide meaning when we say: every recipient of the tonsure is a cleric because of his priestly blessing. St Jerome used the narrow meaning when he said: 'Clerics feed the sheep, I am fed'.* He had in mind bishops and their co-workers to whom has been committed the cure of souls among the people of God. In line with the mediate meaning St Jerome said to a monk living in a monastery: 'Live in the monastery in such a way that you may deserve to be a cleric,' in order, that is, that you may be worthy to serve at the altar.*

*Ep 14.8; CSEL 54:55.

*Ep 125,17;
CSEL 56:136.

[III, 41.] CLUNIAC. What do you have to say about murderers who while in the world performed the public penance which is called *carrina*[30] and whom canonical decrees debar from the clerical status? Having come to conversion of life, they receive in monasteries the mark of the cleric, that is the tonsure. Are they clerics?

CISTERCIAN. Certainly they are clerics, but they cannot ascend to any clerical grade beyond the first. They can only become porters. If written proof is discovered which denies them clerical status, then the words clerical status carry the mediate meaning, it means service at the altar. All tonsured monks are clerics.[31]

[III, 42.] CLUNIAC. Why did you say 'tonsured monks'? Are there now other monks than tonsured ones?

CISTERCIAN. There are those whom we today call brothers, who are, without doubt, cenobitic monks because they are brothers dwelling in unity. In this category there were long ago hermit-monks who lived apart from each other in individual cells and, as country people have today, so they had priests to whom they came with their offering every Sunday to hear Mass and to receive the most holy Communion of the body and blood of Christ. So it is that St Jerome, while he was one of them during his youth (for he was a hermit for four years), wrote to the hermit Heliodorus who had defected from the eremitic life, and among other things he said: 'The case of monks is different from that of clerics. Clerics live from the altar. If I bring no gift to the altar I am as the barren tree which has had the axe laid to its root.'*

*Ep 14:8; CSEL 54:55.

CLUNIAC. For the first time now I understand these words of St Jerome.

[III, 43.] CISTERCIAN. We [Cistercians] now have two monasteries within the precincts of the monastery, one of laybrothers and another of clerics. And therefore even we do not, strictly speaking, call tonsured laymen monks, unless we take 'lay' to mean illiterate.[32]

CLUNIAC. I have not heard these things before.

CISTERCIAN. Who is so silly as to suggest that service at the altar was in olden days denied to the imitators of the Apostles, that is, to cenobitic monks, and that, later on, it was granted to them as a favor? Rather, in their excessive humility they denied it to themselves, judging themselves unworthy of the most holy service of the altar. For this reason, very few men in the cenobitic monasteries in those days were priests.[33]

We read in a letter of St Epiphanius, archbishop of Cyprus,[34] that there was one fairly big monastery which had only two priests.[35] His letter refers to them as holy, and they, because of their excessive humility, had withdrawn themselves from the celebration of Mass. Since the monks could therefore not make their Holy Communion, they went to Epiphanius who was passing through, asking for his counsel and his help. His answer was: 'If you have among you anyone who is worthy of ordination, bring him to me.' And they answered 'We have one who, scared to death of ordination, usually runs and hides himself whenever bishops come. Just now he has not fled, unaware that you are here.' Saint Epiphanius answered: 'Go after him and bring him captive to me; gag his mouth until I ordain him lest he adjure me in the name of Christ. If I am adjured in Christ's name I will not ordain him against his will.'

And so it was done. Because he was a captive and gagged, he was ordained.

[III, 44.] CLUNIAC. The mental outlook of the modern monk is altogether different because all of them, worthy and unworthy, want to be ordained.

CISTERCIAN. In the old days good monks so much loved the quiet life and holy leisure that they hid and ran away from the clerical state. But Christ calls men such as these to the office of preaching and direction, because while the bride rested in her bed, her spouse, knocking [at the door] said, 'Open to me, my sister';* [open to me] the hearts of unbelievers and of those who live evil lives, is understood. He applies the same when he says: 'You, who dwell in gardens, make me hear your voice.'* It is as if he were saying: You, who in monasteries feast your minds on the sweet-smelling flowers of Holy Scripture which you have gathered in your garden, must sow now by preaching to win souls.[36]

[III, 45.] CLUNIAC. I have sufficient evidence that monks who, like the apostles, have left all things for Christ and lived the apostolic (that is, the common) life should, strictly speaking, be chosen for the apostolic office. Since the life of monks is not penitential but apostolic therefore, explain to me what life is properly said to be penitential.

CISTERCIAN. We who are in this vale of tears

*Sg 5:2.

*Sg 8:13.

have to weep. And because we sin every day, we need daily penance. And yet, we are not called penitents precisely on this account. But those who, because of great crimes are forbidden from entering a church, perform public penance, [carrina] and cannot enter a church until they are led in by the bishop on Holy Thursday.[37] They are precisely called penitents and they are to be wholly removed from the service of the altar, even if they are monks and are living extremely exemplary lives in a monastery.

[III, 46.] CLUNIAC. There still remains one item which you have to prove: that the monks' habit is not penitential but angelic.

CISTERCIAN. This does not need proof from me because Pope Boniface proves both that the monk's life is angelic and that his habit is angelic.* For, as it were, he envelops the monk's head in his two wings,* the monk's arms in his two wings, and his body in his two wings. Look, you have a monastic cherubim with six wings in one garment, I mean our cowl but not your cowl because it is sleeveless.

*Decret., D. 89, c. 7.

*alae

[III, 47.] CLUNIAC. We do too have six wing-lengths,* if not in one garment, then in two, that is, in our habit and our cowl.

*A pun: see III, n. 12.

CISTERCIAN. And so does a country boy when he is dressed in a tunic and a cape, and a cleric when he is dressed in a long-sleeved coat and cape. Your habit is not in accordance with the Rule and cannot be justified this way.

CLUNIAC. The Holy Fathers are of the opinion that good monks are to be compared with good angels, bad monks with apostate [angels]. The abbot of Clairvaux expresses the same in these words: *The monastic way of life makes those who profess it and love it like angels and unlike men. Yes, it reforms the divine image in man, shaping our contours to Christ almost as baptism does. We are as though baptized a second time in that, while we mortify our members which are on this earth, we again put on Christ, buried once again with him in the likeness of his death.*

*Pre XVII, 54; SBOp 3:289; CF 1: Cf. Col 3:5, Ga 3:27, Rm 6:5.

[III, 48.] CISTERCIAN. There is also another and still more sacred symbol in our cowl.

CLUNIAC. And what is that?

CISTERCIAN. It is in the exact form of Christ's Cross and, to put it more clearly, our cowl is our cross, as it were, a terrible sign to the powers of darkness. If while he sleeps, he is dressed in his cowl, he is protected by this sign against the power of darkness. Who does not see that this is the most suitable garment for monks? Those who deny themselves by their profession bear in their inmost selves the cross of Christ whose sign is the cross which they carry on their outward selves. The cowl is the sign of perfection, therefore, because as blessed Ambrose bears witness, it has been said to the perfect: *The Lord says, 'If anyone wishes to come after me, let him deny himself, take up his cross and follow me.'** It is safer and seemlier that the monk sleep in his cowl; I think St Benedict did not put that in writing but he understood it in ordering us to sleep as if dressed.*

*Mt 16:24.
Ambrose,
De officiis
ministrorum
II, 3, 9.

*RB 22:5.

[III, 49.] CLUNIAC. Even though we do not sleep in our cowls but only in our shirts, we still sleep dressed, because a shirt is a item of dress.

CISTERCIAN. This is the kind of picayune reasoning I put up with when I was in your order. Would to God you would reason on that level in respect to other precepts of the Rule which you do not obey! Tell me, for example, why do you not wash the guests' feet as the Rule orders?

[III, 50.] CLUNIAC. We have here not a 'picayune reason' but a good reason, because instead of washing the guests' feet as St Benedict ordered to be done for guests, we wash the feet of three poor men and we believe that this is the more pleasing to God.*

*RB 53:13. Cf.
Consuetud. Clun.
2. 37.

CISTERCIAN. Here you have the master, the Rule, whose sworn followers you are, and you scorn it both in words and in deeds. What man, in a sound state of mind, thinks that an offering which is the product of plunder is pleasing to God, when he himself says: 'For I the Lord love judgment and hate plunder in burnt-offerings'?* *Is 61:8.

When we Cistercians are your guests and you refuse to wash our feet, as is our due according to the precepts of our law, even if you give what you refuse us to the poor for God's sake, are you not offering plunder to God? I can never cease to wonder that such manifest disdainers of the holy Rule do not blush to be in our company and in our presence, when we are guests. When you are our guests we accord you the foot-washing and the other things ordered by the Rule.

Because of all this, because you stride on in a highly irregular way, showing contempt for the Rule's precepts and the Apostle's precept about manual labor, we really should not lodge in your monasteries according to that same Apostle's admonition: 'And we charge you, brothers, in the name of our Lord Jesus Christ, to withdraw yourselves from every other brother who lives irregularly.'* *2 Th 3:6.

[III, 51.] CLUNIAC. If you were to stop coming to our houses as guests, what would we thereby lose? There are certainly so many of you coming and going, you come and go so often, that some of our monasteries are weighed down from affording you hospitality. And many of us are so in awe of your being almost always on the road that we say the grey monks are in perpetual motion.

CISTERCIAN. In addition to reasons which are common to both you and to us, we have other special reasons which compel our comings and goings, forcing us to come and go so often, as you reproached us.

CLUNIAC. Such as?

[III, 52.] CISTERCIAN. One principal reason is that our abbots journey every year to the Chapter [General] at Cîteaux to deal with the affairs of our Order, so that they may mutually be proclaimed by each other for any deviations and carelessness in their administration, and that those who are unworthy of their office may be deposed and others be corrected by penances enjoined on them.

A second reason is that each abbot of our Order

must once every year visit each daughter-house of his monastery so that what should be corrected is corrected and our observance is kept intact in all our monasteries.

A third reason is that, since we have neither serfs nor the cash returns which are called census-taxes [on produce of the land and meadows], we have to sell what must be sold and buy what must be bought. We go to the nearest markets to buy cheaper goods; you travel to far-away places to buy dearer goods.

CLUNIAC. Of the three reasons you have mentioned, the first two are praiseworthy while the third is not censurable.

[III, 53.] CISTERCIAN. If you were to love the work prescribed in our Rule, it would become to you a labor of love. Because you do not love it, however, you say we overburden your monasteries. How do we burden them? Whenever we are there, we eat and drink what is ours.

CLUNIAC. Yours? How yours, who never carry your horses' feed with you but get everything from us who supply you ours?[38]

CISTERCIAN. Just as your daily fare is yours because the Holy Spirit—to whom the whole world belongs—speaking in the Rule assigned it to you, so all the things which you supply to us while we are your guests are ours. And they are ours because the same Holy Spirit, the lord of all, speaking in the Rule, assigned them to us and you to serve them to us. Make sure therefore that what you owe us you serve us in humble devotion, because if you were to take from us what is ours, there is no doubt at all that you are perpetrating that theft which is called sacrilege. In fact, I have said 'in humble devotion' so that if we thank you for your services, you do not accept them but say instead: 'We are useless servants. We have done what the Rule ordered, giving you what is yours and nothing more.'*

*Lk 17:10.

[III, 54]. CLUNIAC. Hide that good-for-nothing but extraordinary sermon of yours if you ever want to be made welcome in our monasteries, for if word gets around to us, you will suffer an inglorious rejection. Indeed, if we were to serve as the Rule orders* all the guests who flock in, we would not have the wherewithal to live.

*RB 53:1.

CISTERCIAN. What a great lack of faith. You are afraid that he who issued the order—God, to be precise—would allow you to die of hunger.* You have no confidence in Truth, who both orders and promises in these words: 'Seek first the Kingdom of God and his justice and all things will be added to you.'* Relative to this, blessed Jerome says: 'A faithful man and one of fervent faith considers calculated distribution a kind of lack of faith'.[39]

*Cf. Jerome, Ep 31; CSEL 54:251.

*Mt 6:33.

I hear that you have no particular desire to obey the Rule or the Gospel; you say that you progress simply, in accordance with the way your Order does things. Yet such simplicity is great duplicity, as the Abbot of Clairvaux attests in the very letter you just read. He describes your order succinctly in these words: 'What will not be observed is vowed and what will not be performed is proposed'.*

*Ep 1, 6 (above p. 121).

So then, may the end of our conversation be that you consider a second conversion, so that you may enter that Order in which what is vowed is observed and what is proposed will be performed.

[III, 55.] CLUNIAC. Once again you want to go away from me, but I will not let you go unless you tell me first why you are leaving, without discussing it, the abbot's declaration, in which he said nice things about our Order.

CISTERCIAN. Which things?

CLUNIAC. 'As long as' physical observances which St Benedict instituted 'militate in favor of charity, they are immutably fixed and cannot in any way licitly be modified even by the superiors themselves. But if ever they seem to be contrary to charity, at least by those who have insight and whose duty it is to regulate them, is it not a most manifest justice that the rules which were fashioned for charity's sake should, for charity's sake, when it seems expedient, be either omitted or suspended or modified to something perhaps more profitable?"*

*Pre 2, 5; SBOp 3:257; CF 1:108.

[III, 56.] CISTERCIAN. I had left this whole

quotation untouched because it had, so to say, escaped my memory, but you had your own interests in mind in making me remember it because, if you are not too stubbornly attached to them, a discussion of it will deliver you from your vain hopes. This is a statement not only unfavorable to Cluny's Custom., but so against them that it is decisively destructive of them.*

*Cf. Cassian, Inst. 12, 33, 2, & Conf. 5, 26, 2/3.

CLUNIAC. In positing this opinion, the abbot intended to undergird and stay up our Order: how can you use it to tear it down?

CISTERCIAN. How, you ask? If you keep still you will hear all the more quickly. Tell me, can indiscreet and untempered teaching authority with its lack of discretion ever fight on the side of charity?

CLUNIAC. Never. Lack of discretion is always contrary to charity. It breaks its chain.

CISTERCIAN. The teaching authority of our mistress, that is, the Rule, always fights on the side of charity because it is remarkable for its discretion, as blessed Gregory affirms in speaking of St Benedict: 'He has written a rule of remarkable discretion.'* Discretion, which is the mother of virtues, is the orderer,* not the disrupter, of charity.

*Dial. 2, 36.

*RB 64:19.

[III, 57.] CLUNIAC. Now I see where you are going. You are concluding that the observances of the Rule are immutably fixed according to this statement by the abbot and cannot licitly be changed. But perhaps the founders of our Order were not out to put everything in final form. Possessed of a holy rusticity they modified the observances in their devout simplicity and simple devotion.

CISTERCIAN. Even if I believe they were possessed of holy rusticity, I cannot bring myself to believe that they established that chat which your abbots usually have after Compline with their monastic officials and extern brothers, at which on occasion the affairs of the realm are dealt with right along with the affairs of the monastery while all kinds of gossip crop up. They drag it out so long that after singing their Compline at an unsuitable time they sing the [compline] hymn *To you before the close of day* right along with *Light's dawn reddens the sky** and *Now that the daylight fills the sky*.†

**of Lauds.*
†*of Prime.*

[III, 58.] CLUNIAC. If we were to sing, *Dawn's light reddens the sky* when dawn was reddening it, then we would be cheated of that sweet morning nap in which our Order indulges us.

CISTERCIAN. You lose through that morning sleep, therefore, the riches you acquired from your night vigils, because you sleep during the morning hours contrary to the teaching of the Rule and the examples of holy monks. On this account the prophetic reproach of the psalmist is applicable to you, 'They sleep their sleep and all the rich men found nothing in their hands'.*

**Ps 76:5.*

CLUNIAC. God forbid that the prophet should have prophesied this about our nap.

[III, 59.] CISTERCIAN. Why do the monks of Cluny, who say they imitate Mary in her leisure, not imitate her in keeping night watches, so that at that time in the morning when Christ rose, they might in accordance with the Rule celebrate the office of the resurrection, morning Lauds, at the proper time. In this way they would honor Christ's resurrection by reasonable service.*

**Cf. Rom 12:1.*

Our little discussion must come to a close lest it lose its proper tone by going beyond its measure. As says the poet:

There is a measure in affairs, there are certain limits
    Beyond and below which one cannot keep
        to what is right.*

**Horace,* Serm. *1.1.106-107.*

END OF PART THREE

AN ARGUMENT CONCERNING FOUR QUESTIONS

*Introduction, annotation and translation
by Joseph Leahey*

Translation Consultant: Grace Perigo

ERRATA

Page	Line	Erratum
151	2	READ Whether *the will* alone FOR intention alone
152	16, 21	*the will* alone FOR intention alone
153	13	*the will* alone FOR intention alone
154	9	*the will* alone FOR intention alone
155	36	READ Christ *should* understand FOR would understand
157	21	READ pleasure-seekers *enslave* FOR indulge
157	27	ADD marginal note: Titus 3:3
158	26	READ monks, *followers of the Egyptian fathers* FOR monks of Egypt, followers of the Fathers
166	2	ADD he, *conscience-stricken,* may be built up
166	16	READ *the will* alone FOR intention alone
167	19	READ was asked by *an acquaintance* FOR by a certain well-known person
169	36-7	READ not *just by* any priest but *by* the chief priest
172	10	READ *modesty* FOR moderation
174	35	READ *Damasus* FOR Damascus
178	27	ADD NOTE TO inheritance willed: If one accepted the *testamentum,* he was bound in roman law to remain in his status.
180	6	READ *mourning* FOR morning
185	¶X, 19	READ not let *them* curl their hair
189	15-19	READ But *since* I cannot go on with the discourse, I have undertaken *it* without thinking
218	n. 19	READ CT 3,7,1-3; *8*,1-2.
219	n. 23	ADD Cf. Ovid, *Heroides,* 9.47.
219	n. 26	READ written *before* 1153.
221	n. 62	READ Suetonius
223		ADD DC Charles Du Fresne Sieur Du Cange, *Glossarium Mediae et Infimae Latinitatis,* 10 volumes (1883-87). Reprinted in 5 volumes by the Akademische Druck- und Verlagsanstalt: Graz, 1954

ALTERNATE READINGS

151	23	Men, educated in the liberal arts FOR well-educated
157	13-14	he undertakes a way of life of greater humility FOR he makes a resolution involving greater humility
157	16-18	AMBIGUOUS IN LATIN. MAY ALSO BE READ: The desert and not a public office makes the monk or cleric.
159	16	*abuse* holy things FOR steal holy things
169	24	AMBIGUOUS IN LATIN. MAY ALSO BE READ: persist in its undertaking, except an angel?
177	4	a certain priest was publicly arraigned FOR a priest on trial
180	13-15	whom the diversity of the monastic order is not known, who may become aware of it through this division.
182	¶IX,11-12	'I am not allowed to sit in judgement on a presbyter.'
187	16	*ministers* of Christ FOR servants of Christ.

AN ARGUMENT CONCERNING FOUR QUESTIONS

INTRODUCTION

elatively little is known about the monk Idung who authored both the *Dialogue between a Cluniac and a Cistercian* and the *Argument on the Four Questions*. Perhaps one could say simply that he was one of many discontented persons who found his way into one monastery and then out again, only to enter a different monastery, following some labyrinth of the spirit. In his pursuit he seems to have been very much a bother to himself and a source of ridicule to others. For those who are too soon made glad, there is nothing and no one quite so boring as a man in deadly earnest.

Simply to dismiss Idung as a spiritual tramp is easy but not satisfactory. While his life (as we know it) and his writings (as we have them) reveal wanderings, one is hesitant to raise them to the level of 'spiritual peregrinations' or 'the pilgrimages of a soul'—terms which smack of the *salon*.

From reading the *Argument* and the *Dialogue* one receives the impression of a man who was a sign of contradiction to himself and to others. The literary forms which he adopted are not accidental, but essential. There appears to have continually taken place with Idung both an internal dialogue and an argument. In short, there appear to be at least three levels and three aspects to his life. He was in turn a schoolman, a Cluniac, and finally a Cistercian. Yet, these roles only hint at the man himself.

Idung described himself as 'the least of the poor of Christ', as one 'who was hateful to the three orders', and as 'a sinner monk'. This combination of literary commonplaces, claustral conspicuousness, and conscious confession may surely be viewed as the mere 'spume of words'.[1] His comments on the rule of parishes, on talk, on taverns, and misericords may be regarded as a parody of monastic humility and even as the triumphalism of a neophyte. Is this the residue of a waggish schoolmaster become monk? And yet, in an evocative passage, a fourth or perhaps primary Idung wells forth when he speaks of that great and unconsolable sadness which so often secretly steals into his heart.[2]

One ought not to be led astray, however, by Idung's occasional swooning. It would be too much and would be going too far in the wrong direction to say that here one has the antecedents of Villon's *jeunesse folle*. The *Argument* does not truly provide an opportunity to ask the question of 'where are the snows of yesterday'. After all, Idung was never quite in the dock, though Villon was. Further, more than one literary great or near great—Cicero is only one example—has turned to philosophy after having been helped out of office.

Perhaps this melancholy sentiment of Idung is an instance of what we might call recurring depression or anxiety. Was Idung the spiritual heir (if not descendent) of St Bernard of Clairvaux, lacking in *mel* but rich in *chol*? It would seem not. Rather, Idung provides an example of a conversion late in life to Christ. That he expresses this kairotic experience in the language of his time, and with all the problems of contemporary connotation, makes him more and not less interesting.

Idung of Prüfening was a complex man and a learned monk. Judging by the *Argument*, one would exceed description in describing him as a brilliant author or one of great originality. One will not remember Idung for his *bons mots* or for his profound insights into human nature. This helps us in part to understand the preservation of his work. On the other hand, he was not just a man of simple sensations producing complex thoughts. Perhaps in his move from the schoolroom to Cluny he realized an instinct: that when all is said and done, it was more important for him to live brilliantly than to be brilliant. Of course, one could ask, and not unkindly, what choice he had. This question might also be posed about his later exodus from Cluny to the Cistercians.

His familiarity with antique, patristic, and contemporary culture cannot be questioned. As the text makes clear, he frequently cited St Jerome. His use of Jerome is as much a matter of personality as of practicality. Along with Jerome, Idung shares a love not only of language and a penchant for puns, but also a need to realize his values in others and with others. Both were given, as it was once said of some university professors, to laying down the law on everything—whether it was wanted or not. Idung, like Jerome, is also quite sensitive and sometimes not very sensible; this accounts in part for his often rather extreme language. His sources for the *Argument* do, of course, include Scripture. His predilection, though, is for the philosophical and the legal. In this perhaps he was already a Cistercian before his conversion.

THE TEXT AND TRANSLATION

The critical text upon which this translation is based is that of Professor R.B.C. Huygens: *Le Moine Idung et ses deux ouvrages: Argumentum super quatuor quaestionibus et Dialogus duorum monachorum*. The work, though in the form of a letter, is really a treatise. It is possible that the *Argument* was really an answer or reply to Herbord rather than a request or a treatise alone.

The form in which the letter is cast, the argument, has a long tradition in the history of Latin literature. While Cicero defines a topic as 'the region of an argument, and an argument as a course of reason which firmly establishes a matter about which there is some doubt',[3] Isidore of Seville provides the following definition: There is a 'literary genre between *historia* and *fabula* called *argumenta*, [that is] a report of things which are possible even if they did not happen.'[4] Hugh of St Victor devoted a chapter of his *Didascalion* to the theory of argument and writes that:

> Logic is divided into grammar and argument: argument is divided into demonstration, probable argument, and sophistic: probable argument is divided into dialectic and rhetoric.[5]

In Roman legal usage, the term *argumentum* is associated with *probatio* and *demonstratio*. Among all the different connotations, the primary meaning remains that given by Cicero. Idung, schooled in law and declamation, presented his reasoning on these four questions in written form within a venerable literary tradition.

The *quaestio* has received considerable attention in recent years. Jean Leclercq has written that the object of the monastic *lectio* is wisdom and appreciation, while that of scholasticism is science and knowledge.[6] Thomas Gilby has written that the *quaestio* 'represents an inquiry rather than interrogation.'[7] M.D. Chenu has written on the birth and the evolution of the *quaestio*.[8]

How is the *quaestio* used in Idung's *Argument*? We face here the business of Saul–Paul. That is, it is reasonable to think that Saul did not forget how to make tents when he became Paul, nor did Idung forget the *quaestio* of the schools when he entered the Cluniacs and later the Cistercians. Therefore, Idung's *quaestio* does not exclude the above but it does tend to be the juristic *quaestio* put to monastic use. This element seems to indicate again that Idung's arguments and *Argument* may well have been a response to Herbord rather than an initial letter.

The basic meaning of the title of the *Argumentum* is an argument or mode of reasoning on four cases. The cases at issue are: (1) Whether one and the same person may be a cleric and a monk; (2) Whether intention/the will alone makes a cleric; (3) Whether cloistered nuns and monks while they have the one Rule of St Benedict should also have the same custody of the cloister; (4) Whether it is lawful for a monk to preach in a parish church.

These or similar questions may well have been debated in the classes which Idung held. It would seem that they were questions that had been discussed between Idung and Herbord. In any case, they were the type of question that would have been popular with academics in the mid-twelfth century. The first question has an iceberg quality. On the surface, it is as it appears. In actuality, however, it concerns the relationship of the monastic profession to the clerical state and the conflict, if there is one, between the two. Further, the question points to the antagonism which existed between the secular clergy and the regular clergy on the one hand, and the conflict between the monks and the clergy on the other. Finally, the question is important for it reveals the hard feelings possible between the priests and the *conversi* of the monastic community and the class structures that existed within the monastic establishment. This is somewhat ironic for it is clear from the *Dialogue* that Idung went to 'Cîteaux' as a *conversus*.

The second question, whether the will alone makes one a cleric, is directly associated with the first, but it is really a very different question. Idung treats of the two together. His argument is from authority, but not biblical authority. Perhaps this treatment indicates that the situation was resolved in law but not in fact. It is what Shakespeare implies with 'cakes and ale'.

The third question concerns nuns. Not only does it reveal the contemporary attitude towards women, it illustrates another difficulty: the spiritual direction of nuns, of women observing a rule within a monastery. This was not a small problem, for in the twelfth century many men and women strove to lead religious lives outside monasteries as well as within. They differed from Christians in general by their observation of a rule of life. This could be formal or informal. Numerous distinctions among the religious men and women can be made. There are also degrees and kinds of cloister; some are enclosed (*inclusus*) while others are closed off (*reclusus*). Those outside the monasteries did not necessarily pose more of a problem of jurisdiction, though it would seem that this was the case; rather, they posed a different kind of problem than did those within the walls. Last of all, the connection between affective spirituality, the Cistercians, women religious and the beguines and beghards, is hinted here. Even though Idung reveals some rather interesting traditional and literary views toward women in the *Argument*, it is permissible to say that he went beyond a particular literary tradition? It is clear from the *Dialogue* that he was known to the Abbess of Niedermünster. It might not be permissible, and it might be quite unjust, to take Idung's work in this matter beyond its own purpose.

The fourth question, monks and preaching, was a serious one. One only has to recall the problem of the *gyrovagi*. Were they monks? Were they priests? Were they monk-priests? This problem of preaching monks is connected with not only the *gyrovagi*, but with urban unrest, with the conflicts between the schools in cathedral cities and the schools within the monasteries, and with the universities. Idung was not at a loss to offer a resolution to this question, for he argues that, if a monk has been promoted through the ordinary clerical grades and preaches with the permission of his abbot, then a monk can preach. He does seem, however, to lack enthusiasm.

IDUNG'S SUCCESS

Since the work is an argument on four questions, we may ask whether or not Idung has successfully argued his case. If one evaluates the work on the basis of the statement of the question, the literature available on the topics, the logical coherency of the arguments, and the logic of his conclusions, one would have to admit that Idung's work leaves something to be desired.

Idung advances his *Argumentum* by amassing authorities and authoritative texts, digressions, a lack of economy, and 'in-house' humor. He is given to making puns which are pleasant in Latin but painful to translate. The final measure of Idung's success came in his lifetime. Herbord became a monk. The *Argument* is a pleasant work to read in the Latin and, I hope, also in this English translation which I dedicate to the late Dr and to Mrs Jeremiah F. O'Sullivan.

Joseph Leahey

Mercy College
Dobbs Ferry, New York

NOTES TO INTRODUCTION

1. Thomas Merton, tr., *The Solitary Life: A Letter of Guigo* (Worcester: Stanbrook Abbey Press, 1963) p. 8.
2. *Arg.* p. 166.
3. *Topica,* trans. H. M. Hubbell (Cambridge: Harvard University Press, 1960).
4. Cited in Ernst Robert Curtius, *European Literature and the Latin Middle Ages,* tr. Willard R. Trask (New York: Harper and Row, 1963) p. 452.
5. *Didascalion* 3. 1, tr. *The Didascalion of Hugh of St Victor.* Records of Civilization, Sources and Studies (New York: Columbia University Press, 1968) p. 83.
6. *The Love of Learning and the Desire for God,* tr. Catherine Misrahi (New York: Fordham University Press, 1961) pp. 3, 89, 188, 209.
7. 'Structure of the *Summa*', Appendix I of *Summa Theologiae,* Vol. I (1a.1): *Christian Theology* (New York: McGraw Hill Book Company, 1964) p. 45.
8. *Toward Understanding St Thomas,* trans. A. M. Landry and D. Hughes (Chicago: Regnery, 1964) 85-88, 94.

AN ARGUMENT CONCERNING
FOUR QUESTIONS

Whether one and the same person might be a cleric and a monk[1] ☐ Whether intention alone makes one a cleric[2] ☐ Whether cloistered nuns and monks,[3] although they keep the one Rule of Saint Benedict,[4] should also have the same protection of the cloister* ☐ Whether it is lawful for a monk to preach in church

*i.e., enclosure

To Master Herbord,[5] distinguished gentleman, Idung, the least of the poor men of Christ,[6] strives to present thoughts which are more useful than clever.[7]

Those who, following evangelical and apostolic teaching, are wisely simple and simply wise know no more than is necessary,* give expression to their knowledge with reserve—just as their knowledge is reserved.[8] In this way they avoid unprofitable novel opinions through which simpler readers may err. And so, keeping constantly to the path of reason and authority and having spurned popular opinion, which is accustomed to deviate from reason and authority, they are careful not to give heed to the multitude and so to fall into the error of the multitude.* But what follows will make clear the reason why I have made this premise.

*Cf. Rm 12:3

*Cf. Past. Care
(ACW 11:27),
Dialogues III,15;
FCh 39:140.

Men, well educated it is true, but less expert in sacred law, judge that a cleric once received into the monastic life is not a cleric. And because they either have not read or have not understood[9] the writings of the orthodox fathers on this matter, they irrationally opine and ignorantly teach that the monastic profession precludes the clerical office—as if the monastic way of life were a degradation of the priesthood.

It is not surprising that the common herd, ignorant of letters and law,[10] thinks this way, for it has been taken in by the change involved in tonsure and habit, and it judges only by what the eyes see. How great is that mistake the meaning of the word itself makes clear. And, the steps of the priesthood themselves reveal that monks in no way intrude upon the office of cleric.* Rather, monks who have been appointed in those steps through ordination serve God. I have said 'through ordination' and I say it again, because ordination makes a cleric and not just intention—as some men with deceptive subtlety falsely dogmatize.

*Cf. DCC, I, 3. Decret. D. 67, C. 1.

Indeed, there is one kind which says: 'Just as consent alone makes a marriage and just as that form alone which Christ taught in the Gospel makes the sacrament of baptism, so likewise intention alone makes a cleric.'[11] I say, however, that he who says this in his own heart and believes it, is deceived. And I say that whoever teaches this is a deceiver, because the very meaning of the word [nomen] belies the false inference. Cleric means 'chosen by lot' or 'adopted'. And from this the name is taken because the Apostles elected or adopted Matthias by casting lots.* Today this election or adoption does not and should not take place by lot, but by that ordination which canonical authority has established.* Without ordination, as much as you would like to be a cleric, you neither are nor should be called a cleric. For, as I should have said, a humble disinclination rather than a self-seeking intention makes a cleric.*

*Ac 1:26.

*Decret. D. 23, c. 8.

*See DCC, III, 36, 39, 43.

Indeed, we read in a certain reliable history[12] that some holy monks who were living an anchoretic life and fleeing the honor of the clerical office because of an excessive humility, because they were necessary to the church, were seized and bound, and, amazingly, as they resisted, they were ordained. One of them cut off his own ear in order by so doing to evade the clerical office.[13] And Jerome in the letter which is entitled 'The Funeral Oration in Honor of Nepotian' bears witness that this same Nepotian, a monk, was ordained against his will by his uncle Heliodorus, who was a bishop and a monk. He praises him in these terms: *Having been made a cleric, he is ordained a priest through the usual grades. Good Jesus! He groaned and wailed! Then, for the first and only time he became angry with his uncle. But the more he resisted, the more he stirred everyone's enthusiasm for him. By his refusal he deserved the status he did not want.** Therefore the view expressed in the words 'intention alone makes a cleric', should not be held, nor the opinion or the phrase be given wide circulation, because it gives rise to a disordered understanding in the minds of their inquisitive students, who seek their own teaching and not that of Jesus Christ.* This I have learned through experience.

*Jerome, Ep 52, 10.

*Ph 2:21

Nor can this mistaken notion be supported by the fact that Jerome, writing to Oceanus, says 'It is not soft clothes that make the cleric and priest, but the chaste intention of the mind'.* He says that a chaste intention of mind makes a cleric; that is, worthy of the clerical office. If the letter is understood simply and literally, a foolish conclusion is reached through that literal understanding—this is shown by the following reasoning. If a chaste intention of mind makes a cleric, it follows that he who does not have a chaste intention of mind is not a cleric. If he is not a cleric, then he is not a presbyter. If he is not a presbyter, then he is not able to make the body of Christ. Therefore, he who is not chaste does not make the body of Christ. Who does not see that this error is tremendously absurd?[14] He who aids and abets this error clearly is speaking not of someone who has devised evil in his heart,[15] but of someone who has lapsed through a bodily sin [when he says]: 'A priest who has lapsed in secret and has therefore lost his office, if he celebrates masses, will not be able to make the body of Christ because he is cut off from the office, and it can only be restored to him by the bishop.'[16]

*Ps Jerome, Ep 42,4.

But let the present discussion override this heresy which was the cause of enough excitement in the time of Bishop Cuno of blessed memory and has been sufficiently refuted.[17] We have said that St Jerome's words 'a chaste intention of mind makes a cleric' are to be understood in the following manner: 'makes a cleric, that is worthy of the clerical office'. The very same can be said of the words: 'intention alone makes a cleric' so that the meaning is as follows: 'The value of a good intention is that it makes him who is to be ordained fit for the honor of the clerical office.

II.

Jerome's authority proves, however, that the clerical and the monastic states may very well come together in one and the same person because they are not opposites but diverse.[18] And furthermore, if conjointly they be predicated of one and the same subject, the predication will not be accidental.* When writing to a monk he says: 'You should live in a monastery in such a way that you deserve to be a cleric.'* Likewise, when writing to Heliodorus, who was then only a monk (afterwards he was made both a cleric and a bishop), he says the same thing: 'If the devout flatteries of your brothers urge you to the honor of the clerical office, I shall rejoice in your elevation and I shall fear for your fall'.* In these words he points out the practice in well-ordered monasteries; namely, that a monk who possesses more fervent zeal in the monastic way of life may be chosen to the honor of the clerical office. And once he has been made a cleric he is to be respected more and given a higher place in choir in respect for his rank. If he is later found to be lukewarm and, after having been admonished according to the Rule [of Saint Benedict] he still does not mend his ways, he is to be suspended from his place [in choir] and from the office of holy orders,* which do not make him holy but demand that he be holy.* For indeed, if a man who is guilty of a crime has received holy orders, he is guilty of sacrilege;† for, as authority

*Cf. DCC, II, 24, 25.

*Jerome, Ep 125, 17. Cf. DCC, III, 40.

*Ep 14,8.

*RB 62:9-10.
*CT 16,2,16. DCC, II,57,59.
†CT 6,5,1,2; 6,35, 13; 16,2,25.

bears witness, he usurps a holy thing to himself.*

The unique privilege of holy orders should be noted because it does not admit a bigamist[19] no matter how holy he may be, nor even a monogamist[20] who has married a widow or a cast-off wife.[21] St Ambrose gives the reason for this in his book *On the Duties of the Ministers: Regarding wedlock itself, the law is that marriage is not to be repeated nor is a marriage to a second spouse to be undertaken. It may seem strange to many that there should be put forth as impediments to the gift of ordination a second marriage contracted before baptism when even crimes are not considered a hindrance if they have been remitted by the sacrament of baptism. But we must realize that while in baptism a fault can be blotted out, the law cannot be abolished. There is no fault in the marriage, but this is the law. In this marriage, whatever fault there is is remitted in baptism; whatever pertains to law is not undone [by baptism]. Therefore, how is one able to encourage widowhood when one has made a second marriage?* *

Here I have inserted at great length those things which St Jerome wrote to Nepotian, who was both a cleric and a monk, because in a special way they provide a remedy in law for the case which I have undertaken to plead. He says: *I know that from your uncle the blessed Heliodorus, who is now a bishop of Christ, you have learned and daily are learning which things are holy, and that you have the norm of his life as an example of virtue. But accept also this little book and my words, however poor, in addition to his, so that when he has instructed you as a monk, this might teach you to be a perfect cleric. Accordingly, the cleric who serves the church of Christ would understand first of all what he is called and, once the name has been defined, let him strive to be what he is called,* KLERIKOS. *For if the word* cleros *in Greek is called* sors *in Latin, then clerics are called this either because they belong by lot to the Lord, or because the Lord himself is their lot, that is, their portion, the allotted portion of clerics. He*

*Cf. Council of Aquileia (381); Mansi 3:621.

*De officiis ministrorum, I. 50. 248. Cf. Decret. D. 26, c. 4.

who is the Lord's allotted portion or who has the Lord as his allotted portion, should show himself to be someone who possesses the Lord and is possessed by the Lord. He who possesses the Lord and says with the prophet: 'The Lord is my portion',* can possess nothing that is not the Lord. But if he possesses something besides the Lord, the Lord will not be his portion. For example, if he has gold, silver, or possessions, or inlaid furniture, the Lord will not deign to be his portion along with these portions. For if I am the Lord's portion and the lot of his inheritance, I do not receive a portion among the other tribes; but, just as a levite and a priest, I live from the tithes and, serving the altar, I am sustained by the offerings of the altar. Having food and clothing, I will be content with these and naked I will follow the naked cross. Therefore I implore you and I admonish you 'repeating again and again'* not to think that the office of cleric is a kind of ancient military service. That is, you should not seek worldly gain in the army of Christ, nor should you possess more than when you undertook to be a cleric. Let it be said of you, 'Their portions profit them not'.* The poor, pilgrims, and Christ, their fellow-guest, shall know your table. Flee, flee, as you would the plague, the clerical businessman and the one who is rich off the poverty-stricken, vainglorious, though of low birth.*

*Ps 73:26. Cf. Decret. C. 12, q. 1, c. 7.

*Cf. Vergil, Aeneid 3:436.

*Jr 12:13.

*Ep 52, 4-5.

The same author says further on in the same letter: *We blush at the witticisms and the other absurdities of lovers in comedies. We deprecate them in men of the world, how much more so in clerics and in monk-clerics whose way of life is adorned by priesthood and whose priesthood is adorned by their way of life? I do not say this because I am afraid of such dreadful behaviour in you or in holy men, but because in every way of life, in every rank and sex, both good persons and evil are to be found, and the condemnation of evil is the praise of the good. One is ashamed to say it: Priests of idols, actors, charioteers and harlots take possession of inheritances, yet by law the same is forbidden to clerics and monks alone. And it is christian emperors and not persecutors who forbade this.*[22] *I do not complain about the law, but I do grieve that we merited this law. It is a good cautery, but where does the wound come from that I require a cautery? Prudent and strict is the written bond of the law, and yet by it is avarice not restrained.**

**Ep 52:5-6.*

Regard the words of St Jerome. They express the way in which clerics ought to live,* and adequately settle the question under discussion—even though the reasoning previously advanced and that which follows were legally invalid. It is this:

**Cf.* Decret. *D. 23, c. 3.*

III.

When a cleric becomes a monk, he makes a resolution involving greater humility, greater obedience, greater abstinence. These are the makings and not the un-makings of clerics, for Jerome says: 'The desert makes the monk or the cleric and not the man of affairs.'* And because he who has made this profession uses neither meat nor baths nor multi-hued tunics and squirrel furs nor other things through which pleasure-seekers indulge their own bodies, what man of sound mind would say that he had lost his clerical status, when neither the monastic nor the clerical obligation demands the use of these things?

**Ps.-Jerome, Ep 42,9; PL 30: 300.*

Those who in their desires pursue indulgence of the flesh and serve not their needs but their pleasures, contrary to the apostolic precept, are only slaves of the body and bondsmen of the flesh. Because their God is their belly, they set their supreme good in pleasure and they do not eat and drink to live but live to eat and drink.* Therefore, the judgment of philosophy convicts them of not really living. Pythagoras says: 'He does not live whose only thought is to live, [for] an inglorious life is death's accomplice'.* With what contempt such men as these are held even by heathen philosophers is attested by Boethius, who says in the person of Philosophy: 'Who would not cast off the slave of that most vile thing, the body?'* And when

**Caecilius Balbus, De nugis philosophorum, I,11. (Cf. Ph 3:19)*

**Ibid.*

**Consolation of Philosophy, 3, pr. 8,6; Stewart III, vii, 12-13.*

Pythagoras heard a certain pleasure-seeker saying, 'I would rather live with women than with philosophers', he answered, 'And pigs would rather stay in muck than in clean water'.* Socrates showed what he meant by muck, saying: 'A beautiful woman is a shrine built over a sewer.'* Another philosopher expressed what they felt about those who despised them by saying: 'Men despise me and simpletons despise them, but they do not worry about the simpletons, nor I about them.'*

*Caecilius Balbus, I, 7.

*Ibid.

*Ibid. See Huygens, notes, pp. 347-8.

Therefore, since it is well-known that heathen philosophers, in order to devote their time to philosophy,[23] despised the riches and the pleasures of the world, and, because of this and this alone, were despised by men, is the spirit of the Christian not consequently crushed by the utterly wretched misery—the Christian who is not willing to despise the unhappy happiness of this world for the sake of the kingdom of heaven promised to him by Truth,* but who, with his whole heart, seeks after the pomps of Satan which he renounced at baptism, not afraid to be found guilty of sacrilegious falsity for which eternal suffering is justly due.

*Mt 5:3.

But, as Jerome says, Christians have their own philosophers. The most eminent among them are the monks of Egypt, followers of the Fathers.* They also have their own Epicureans, foremost among them monks of that kind which is worse than Sarabites†—the worldlings—indeed the carnal clergy, who misappropriate the inheritance of Christ's poor by their sacrilegious pleasures. At great expense they purchase for themselves the soft skins of the ermine[24] which, no one but the coddled denies, are suitable only for mollycoddles.

*Jerome, De viris illustribus (Prologue), and Ep 130, 19; PL 23:768.

†RB 1:6-9.

The abbot of Clairvaux supports the judgment of these words in his twenty-third Sermon on the Song Songs. He explains the words of the prophet by saying: 'Though we pity the godless man, he will not learn righteousness. He has worked evil in the land of the saints and will not see the glory of the Lord.'* Especially to be feared is that which we read about such a person in the prophet, where, in speaking to

*Is 26:10.

his angels he says, 'Although we pity the godless man'. And to those who ask in dismay, 'Will he not therefore learn righteousness?', he answers, 'No'. And he gives the reason; saying, 'In the land of the saints he has wrought evil deeds and he will not see the glory of the Lord.' Let clerics beware. Let the ministers of the church in the lands of the saints, which they possess and wherein they work evil beware. Not content with the stipends which should suffice them,[25] they wickedly and impiously keep for themselves the surplus with which the destitute should be fed, and for the sake of their own pride and luxury, they are not afraid to squander the food of the poor. Surely they commit a double sin, and they despoil the belongings of another and they steal holy things for their own vanities and infamies.* For this reason it is remarked that 'he whose many judgments are of unfathomable depth'* may be merciful to and may spare the like of these for the present—but not forever. Should one look for rest in this place?*

*Cf. DCC, III, 53.
*Ps 36:6.

*SC 23, 12-13; CF 7:36.

You should not marvel that that contemporary writer,[26] who possesses the zeal and knowledge of God* has dared so freely to cast in the teeth of priests and ministers of the church their base deeds and sacrilege, because where the spirit of God is, there is liberty.* And the spiritual man judges all things and is judged by no one.* And who would hide someone who does not allow himself to be hidden, who goes to great expense so as not to be hidden?

*Cf. Ps 69:9, Jn 2:17, Rm 10:2.

*2 Co 3:17.
*1 Co 2:15.

That soft and costly garment of which we spoke above reveals a softness and emptiness of mind; and while it covers the private parts of the body, it lays bare the shameful recesses of the mind. Ovid says of the fiery Phaeton: 'There was something useful in that calamity,' (and uses 'useful' instead of 'beneficial').* And there is a common saying: 'There is no evil in which there is not some good'. However, I find nothing good in expensive and luxurious clothing except that the red-dyed pelisses* by their fiery color warn of the fire of hell.

*Metamorphoses, 2, 332.

*gulae rubricatae: animal skins, dyed red or fustian.

Still, that remarkable and memorable response of Master Anselm of Laon comes to my mind. Having been petitioned by his brothers to reprove one of his students who was conspicuous for the surpassing prodigality of his riotous dress, he answered: 'And where would I find a herald to go ahead of him through the highways and the byways* crying out: 'Here comes the lecher! Watch out for his lechery'? His dress is not quiet; it screams, it broadcasts it.'[27]

*Lk 14:21.

IV.

On another occasion, the aforesaid abbot again, with greater freedom (zeal for the house of God was eating him up),* gracefully reproved even cardinals. It will not be profitless to know this reproof. For, writing to the bishop of Soissons,[28] he says: *The Romans do not care very much how a case is adjudicated, but because they are very fond of gifts, they seek recompense.* I speak openly of open things. I am not making public something which should be private, but I expose what is flaunted. Would that these things were done privately in chambers.*[29] *Would that we alone had seen and heard them! Would that those who tell of them were not believed! Would that contemporaries had left behind a Noah for us, so that we could cover them up to some extent!* But now that the whole world knows the tale, shall we alone keep silence? My head has been severely shattered; and should I, with blood bubbling up all about me, have thought that it should be covered up? Anything I put over it will get blood-stained. And greater confusion will be the result of having wished to cover up what cannot be covered.**

*Ps 69:9, Jn 2:17.

*See DCC, II, 48.

*Gen 9:20-24.

*Mor [Ep 42] 7, 29, Cf. DCC II, 48.

Look. The lover and the beloved have a special intimacy and he does not spare the roman curia for, as the saying of the wise man has it: 'Better are the wounds of a lover than the deceitful kisses of an enemy'.* Yet no one has a just cause for becoming furious, and is not furious because of a reproof directed at no one in particular—except the person of whom it is said: 'The self-conscious man thinks that

*Pr 27:6.

everything is said about him.'* Therefore, anyone who is offended by what is being said without any definite mention of names betrays himself and by his impatience he shows himself to be guilty. [*Disticha Catonis, I. 17, 2.]

We may add a few things to the previous words of the abbot: A cleric should not be a mercenary of Christ but an officer.³⁰ By what effrontery does he dare to accept the stipends due for clerical service, if he is ashamed of that service and refuses to bear on his head the sign that not only gives him title to, but also symbolizes, the kingdom and priesthood of his king? When he was appointed to a church he ought to have received that sign; yet if he never bore it because he refused to bear it, he was never a cleric. But he who has been chosen by clerical election and has borne it and has abandoned it because of his frivolity, is said not to be a cleric but a julianist.* [*An apostate.]

The venerable authority of the canons says that the tonsure of a small crown* is a sign of disgrace and that a cleric so tonsured is an offender against the Catholic faith. The fortieth chapter of the Council of Toledo bears witness to this in these words: *All clerics, even lectors, just as deacons and priests, having shaved all the upper part of the head, shall leave below it only a crown. And they are not to do as lectors seem to do in this part of Gaul; for they have a small circle only on the crown of the head and have flowing hair like laymen.*³¹ That was the usage of heretics in Spain. Wherefore it is fitting for the removal of scandal that this disgraceful sign be put aside and that there be one tonsure or style as is the custom in the whole of Spain. He who does not observe this will be an offender against the Catholic faith.* [*corona] [*The Council of Toledo IV (633 AD); Mansi 10:630.]

And it is especially amazing that they are not afraid to be branded with the iron of anti-Christ, while because of their worldly embarrassment they are ashamed to be signed with the sign of Christ's Calvary, in which they ought to glory. As the Apostle says: 'Let me not glory save in the cross of Our Lord Jesus Christ.'* Moreover, are not robes which are split up the front, skirts with almost no [*Ga 6:14.]

tail, and tonsures either non-existent or so small that if one wishes he may cover it with near-by hair palpable proofs by which everyone is given to understand that if he could have the benefits attached to the clerical office without the clerical office he would wish neither to be nor be called a cleric? And since in the spiritual warfare he is seeking carnal rather than spiritual riches,* setting the creature before the Creator, he becomes an idolater of the fifth kind of idolatry, which, as Augustine bears witness, is avarice.* The opinions of the masters bear witness to the same: The greedy man loves a penny more than God.†

*1 Tm 4:8.

*Rm 1:25; Cf. Augustine, Sermo 107,7,8; PL 38:630.

†Cf. Mt 6:24; 7:26.

Nor should what we say seem remarkable since Christ himself excludes from his army those clothed in soft raiment. He says: 'Behold, those who are clothed in soft raiment are in king's houses.* Gregory says: *What does it mean: 'Behold those clothed in soft raiment are in kings' houses', if it does not define by a clear judgment that these men are fighting not for a heavenly but for an earthly king. Being given up to outward things, they flee suffering hardships for God's sake and they seek only the comfort and the pleasure of the present life.*

*Mt 11:8. Cf. DCC III, 23.

Therefore, let no one think that there is no sin in the dissolute desire for expensive clothes; for if this were not a sin the Lord would certainly not have commended John for the harshness of his garment.* If this were not a fault, the Apostle Peter would never in his letter have curbed women from desiring costly clothes by saying: '[Dress] not in expensive clothes?'* Consider, therefore, what fault there is that men should also desire the very thing which the shepherd of the church carefully prohibited to women.*

*Mt 3:4.

*1 Tm 2:9.

*Gregory the Great, XL homiliarum in evangelia libri duo, I, 6, 3; PL 76:1097.

Here then is the rule concerning dress for all Christians. And because this is a general rule agreeable with the law of Christianity, what should be understood concerning clerics and monks, whose order in particular requires that they carry the cross of Christ not in constrained but in voluntary poverty?[32] From this it is evident that whenever an expensive garment is purchased through unlawful and ill-gotten gain and by plundering the poor a sin is committed. By this, as St Gregory says in the *Moralia:* 'Since the garment is put on because of pride, no one wears it where it will not be seen.'*

If indeed, as St Augustine says, it is a sacrilege to give the property of the poor to the rich, it follows that it is a sacrilege for the rich to accept the property of the poor. For both these things fall under the same reckoning of sin. It is for this reason that the writer of the *Rule for Canons* says: 'Those who have enough of their own take with great danger to their souls that on which the poor would live.'* And lest they wrongly interpret that 'having enough', he adds: 'Having food and clothing they should be content.'* For the Apostle said: 'Those who serve the altar should live from the altar.'† He did not say, 'They should become rich.'³³

Jerome says: 'It is praiseworthy for poor bishops to take thought for food, but it is disgraceful for all priests to be zealous for their own riches.'* It is dangerous (in fact it is apostasy) for priests to be zealous for their own riches; indeed it is exceedingly dangerous for all Christians because apostolic authority declares generally and for all: 'Those who wish to get rich fall into the snare of the devil.'* And Truth Himself says: 'Woe to you rich men, you have your consolation.'* And in the Gospel according to Mark, Truth says: 'It is easier for a camel to pass through the eye of a needle than for a rich man to enter the kingdom of God.'* This gospel text demands that we mean not only the person who has riches, but also him who does not and gladly would. The text continues: 'Those who were hearing this were even more amazed. And they said to themselves: "Who then can be saved?" '* Bede says: 'What does that reply mean, for incomparably greater was the crowd of the poor, who because they had lost their riches were able to be saved? [What can it mean] except that they understood that all who love riches, even if they are unable to acquire them, are to be reckoned among the number of the rich.'*

**Gregory the Great,* XL homiliarum . . . . *2,40; PL 76: 1305.*

**DCC, I, 31,32.*

**Concilium Aquisgranense (816), cap. 107; MGH, Legum III Concilia II, 1, p. 382.*
†*1 Co 9:13.*
**Ep 52,6.*

**1 Tm 6:9.*

**Lk 6:24.*

**Mk 10:25-29.*

**Mk 10:26.*

**In Marcum, 3,10,26; CCh 120:802-805.*

V.

However, there are certain profits which seem to those who are ignorant of the canons,[34] to be lawful but which are unlawful—for example, the rents of fields and vineyards which they call by the more honorable name, 'benefice rents'.* But at the Council of Chalcedon, which is one of those four councils to which St Gregory assigns evangelical authority, the holy fathers forbid such rents to all clerics as base gain.* And no wonder, for the precept of ethical discipline is this: 'Avoid sordid gain as if it were loss.'† Well-considered reason upon the matter of clerical benefice rents will answer: 'It is sordid for lawful soldiers to be paid from benefice rents which are proper to countrymen alone[35] because a practical honesty does not take what greedy self-interest slyly urges.' But which of the seculars[36] will agree to that verdict, which is based on reason and authority?*

Well then, who can detect his own failings?† Surely only that man who fears God and 'diligently searches out his will in the holy scriptures'.* And confronting himself both as defender and prosecutor, he argues with himself and against himself** in this or in a similar manner: 'Oh, sinner! Perhaps you think there is such a thing as a small sin?' Would that the severe Judge thought any sin were small! But woe is me! Does not every sin dishonor God by deviating from the law? What sin will the sinner dare to call small? When is it a small thing to dishonor God?* O dry and useless wood, deserving of eternal fires!** What will you answer on that day when an accounting is demanded of how you have spent all the time of living meted out to you, down to the last winking of an eye?†

'Surely at that time, your every idle deed or idle word* or silence—down to the smallest thought**—will be condemned if it was not directed according to the will of God. Woe! How many sins will spring up which you do not see

*censualia beneficia.

*Gregory the Great, Ep 1,24; MGH Epp I,19-22, p. 36, Decret. D.15, C.2. Cf. DCC, 1,50,54.
†Caecilius Balbus, I,3, p.18,6.

*Cf. DCC,II,30.
†Ps 19:12.

*Augustine, De doctrina christiana, 2,9,14; CCh 32:40,1-2. Cf. DCC,I,51.

**Cf. Ps 50:22.

*Cf. Si 10:16 & Bernard, PP I,3; SBOp 5:1920, 2-3. Cf. Rm 4:15, Ga 2:18.
**Cf. Is 56:3, Si 6:3.
†in ictu oculi: Cf. 1 Co 15:22.
*Cf. DCC,III,22.
**Cf. 2 Co 5:10, DCC,I,51.

now!* Assuredly, there are more numerous and perhaps more dreadful things than these which you now see and you think are not evil (which you believe to be good) and which, when they appear undisguised, will be seen as the blackest of sins. There you will undoubtedly receive in proportion as you have behaved in the flesh, at a time when there will be no place for mercy, when penance will not be accepted nor amendment of life be hoped for.

'Here [and now] give thought to what you have done and how it behooves you to reform yourself. If you have done many good and few evil deeds, greatly rejoice; if many evil and few good deeds, greatly grieve. Unprofitable sinner! Are these thoughts not enough to make you howl aloud?* Are they not enough to turn blood and marrow into tears?* Woe, amazing hardness [of heart] which blows so heavy are too light to break up.* O sluggishness insensible! Sharp goads are too blunt to bestir the likes of you!'*

Augustine (who is Catholic in all of his writings and whose words it is uncatholic to disobey for they are faithful) also denies that those who live a worldly life can know the truth. He calls 'wickedness' the worldly life which in the book *De agone christiano* he describes in this way: *Anyone who thinks that he can know the truth while he is still living a profligate life errs. It is wickedness to love the world and to value those things which come to be and which pass away, and to strive to acquire them and to rejoice when they abound and to grieve when they are lost.*

Surely, anyone who has been so lulled to sleep amid earthly cares that he cannot be awakened by these words of St Augustine is not asleep but dead,* and unless life-making grace deigns to be present to him,* he will not be able to hear the apostle crying out: 'Now is the hour for us to arise from sleep. Let us cast off the works of darkness' and so forth.† The reason for this present writing and the intention of the writer is that, if this writing should perhaps come into the hands of anyone

*Cf. Rv 9:12, 11:14.

*Cf. Jb 6.
*Cf. DCC, III, 45.

*Cf. Pr 19:29.

*Cf. Col 4:24,21.

*De agone christiano, XIII, XIV; CSEL 41:118.
*Cf. Mk 5:39, Lk 8:52.
*Cf. Prosper of Aquitaine, 'De ingratis' Carmen in quatuor partes, II,153,504; PL 51:121.
*Rm 13:11-12.

living a worldly life yet not disdaining to read this little something,* he may be built up† by the authorities here assembled—through the inspiration of the One who inspires wheresoever he will.** He is always ready to help those who hope in him so that they may be inspired to resolve to live the spiritual life.

*Cf. Cicero, De inventione, I, 53, 110.
†Cf. 1 Co 8:1, 16:23, 14:4.
**Jn 3:8.

VI.

However, I have taken the opportunity to write those four [questions], concerning which your opinions[37] seem to dissent both from reason and from authority, and which, because of their very subtlety,[38] are not of much use to weak [minded] auditors. These are the four questions: Whether one and the same person may be both cleric and monk; whether intention alone makes a cleric; whether cloistered nuns and monks although they keep the one Rule of St Benedict should also have the same guardianship of the cloister; whether it is lawful for a monk to preach in church.

On two of these [questions] I have already spoken with that meagre eloquence of mine which can be called 'eloquence' only through exaggeration and is in keeping with my feeble intelligence.[39] Always, as I freely acknowledge, have I been and am I speechless, as my wicked life demands; even more so when the requirement of honest business or necessity demands a discourse.* Because of this, very often a great sadness steals into my heart, but sometimes a kind of consolation follows it. The reason for this is because many have been puffed up through their own eloquence and have fallen headlong into pride and because it is [always] safer to hear a sermon than to give one.

*Cf. Past. Care, I,9; ACW 11:37

Wherefore St Ambrose says in his book *On Duties: I have seen many fall into sin through speaking and scarcely anyone through keeping silence. Therefore it is harder to know how to be silent than how to speak. I know that many speak because they do not know how to be silent.** And according to Jerome, as

*De officiis ministrorum I, 2. 5. Cf. Decretum. C.17, q.5, c.20. DCC I, 20.

often as we do not in speaking observe the 'circumstances of speech' namely: 'What, to whom, why, in what manner, where, when', just as often does an evil word proceed from our mouth.* *Comment. in Ep. ad Ephes, 4:29; PL 26:546, Cf. Decretum. C.22, q.5, e.21.

Holy Agathon, one of the Fathers, fearing this, carried a pebble in his mouth for three years in order to learn to refrain from speaking.† And another, because he was illiterate, went up to a certain man to be taught a psalm. When he had heard the first verse of the thirty-eighth psalm: 'I have said: I will guard my ways, that I sin not with my tongue',* did not allow himself to hear the second verse, and said [to himself]: 'If I can carry this out in action, then this verse alone is sufficient for me.' When the sage who had taught him the verse[40] reproved him for not having come to him at all for six months, he answered: 'Because I have not fulfilled that verse yet.'*

*Vitae patrum V: Verba seniorum, 4,7; PL 73:865.

*Ps 39:1 (38 LXX)

*Source unknown.

But later, when he had lived many more years, he was asked by a certain well-known person whether he had learned the verse. He said: 'In forty-nine years I have hardly been able to carry it out.' It is not surprising that they used to take such pains to guard the lips because Truth, which cannot lie, says: 'For every idle word that men have spoken, they shall render account on the day of judgment.'* But enough of this for now.

*Mt 12:36.

Now our little discourse* may be continued to a consideration of the third question, which is this: Whether cloistered nuns and monks, since they keep the same Rule of St Benedict, should also have the same guardianship of the cloister. Here the natural differences between the sexes might provide good support of reason, if the reasoner's ability is of a kind which enables him by his very shrewdness to draw forth arguments relevant to this matter.[41] But because I am naturally thick-headed, my ingenuity is dull and my abilities are dealing kindly with me if—by my slow dull wit—I have said anything consonant with reason and authority.* Do you think that those things which I just said I said in order to reprove them? God forbid that I should reprove with any sarcasm their foolish wisdom.[42] They have

*Cf. Cicero, De oratore, 2, 38, 159.

*Cf. Horace, Ep 2. 1. 244 & Serm. 2. 2. 3. Cicero, Tusc. 5. 15. 45. See Curtius, pp. 410-11.

been 'funning' rather than philosophizing. But I firmly hold and do not doubt that every good thought, and speech, and action, is his gift* of whom the apostle says: 'The one and the same spirit who works all things allots to each as he will'.*

*Cf. DCC II, 9.

*1 Co 12:11.

But to return to our subject:[43] In the first place it must be said that, because the feminine sex is weak, it needs greater protection and stricter enclosure. The church testifies to the weakness of that sex when it prays on the feast of a virgin-martyr, 'O, God, who, among the signs of your power, has also conferred the victory of martyrdom even on the weak sex.'[44] What protection of the cloister will ever be sufficient for this sex, seeing that King Acrisius was unable to protect his Danae though she was enclosed in the highest tower?* We need not be concerned over the fable which is only a fable, but the commentators on sacred scripture allow moral stories, indeed myths (that is, the meanings of fables) when they are suitable.* And so Horace is not said to be a liar when he (intending not to lie but to instruct) introduced a country mouse and a city mouse who talked with one another.* Augustine defines a lie in this way: 'A lie is a false interpretation intended to deceive.'*

*Horace, Carmina, 3, 16.

*Cf. Aug., De doctrina christiana, IV, iv.

*Horace, Serm. 2,6,80-117.

*De mendacio, 4; CSEL 41, p. 416, 10-11.

The feminine sex (whose protection is now being treated) has four formidable and declared enemies. Two are within the sex itself: lust of the flesh and frivolous feminine inquisitiveness.* Two are without: the casual lechery of the masculine sex and the wicked envy of the devil. To these are added [the fact] that a woman can lose her virginity by violence —a thing which in the masculine sex nature itself prevents. Here it should be noted that, according to blessed Jerome, chastity is the only thing for which it is lawful for a man to lay violent hands upon himself, if he cannot escape the violator in any other way.* And lest we seem to consider such a matter at too great length, let us say simply and in an ordinary way: 'The more fragile the vessel, the more diligent the care it needs lest the vessel be broken, and that kind of care which would prevent its being

*Cf. Cicero, Philippics; Ker. 7,3.9.

*In Ionam, I,2, cf. Decretum., C. 23, q. 5, c. 11.

carried off through theft or pillage, a protection which golden vessels require more than glass'.

A consecrated woman requires both kinds of protection for she can, metaphorically, be called a glass vessel because of her fragile sex and a golden vessel because of the ideal of the office of virgin.* The reader should not wonder that I do not use the customary word, that is *monialis* [alone—feminine].† I am observing the rule of grammar[45] according to which *monialis* is nothing. *Sanctimonialis* [consecrated woman], however, can be used, because it is something. But it cannot be used without qualification, because it is an adjective.* When therefore we say (following the grammarians) 'a consecrated woman', the full meaning will include both [concepts]:* namely, the fragile sex and the intention of holy virginity. Virgil describes the one in this way: 'Fickle and forever changeable is a woman.'† The apostle describes the other when he says: 'A virgin takes thought for the things of the Lord, that she may be holy in body and in spirit.'* When these two qualities coincide in one person, who can devise a suitable protection by which the fragile sex might persist in its undertaking—which is to be an angel?

Therefore, Jerome says to Principia, the Roman virgin: 'Sex is forgotten by a virgin who carries Christ in her body and who already possesses what she will be.'† It is not remarkable if Jerome said this, for [a virgin] lives in the flesh beyond the flesh. She lives on earth the heavenly life which Christ has promised, saying: 'In the resurrection they will neither marry nor be married, but they will be as the angels of God.* This heavenly spouse, because she must have very careful protection and must be removed from public gaze, is marked out by this, that she is veiled not only from every priest but equally from the chief priest.* By a dark robe and by a dark veil is she covered, because every earthly ornament is unworthy to touch her, for her every glory is that of the daughter and spouse of the heavenly king within.*

The excellence and dignity of this glory Jerome shows in writing to Eustochium the virgin, saying:

*See DCC,III,31 & DC,VII,298: sanctimoniales.

†Cf. Augustine, De verbo domini, Sermo XXII,cap. I.

*See Cicero, De finibus, 4,20,57.

*See Cicero, De partitione oratoriae, 12,41.

†Aeneid, IV, 569-570.

*1 Co 7:34.

†Ep 65,1.

*Mt 22:30.

*Cf. Ovid, Metamorphoses 9:261.

*Ps 45:14.

'O my lady Eustochium'.* By having said this—because he called her his lady—he proves that he had spoken the truth, for he says: 'I ought to call the Lord's spouse "my lady" '.* Through the following story Jerome, speaking of the same Eustochium, shows that it was not permissable for her to be decorated with any worldly ornament. *Once upon a time a most noble woman, Pretexta, changed her appearance and style of dress and arranged her disordered hair in a worldly manner. She did all this at the command of her husband Emicius, who was the paternal uncle of the virgin Eustochium. And lo! That very night, while she slept, she saw an angel of terrible mien come to her, threatening her with punishment in these words: 'Did you dare to prefer your husband's bidding and to touch with sacrilegious hands the head of God's virgin? Even now those hands are withering, so that you may perceive in agony what you have done. And at the end of five months you shall be led to hell bereft of your husband and children.' In due course everything was fulfilled and death swiftly sealed the belated penitence of the wretched woman. In such a way is Christ avenged against the violators of his temple.**

* *Ep 22,2.*

* *Ibid.*

* *Ep 107,5. abridged.*

VII.

But the ornaments which Christ looks for in his spouse and by which she is recognized to be his are those marks which reveal the holy virginity of a glorious soul, of which the psalmist beautifully and expressly said not 'within' [*intus*] but 'from within' [*abintus*];* for holy virginity is in the heart [*in mente*] in such a way that it gives forth its own signs.[46] These are: a face made pale and lean; modesty in speaking; obedience in listening; frugality in food; soberness in drinking;* gravity in gait; cheapness in clothing; a skin toughened by hair-shirts and not pampered by baths. Jerome says: 'A glossy skin betokens a dirty soul.'*

* *Ps 44:14 Vulg.*

* *Cf. 1 Tm 2:9.*

* *Ep 117,6.*

He says the same again about the education of a virgin: *For the full-grown virgin*[47] *I object utterly to*

baths. She ought to be ashamed, and should not be able, to see herself naked. If she has indeed weakened her body and brought it into subjection by fasts and vigils, if by the chill of chastity she desires to extinguish the flame of lust and the smolderings of her hot years; if by a calculated squalor she hastens to soil her natural beauty, why then does she contrariwise stir up sleeping fires with the warmth of baths?* *Ep 107,11.
Cf. Ep 66,7.

Authority sets the limit of moderation in eating and soberness in drinking which the spouse of Christ should have. Jerome says: *If those with emaciated bodies are assailed only by their thoughts, what does a girl suffer who [still] enjoys delicacies? Surely as the apostle says: 'She is dead though still alive.'** However, if I am in any way discreet, if one already tested is to be believed, this is the first advice I give, this I admonish: that the spouse of Christ should flee wine as poison.*[48]* These are the devils' chief weapons against youth. Avarice does not so much disturb nor pride puff up nor ambition entice them. Easily do we abstain from other vices, but this enemy is enclosed within us. Wherever we wander, we carry the enemy with us. Wine and youth are the twin fires of passion. Why do we add oil to the flame? Why do we add fuel to the burning body?**

*1 Tm 5:6.

*Ep 22,8.

Again he says: *Let her nourishment be a small cabbage and occasionally a little fish. And not to draw out the teaching on gluttony, which I have spoken of more fully in another place, let her eat in such a way that she is always hungry, so that immediately after eating, she can read, pray and chant the psalms. Let reading follow prayer, prayer follow reading.*[49] It seems only a short time that she is busy with such a variety of works.

Let her also learn to weave wool, to hold the distaff, to place a wool basket on her lap, to turn the spindle, to guide the threads with her thumb. Let her spurn silken chinese stuff [50] *and the weaving of wool and gold into the threads, let her make clothes by which the cold is kept out and not those by which a body clothed is laid bare [to cold weather].** Again

*Ep 107: 10, 9, 10.

he says: *If you want to reply that you are sprung of noble stock, always brought up in luxury and featherbeds, that you cannot do without wine and appetizing foods, and that you cannot live more strictly by these rules, I shall answer: 'Well then, live by your own law, you who cannot live by the law of God.** *It is not that God, the Lord Creator of the whole world, takes delight in the rumblings of our stomach, in the emptiness of the belly, and in the burning of the lungs, but rather that in this way moderation may be preserved.'**

The spouse of Christ should also have such an uninterrupted stability in her cell or in her monastery that she does not go out to visit a prince's wife, even if she lives near the monastery. This is for two reasons. One of them is a holy pride, of which Jerome says: *O Spouse of Christ! Why do you treat your husband unjustly? Spouse of God, do you rush off to the wife of a man? Learn in this respect a holy pride. Know that you are better than they.** There is another reason which is indicated by the story of Dinah.†

When she went out to see the women of that neighborhood, she was seized by Shechem the son of Hamor and raped. About this matter we have previously spoken a little. Jerome says:* *The spouse of Christ should never go out of doors, nor should those who stroll around the city come upon her lest they strike her and wound her and, carrying off the garment of her modesty, they leave her naked and bleeding. Instead, when anyone knocks on her door, let her say, 'I am a wall and my breasts a tower. I have washed my feet and I cannot soil them.'**

Again [he says] to Eustochium: *Take care not to leave the house. Dinah went out and was despoiled. Your husband is a jealous spouse and does not want your face to be seen by others.** Likewise in a letter to Oceanus: *What I say will be for your edification, holy virgin.* In the Life of Saint Martin recounted by Sulpicius we read that St Martin, while passing by, wished to go to see a certain virgin who was esteemed for her way of life and chastity. She was

**Cf. Bernard's Letter to Robert, cited in DCC III,32.*

**Ep 22,11.*

**Ep 22,16.*
†*Gn 34:1-2. See Gregory the Great, Past. Care, III,28; ACW 11:200.*

**Ep 107,7.*

**Sg 8:10, 5:3.*

**Ep 22,25.*

unwilling *[to receive him]*, but sent him a gift. Looking at him through the window, she said to the holy man: *'Pray out there, father, for I have never been visited by a man.'* St Martin thanked God that she, who had been trained in such a way, kept resolute her chaste will. And he blessed her and went away filled with joy.*

I will come to the end of my instruction by a brief summing up.[51] Reason, authority, precedents, the veiling of the head, the consecration, the betrothal itself (which is signified by the pledge of the ring and which is so important that, as we have already said, only the bishop and not just any priest should officiate)—what do all these things imply but that the heavenly bride should be protected by enclosure so careful that she be not leered at by an immodest eye, the messenger of a lecherous heart, lest her glory should become her shame by that wretched downfall which the prophet laments.*

Jerome says to Eustochium: *Beware, I beg you, lest someday God should say of you, 'The Virgin Israel has fallen and there is none who might raise her up.'** I speak boldly: Although God can do all things, he cannot raise up a virgin after her ruination. He has the power to free her from punishment, but he does not will to crown a despoiled maiden.* Let us fear lest that prophecy be fulfilled in us: *'Good virgins shall fail'.** Observe that he says, 'Good virgins shall fail', for there are bad virgins as well. He says: *'He who looks upon a woman with lust has already sinned against her in his heart.'** Therefore, virginity is lost in the mind.

These are bad virgins, virgins in the flesh and not in the spirit, foolish virgins who, because they do not have oil, are shut out by the bridegroom.* But if those who are virgins are not saved from other faults by their bodily virginity, what shall happen to those who have prostituted the members of Christ and have changed the temple of the Holy Spirit into a brothel?* They shall hear on the spot: *'Go down, sit on the ground, virgin daughter of Babylon. Sit on the ground. There is no throne for the daughter of the*

**Ps. Jerome, Ep 42, 10* ad Oceanum de vita clericorum; *PL* 30:300-301.

*Am 5:2, 1 *M* 1:42.

*Am 5:2.

**Cf. Si* 42:10.

*Am 8:13.

*Mt 5:28.

*Mt 25:1-13.

**Cf. 1 Co* 6:19.

Chaldeans. No more shall you be called soft and delicate. Take up the millstone and grind the meal. Take off your veil, bare your legs, cross the rivers. Your shame will be revealed and your disgrace become plain.* And this, after the bridal chamber of the Son of God, after the kisses of your brother and spouse.* She, of whom the word of the prophet rang out: 'The queen stands at your right hand in vesture of gold wrought about with diverse colors,'* she will be stripped bare and her backside will be turned toward his face.[52] She will sit near the waters of deep solitude,† and she will spread her feet for anyone who passed by and will be defiled from head to foot.*

*Is 47:1-5.

*Sg 4:10; 5:1.

*Ps 45:10.

*Cf. Jl. 4:19, Ho 2:3, 9:1.
*Ep 22, 5-6.

To unravel the case before us, I have used only the abundant authority of St Jerome as a special advocate of our case. Anyone who wishes to know the reason for this will recognize that our purpose in this is to show that the protection afforded by stricter enclosure is more necessary for consecrated virgins than for monks. While others have written in praise of holy virginity, he has written on its protection.[53] Others have written on the glory of virginity preserved, he on the shame of virginity lost.[54] Who does not see that his witness supports our own thesis?

But lest what we say be ambiguous, let us hear what Jerome himself says to Eustochium:* *At the beginning of the booklet, I said that I was going to say little or nothing about the trials of marriage. And now I advise the same thing: that if you wish to know how many worries a virgin is free of, how many a wife is bound to, you ought to read Tertullian's 'To a Philosopher and a Friend'* and other little books on virginity. And [you ought to read] the first-rate book of St Cyprian,† and what Pope Damascus has written in prose and in verse on the subject.** And [you ought to read] also the short works of our Ambrose which he wrote to his sister not long ago. In them, he exerted himself so eloquently that he has excellently considered, expressed, and set in order everything which pertains to the praise of virgins.*

*Ep 22, 22-23.

*Liber ad amicum philosophum, (before 197) is not extant.

†Liber de habitu virginum; PL 4:451-478, based on Tertullian, De virginibus velandis; PL 2:935-62.

**No longer extant.

A different course has been taken by us: not only

do we extol virginity, we preserve it. It is not enough to know what is good unless what is chosen is guarded very carefully, because the one is a matter of judgment, the other of action. The one is common to many, the other to but a few. 'He who perseveres to the end,' he says, 'will be saved'.* And, 'many are called but few are chosen'.* And so I call you to witness in the presence of God and of Christ Jesus and his chosen angels,* not to display lightly in public the vessels of the temple (which it is granted only the priests to see), lest any profane person should look into God's holy place.⁵⁵

*Mt 10:22.
*Mt 20:16, 22:14.

*Cf. 1 Tm 5:21.

Uzzah, drawing near the ark (an unlawful thing to do) was struck down by sudden death.* Yet no gold or silver vessel was ever as dear to God as the temple of a virginal body.* The dark cloud came first; now there is truth.† You, however, speak in a simple manner and, being kindly, do not despise those who are of ignoble birth. But lewd eyes see differently. They do not know how to regard beauty of soul, but only physical beauty. Hezekiah shows the treasury of God to the Assyrians, but the Assyrians should not have seen what they desired.*

*2 S 6:6-7.

*2 Co 11:2.
*Ex 14:20,20:21, 1 Co 13:12.

*Cf. 2 K 18:15-16.

Notice that in these words he proves on the authority of the Old Testament that the spouse of Christ, God's most precious treasure, ought to be guarded and enclosed as if under a seal,* lest the Assyrians, that is the lewd eye, be able to gawk at her. Therefore, the protection of enclosure which the Rule of St Benedict requires is unlike and less than that which is due the bride of Christ.

*Cf. Rv 20:3, Sg 4:12.

St Benedict did not write his rule for consecrated virgins but only for monks.* In it a monk is permitted to be sent out on a journey in answer to some call, to sell at the market and buy what the needs and requirements of the monastery demand.* Now no one doubts that this is unfitting (and wholly unbecoming) for any reason for the spouse of an earthly king, much less for the bride of the King of heaven. Many other things as well which do not apply to that sex are in that same Rule which was written, all agree, only for monks, because in it there is no

*Dial. II:36; FCh 39:107.

*RB 51:1.

mention of virgins.

If he who 'of all the just was filled with the spirit', as the *Dialogues* of Gregory attest,* had written a Rule for them, do you really think that he would with dangerous license have allowed that sex to appear in public? It would be contrary to the words and the examples of the fathers and contrary to his own example; for he himself visited his own sister St Scholastica, a woman consecrated to a life of holiness,* only once a year.

*Dial. II, 8; FCh 39:72.

*Dial. II, 23; FCh 39:102-104.

He wrote no rule for consecrated virgins nor was it necessary to write any, because in those times monasteries of virgins existed only under the guardianship of abbots. And with good reason![56] It is not expedient for that sex to enjoy the freedom of having its own governance—because of its natural fickleness and also because of outside temptations which womanly weakness is not strong enough to resist.

The examples of holy monks bear witness, however, to what we spoke of a little while ago: that the Rule permits a monk to go to the market for the needs of the monastery. Of these [holy monks] we read in the *Vita patrum* that, in the markets where they used to sell their own products, they actually worked miracles through the power of Christ. And what has been said on the third question can prove (unless the contrary is proved) that the protection of an unbroken enclosure is more necessary for women than for men, for dedicated holy women than for monks.

VIII.

Now, taking the counsel of both reason and authority, let us look closely at the question at hand: whether it is lawful for a monk to preach in church.[57] There are some clerics who, boasting of their office and despising the monastic order,* say it is contrary to both reason and authority for a monk who is dead to the world to open his mouth to preach 'in the midst of the church.'* The priests of the country villages, agreeing heartily with this opinion in the days of

*Cf. Ezk 35:13.

*Si 15:5; the antiphon to the introit of the Mass for Doctors of the Church.

Bishop Hartwick of blessed memory,* did not allow any monk to take part in one of their synods, which they call a chapter.

*Hartwick died in 1126.

Indeed, there was a certain priest on trial there, who, on the advice of his fellow priests, complained when he saw some monk present that this was a mean trick. And through his advocate he answered the charges not by argument but rather by asserting that a cleric's case ought not to be brought up in a dead man's presence. When this got around, a miracle took place: that dead man arose and went out of the assembly. But when Bishop Hartwick died three years later, the monk Cuno succeeded him as bishop. He who was dead to their way of thinking heard their cases and judged their lawsuits. In this way, divine providence turned to folly their foolish wisdom and confounded their unjust justice.

But because a dispute about the death of a monk has arisen, let us see what is the death by which a monk is said to have died. There is one death of the body, another of the soul, another of sins, and another according to which someone is said to have died to the world. The death of the body is the separation of the soul from the body.* The death of the soul is its separation from God. The death of sins takes place in baptism where all sins are so blotted out that not one remains, just as all the Egyptians pursuing Israel were drowned in the Red Sea so that not one remained*—this is a figure of baptism. Concerning this death the Apostle says: 'All of us who have been baptized into Christ Jesus have been baptized into his very death, and we are buried with him through baptism.'*

*Dial. IV, 47; FCh 39:258.

*Ex 14:22-27.

*Rm 6:3-4.

There is no dispute here about these three [deaths]. The fourth is understood in two ways as follows: 'dead to the world', that is, separated from worldly but not from ecclesiastical concerns. By this death both cleric and monk ought to have died, because they are soldiers of Christ—and not mercenaries but knights.* Of these the apostle says: 'No one who serves as God's soldier entangles himself in the affairs of the world.'* Consequently, they too

*Cf. above IV.

*2 Tm 2:4.

ought to live from tithes and the offerings at the altar. These are the portions of the God for whom they do battle.[58] This is the reason why the canons forbid to clerics all secular transactions except the care of pupils, if necessity happens to require this.

Death to the world is understood in a second way: that is, separation from men by the solitary life, living alone for God alone, which is the death characteristic of the second kind of monks.* Isidore of the *Etymologies* distinguishes these two kinds as follows. He says: 'The hermits seek to resemble* Elijah and John. The cenobites seek to resemble the apostles.'* And St Benedict in the *Rule* says: *The first kind are the cenobites, that is, those who belong to monasteries and serve under a rule and under an abbot. The second kind are the anchorites, hermits, that is, who are not in the first fervor of religious life, but who by day-by-day testing in the monastery have learned, with the help and the encouragement of others, to fight against the devil. And they go forth from the ranks of their brethren to the solitary combat of the desert. They are now serene without the encouragement of others. They can now, with God's help, do battle against the weaknesses of the flesh and of the mind.**

By this death died blessed Arsenius.* After his parents died, he refused the inheritance willed to him, saying: 'I died before they did'. And St Benedict [was dead this way] for three years, and St Jerome, indeed, for four.* It is profitable to listen to how Jerome himself describes his own death because he has in mind both the edification of the reader and the solution of the prior question. He says: *O, how often, when I was stationed in that vast desert*[59] *which, burnt up by the sun's rays, affords monks a savage habitation, did I imagine that I was in the midst of roman luxuries! I used to sit there alone, for I was filled with bitterness. Misshapen limbs were roughened by sack-cloth and a filthy skin concealed the filthiness of an ethiopian flesh.*[60] *Every day tears and every day groanings! And if sleep threatened to overwhelm me who was always fighting against it,*

---

*RB 1:3-5.

*imitantur.

*Isidore of Seville, Etym. 7,13,3. See DCC, II, 44.

*RB 1:2-5.

*Vitae Patrum V: Verba Seniorum, 6,7; PL 73:888.

*Cf. Dial. II,1 (FCh 39:57). Cf. DCC, II,42.

I would dash to the bare ground my bruised bones and limbs that hardly stuck together.

About food and drink I say nothing, for those who are wasting away are used to taking cold water and to take anything cooked is an indulgence. Therefore I myself, who for fear of hell had condemned myself to this prison, I the companion only of scorpions and of wild beasts, often found myself in the midst of maidens' dances. My face grew pale with fastings and my mind seethed with desire. In my cold body and in my flesh which alone had decayed, the flames of lust shot up.

And so, destitute of all aid, I lay at Jesus' feet, I wet them with my tears and wiped them dry with my hair.* And I subdued my warring flesh with a week's fast. I am not ashamed of my wretchedness; rather, I lament that I am not what I might have been. I remember crying out that I had joined day to night and I did not stop beating my breast until, at the Lord's command, peace returned.   **Lk 7:38.*

I was afraid even of my little cell as if I knew my own thoughts. And enraged at and stern with myself, I went deep into the desert.[61] *Wherever I looked I saw only the hollow valleys, the jagged peaks of mountains, rocky precipices. There was the place of my prayer. In that house of correction I subdued the wretched flesh.*[62] *And as the Lord himself is my witness, after many tears, while fixing my eyes on heaven, I thought afterwards that I was among ranks of angels. Gladly and joyfully I sang: 'For the perfume of your ointments we run after you.'**   **Sg 1:3.*

Now if those who are attached only by thoughts endure this (since the body has been worn out), what does a girl endure who enjoys luxuries? The Apostle says: 'Though living, she is dead.'* However, if I may offer any counsel: if one already put to the test is to be believed, this is my first admonition, this do I beseech: the spouse of Christ should avoid wine like poison.*   **1 Tm 5:6.*

    *Ep 22,7-8. Cf. DCC, III, 32.

Look at St Jerome. Because he was a monk of both kinds,* he was dead to the world in both ways. And although he had died to worldly concerns, but   **Cf. DCC III,42.*

not to those of the church, he deserved to be counted among the most distinguished doctors. For his whole life was spent not only in teaching but also in writing, teaching that will abide. How, then, does he not contradict himself in teaching that, 'The monk has the office not of teaching but of morning, for he mourns for himself and for the world'?* And how does the apostolic see not contradict itself even in its decrees* when it prohibits a monk, however learned he may be, from preaching—and yet comes out in favor of a monk preaching? Therefore it is essential that one realize that this may blind someone to whom the distinction in the monastic order is not known, who yet may become aware of it through this distinction.

*Cf. Contra Vigilantium, 15: PL 23:367.

*See DCC, II, 16.

One monk is called a cenobite, another a hermit, that is, an anchorite who is properly—according to the etymology of the word—called a monk. For *monos* in Greek is translated into Latin as *one* or *alone*—hence, *monk*, that is, one living alone, and *monastery*, that is, the dwelling of one living alone. Now *cenobite* is from the Greek *cenon*, that is, *in common*, and is translated as *living in common*. Cenobium is the dwelling place of those living in common. And this name *monk* is common to cenobites as to hermits but with a different meaning.* For in the case of hermits it means a single person living by himself. In the case of cenobites, it means the one spirit of the many who seek to resemble those of whom it was written: 'All the believers were of one heart and one soul; nor did any of them say anything was his own, but they held all things were common. Nor was any of them in want. To each one was given according to his need.'*

*See DCC, II 42,43,49.

*Ac 4:32,34-35. Cf. DCC II,38.

Anyone who does not like equivocation[63] can say that cenobites and hermits should not both be called by the same name, *monk*. But one-ness is meant in a different way in each case: in hermits, one-ness of person; in cenobites, one-ness of spirit. The Holy Spirit, its author, has reserved this unity of the brethren dwelling together as his own excellent gift for a time of grace, and by bringing into being from himself the glowing first-fruits of the infant church by describing this unity, by means of charity He shaped it to be a teacher. In order to commend more fully the excellence of this precept, the same author, the Holy Spirit, described it in fine terms in the Old Testament through the prophet king and in describing prophesied, saying: 'Behold how good and how pleasant it is for brothers to live in unity.'*

*Ps 133:1.

The personal and private homes of the canons contradict both this pleasant good and that goodly pleasantness. Since they have, and ought to have according to their rule,* a common refectory and a common dormitory and other common workshops, I do not see why personal and private manses are necessary, unless it is so that the pleasant good (that is, the brethren living in unity) may be broken up and place given to the devil, who by the opportunity the place offers can advocate things which must be passed over in silence here. Faithful reader, to use St Jerome's words, you understand (as I do) what I am silent about and what I say better by saying nothing.

*See *Concilium Aquisgranense (816)*, c. 117; MGH, Legum III Concilia II, 1 (1906) p. 398.

But what part of the body is not a slave to pleasure if it has a pleasure-loving head? For, according to the reckoning of natural philosophy, the individual limbs derive their power of sensation from the head?* If a bishop is given over to pleasure, therefore, what wonder is it if his clerics live frivolous and fickle lives? And what will the quality of the life of laymen be but thoroughly dissolute? For this reason, St Gregory in the *Moralia* speaks this way: *It is necessary that we understand that anything done wantonly by men of inferior rank should be held in check by the discipline of men of greater rank. But when the men of greater rank become slaves to passion, the reins of wantonness are loosed on those of lesser rank. For who would willingly restrain himself under the tight rein of discipline when those who are recipients of the right to apply disciple have let themselves go?**

**Past. Care III,10*, Admonition 11.

**Moralia,2,16,27*; PL 75:568.

To cover up shameful things, however, we can say

this without violating integrity:[64] that it is greatly to be feared that a canon, who ought to serve as Christ's soldier, does not, if he has been split asunder for the sake of patrimony, which requires a dwelling of one's own just as a private manse requires administration. He serves the world in part and God in part—if indeed he serves God, for Truth says: 'No one is able to serve two masters. You are not able to serve God and Mammon.'* But lest in dwelling on these matters we offend the lovers of pleasure and of possessions, let us return now to the sequence of the yet-incomplete division.

*Mt 6:24.

IX.

We have spoken of the division of that name, *monk*, and we have given a description of its separate parts. Likewise, each part is subdivided in this way: cenobite or hermit, a cleric is one thing, a layman another, that is, a non-cleric. That person is a cleric who has been established in some clerical grade through ordination. That person is a layman who does not have clerical rank; custom calls him a *conversus*.* And he is a monk of the kind to whom Saint Jerome wrote that letter and in whose person he said there: 'I am not allowed to sit in the presence of a presbyter,'[65] although the very man who said this was a priest and the one to whom he said it was not even an acolyte. Consequently, anxious to be understood, he said in another place: 'A monk does not have the office of teaching but of weeping.'* The apostolic see, in the interests of the greater good, has also forbidden by law the office of preaching to the monk who is only a monk and not a cleric, because many lay monks of that time were anthropomorphites[66] and were mistaken in their belief concerning the body of Christ which is presented on the altar.

*Cf. DCC, I, 23.

*See DCC II, 41.

It is not enough to know what is said in the decrees unless one also knows to whom and why and when it said.* And it is necessary to understand, by logical reflection, that the clerical state and the lay state are

*See Decret. I, D. 29, cc. 1-3. Cicero, De partitione oratoria, VIII, 32.

contraries, for they are not able to exist at the same time in the same person. And they are immediate contraries in respect to a third 'something', that is, a Catholic is either a cleric or a layman.

But the monastic state and the clerical state are not contraries; rather, both are additional and further offices and can exist in the same man.[67]

One and the same man is indeed both cleric and monk: monk because he made the monk's profession; cleric because he holds the office of cleric. Cleric is the name of an office and not something in nature.* And what wonder if one and the same man is both a cleric and a monk, when one and the same man, from different points of view, may be both a father and a son: a father because he has a son; a son because he has a father. I think a conclusion has been reached on how Jerome does not contradict himself and how the apostolic see does not contradict itself in its decrees.

*See DCC II,16.

Concerning the Sarabites and the gyrovague monks (that is, the third and the fourth kinds of monks), we have said nothing, for as St Benedict says: 'Concerning their thoroughly wretched manner of life, it is better to say nothing than to say anything.'* Master Lanfranc was by no means unacquainted with those things which we have said about the diversity of the monastic order. He was a man very learned in divine and human knowledge. When made a monk, he wrote to Master Berengarius against his heresy.[68] In that writing, he made a similar division: 'The Catholic Church is divided into clerical and lay orders.'* This division would be extremely faulty unless one monk might be a cleric and another a layman. I have said 'division', for in its meaning it is equivalent to that division set by the rule: 'Some Catholics are clerics and some are laymen.'

*RB, 1, 12.

*De corpore et sanguine domini, 4

And a teacher in speaking as a teacher and a dialectician as a dialectician, even as a heretic though still an expert in logical divisions, would not divide the catholic church in an uncatholic way if he either posited that monks are outside the catholic church or reckoned a bishop-monk among laymen.[69]

We spoke above of a certain case where a decree of the apostolic see removes from the office of preaching the monk who is a layman.* Nevertheless, there is that very telling point which the apostle sets forth when he says: 'How shall they preach unless they be sent.'*

*See Decret., Pars II, c. 16, q. 1, c. 19.

*Rm 10:15. Cf. DCC II, 49.

No one, surely, holds the office of preaching unless he has been sent by the person who has the power of sending.* Clerics, when they are ordained, are invested with the office of the altar and of preaching.[70] Therefore, because monks are themselves also ordained in the same way as clerics are in every respect, whatever a cleric receives in ordination through the ordaining bishop, the monk also receives the very same thing.[71]

*Cf. DCC II, 45.

Therefore the monk who is simply a monk, that is, not ordained, however learned and however holy he is, will be presumptuous if he usurps to himself the office of preaching. Saint Wolfgang, who was not unfamiliar with this—as one reads in his *Life*[72]—when he had received the permission of his own abbot, left his monastery but not his monk-ness.* And because he was a priest, he took the road to preach the Gospel to the Pannonians.[73] Nevertheless, no one, even if ordained, should put his scythe to another's harvest, that is, preach to another's parishioners without the permission of the one whose parishioners they are. Accordingly, St Wolfgang had resolved to preach not to Christians but to pagans.[74]

*See DCC, I, 47.

If the things which have been said so far are weighed by careful consideration, they affirm, unless I am mistaken, through the firm support of reason and authority, that the monk once invested by ordination with the same office and in the same way as a cleric should be called by the name of the same office, that is, cleric. And he ought to be paid by the benefice which is due to the same office, which means he ought to live from the tithes and the offerings of the faithful.

And I would say even more if I could do so without offending certain people. And I would say that he has a better right than a secular cleric who possesses an earthly inheritance† and earthly possessions by earthly right.* As the authority of the Old Testament bears witness, the Lord ordained that tithes be given to the Levites, that is, to the ministers of the altar, but on this condition: that they receive no portion in the distribution of the land among the other tribes. He [the Lord] says: 'I will be their portion', as if he were to say: 'Tithes are mine. I want only those to have them whose portion I am, that is, those men who possess nothing on earth but me'. Therefore Jerome, a monk and a cleric, because he was a priest spoke with certainty and not tentatively: *If I am the Lord's portion and the share of his inheritance, I do not receive a portion among the other tribes, but as a levite and a priest, I live from the tithes and, serving the altar, I am supported by the offerings of the altar. Having food and clothing, I will be content with these and naked I will follow the naked cross.* **

†Whether or not clerics should possess anything was a much debated question. Some idea of the problem may be gained from Gratian, Decret. *Pars II, c. 12, q. 1, Pars I, Pars II.*

*terreno iure: This phrase should not be placed in opposition to 'heavenly law' or 'celestial law'. Rather, terreno iure might accurately be placed in parallel to iure ecclesiastico, if not in opposition.

**Ep 52,4.

X.

If you should object to this, saying, 'Priests, the rectors of parishes to whom has been entrusted the care of souls, ought to have tithes, but not monks who are for no reason at all permitted to rule parishes', I shall respond: If it is permitted for monks to rule large parishes, why is it not permitted for them to rule small parishes, since this would be even more in keeping with monastic humility? What is a bishopric if not a large parish?[75]

St Jerome wrote to Nepotian the monk a letter in which he instructed him in the ruling of his own parish, as the words of that letter insinuate: *If in discharging your clerical office you visit either a widow or a virgin, you should never enter the home unaccompanied but take as your companions those by whose attendance you will not be dishonored. If a lector, if an acolyte, if a psalmist accompanies you, let him be well-mannered and not well-dressed; do not let him curl their hair with a curling-iron, but rather let their deportment proclaim their modesty.*

Nor should you sit down with a woman by yourself in a private room without a third party or witness. If something of a more intimate nature has to be said, she has a nurse, an older virgin of the house, a widow or a married woman [to speak to]. She is not so god-like[76] that she has no one but you in whom she is duty-bound to confide. Beware of every suspicion, and whatever might credibly be dreamed up; avoid it beforehand, lest it be dreamed up.* *Ep 52,5. Cf. DCC, I, 16,17.

Likewise: Either rarely or never let women's feet visit your humble lodging. Either equally ignore or equally love all the maidens and virgins of Christ. Do not stay under the same roof and do not trust confidently in past chastity. You cannot be stronger than Samson or holier than David or wiser than Solomon.* Always remember that a woman drove its first inhabitant from the possession of Paradise. If you are sick, let some holy brother attend you, or your sister or mother or a well-proven woman of the faith. But if there are no persons of blood-kinship and purity of character, the church supports many old women who furnish the office and receive payment for the service of ministering. In this way your infirmity may also bear the fruit of alms-giving. I know some who have grown strong in body and begun to weaken in spirit. She serves you dangerously whose face you frequently consider.* *DCC, III, 32. Bernard of Clairvaux, Ep 1, 3. / *Ep 52,5.

Likewise: Let what you do not subvert what you say, lest when you speak in church someone may say to himself, 'Why do you not then yourself do as you say?' Even a thief can bring a charge of covetousness; the mouth of a priest should agree with his thoughts. Be subject to your bishop and accept him as the parent of your soul.* *Ep 52,7.

Likewise: When you teach in the church, do not excite the people's applause but their groans. And let the tears of those who hear you be your praise. The priest's sermon should be based on the reading of the scriptures.* *Ep 52,8.

These sayings of St Jerome instructing the priests of common people* and the whole exhortatory letter advocates this: that priests to whom the care *sacerdotes plebium not sacerdotes populi.

of souls has been entrusted should guard most carefully their own reputation, without which their preaching has little or no effect. For if one's reputation is disregarded, that saying of Gregory still holds: that 'if a man's life is despised, his preaching is scorned.'*

Nor should we pass over in silence St Jerome's judgement in the same letter against the golden ornaments of the church as things which should be rejected along with the other jewish superstitions. The careful reader will be able to gather this from his words when he says: *Many persons build walls and purloin the church's columns. Marble gleams, panelled ceilings glitter with gold, the altar is set off by precious stones, and yet there is no election for the servants of Christ. And let no rich man cite in refutation the temple in Judaea, the table, the oil-lamps, the censers, the offering dishes, the goblets, the mortars, and other things made of gold. These things were approved by the Lord at a time when the priests sacrificed victims and when the blood of beasts was the remission of sins.** *(Though all these things happened to them as a foreshadowing: 'they were written for our correction, to whom the final age of the world has come').**

But now, since the Lord, a poor man, has consecrated the poverty of his own home, let us consider his cross (which we ought to carry) and we will regard riches as filth. Why should we wonder that Christ calls mammon 'wicked'? Why do we hug and love what Peter declares he does not possess? Besides, if we follow only the letter and the bare narrative about gold and riches delights us, we ought also to regard other things as well: Let bishops take as wives virgins of Christ. However well-intentioned he is, the man who is deformed, who has a scar, is to be deprived of the priesthood. Let leprosy of the body be preferred to vices of the soul.* *Let us increase, let us multiply and fill the earth, and let us not sacrifice a lamb or celebrate the mystic pasch, for these are forbidden by law to take place away from the temple. And in the seventh month, let us set up the*

*Hom. in Evang., 1,12,1; PL 76: 1119.

*Cf. Heb 9:22.

*1 Co 10:11.

*Cf. Cyprian, The Unity of the Catholic Church, c. 18 (ACW 25; 60-61)

tabernacle and announce the solemn fast with a trumpet.*

*The Feast of Tabernacles. See Ez 3:1-4.

But if we compare all these things, the spiritual with the spiritual, and know with Paul that the law is spiritual, and with David sing the words, 'Take away the veil from my eyes and I shall ponder the wonders of your law',* we ought then to understand, even as Our Lord understood and interpreted the Sabbath. And we should either reject gold and the other jewish superstitions, or, if gold pleases [us], then the Jews also should please us; along with the gold we must either approve or condemn them.*

*Ps 119:18.

*Ep 52,10.

That outstanding teacher, who was highly expert in the three languages of sacred scripture, would certainly not have written such things if he had discovered in any authentic scripture that golden ornaments were enjoined on Christians either by precept or by counsel. If we have scant confidence in him, let us hear what St Ambrose says on this same subject. In the book *On Duties*, where he discusses the works of mercy, he says this: *Why is it necessary to guard what gives no help? Will the Lord not say: 'Why have you allowed the needy to die of hunger? Surely you had gold, you should have given alms. It would be better for you to save vessels of living flesh than of metal.' To this no reply can be made. What indeed could you say—'I was afraid that the temple of God would have no ornament'? He would answer: 'The sacraments need no gold, nor do they, not bought with gold, give satisfaction to gold. The adornment of the sacraments is the ransoming of captives'.*

*De officiis, 2,28,137-138.

Again he says: *What better treasure has Christ than those in whom he says he dwells? So it is written: 'I was hungry and you gave me [food] to eat; I was thirsty and you gave me drink'.* Again he says: *Take care lest you keep in your money-box the salvation of the needy and bury as if in tombs the life of the poor. You, what do you give to the poor man? Money. And he, what does he receive? His life.*

*Mt 25:35. De officiis, 2,28,140.

*De officiis, 2, 16, 78.

And because it is written, 'Every charge will depend on the word of two or three witnesses,'* after we have heard two reliable witnesses, let a third witness, who is not less reliable, also be heard, namely, St Basil. He explains the apostle's words: 'Charity does no wrong,'* by saying: 'Whatever is done not for some necessary purpose but for embellishment or decoration, this is wrong.'*

Therefore, what greater evil is there than with labor and expense to beat into gold-leaf, to spin and weave into thread that gold by which hunger and cold could so easily be driven from the living temple of God—all so that gold orphreys can be embroidered and then sewn onto sacred vestments and can attract to themselves the attention of those praying in the oratory and become a hindrance to their loving prayer? Although I cannot go on with the discourse I have undertaken without thinking of that comic line, 'If you go on saying what you wish, you will hear what you don't wish,'* I will say what I think, that those who set such store in superstition either have no zeal for God or have no knowledge.*

For who would say he has zeal for God according to knowledge who prefers to clothe wood and fibres with the gold that he has rather than to come to the aid of the naked and hungry Christ, although he himself has said, 'Whatever you did to one of the least of mine, you did to me'?* Likewise: 'Martin, while still a catechumen, has covered me with this garment.'* Where do we read that he appeared to anyone saying, 'You have honored me with this gold orphrey'? At the judgment, the strict judge will make a strict examination not of apparelled chasubles, but of the works of mercy.'*

*Dt 19:15.

*1 Co 13:14.

*Interrogatio, No. 142; PL 103:537D.

*Terence, Andria 920 (5,4,17). Cf. DCC II, 36.
*Cf. DCC, I, 19.

*Mt 25:20.

*Sulpicius Severus, Vie de Saint Martin; ed. Fontaine, I (1967), 3,3.

*Cf. DCC, I, 38.

XI.

Because I have written to you concerning our four doubtful matters—perhaps not eloquently yet for all that adequately, I think—I advise you to remember that 'better are the wounds of a lover than the fraudulent kisses of an enemy',* and that, according to the counsel of Diogenes, to improve yourself, you should have either a very good friend or a very

*Prov 27:6.

great enemy.* Minister to my unhappiness by taking thought for your happiness. Do not put off your conversion until that moment when either you cannot be converted or, having been converted, you become a sacrifice not offered through love, but one wrenched out by the fear of death.⁷⁷

*Caecilius Balbus, 5,2,p.21,6-8.

*Cf. Vergil, Aeneid, XI,283.

Believe me, a wretch already put to the test,* that the fruit of a life of wantonness is thoroughly wretched. For fleeting pleasure passes away and cannot be recalled, and yet the penalty to be paid for wantonness is inescapable—either man himself or God punishes. And while even the most corrupt people can be saved through sincere penitence, nevertheless that glory which is lost through a corrupt lifestyle is beyond recall. 'He who sows sparingly will reap bountifully.'*

*2 Co 9:6.

Keep this three-fold consideration in mind as a kind of seedplot for your correction.⁷⁸ It will convince you by a credible and compelling argument that nothing is more foolish than putting off conversion, since one does not know at what hour a thief will come to break into the house.* And, lest you search for distant examples, let the sudden death and the unexpected and dreadful end of your two brothers recently departed bear witness to the very same thing. Flee, therefore, flee that intercourse which surpasses madness, that is to say, that utterly wretched exchange which lovers of wantonness make. For the sake of temporal, fleeting and false joy they lose true and eternal joy.

*Mt 24:43, Lk 12:39.

No one, as St Gregory says, no one will be able to rejoice with the world here [on earth] and reign with Christ there [in heaven].* And blessed Pope Leo in one of his sermons says: 'These two times succeed themselves each in their own order: a time for weeping and a time for laughing.* Brothers, let no one deceive himself. In this world there is no time for laughing.'* One of the Fathers, firmly believing this, upbraided another when he saw him laughing and said: 'We are going to have to render an account of our whole life before heaven and earth, and you are laughing?'*

*Not identified.

*Cf. Qo 3:4.

*Not identified.

*Vitae Patrum sive Hist. Erem. Libri Decem, V: Verba Seniorum,3,23; PL 73:864.

But because the Apostle says, 'The sadness of the world works death,'* we ought to ask of our father tears,[79] typified by the lower and higher springs which Achsah, the daughter of Caleb, asked from her father.* One of the Fathers said to the person who brought him news of his father's death: 'Be silent; do not blaspheme. My father is immortal.'* We ought therefore humbly to beseech him, our immortal father, to give us tears to water our parched land, tears with which to weep over our sins in the first place, and then, loathing earthly exile, to say weeping: 'Woe to me that my sojourn is prolonged.'* And in this way, through ardent longing for the heavenly country, let us go up to the higher spring, so that out of great longing and desire for the vision of God, who truly is our Father, having a well-spring of tears, we can say truthfully, 'Day and night my tears have been my bread, while daily they say to me: Where is your God?'*

*2 Co 7:10.

*Josh 15:16-19, Jg 1:12-13.

*Vitae Patrum, V: Verba Seniorum, 1,5; PL 73:855.

*Ps 120:5.

*Ps 42:3.

The best workshop for producing these tears is the monastery and the fellowship of brothers living according to a rule. They imitate those of whom the apostle says: 'Having nothing and possessing all things.'*

*2 Co 6:10.

Oh, worthiest intention of the common life and whole-heartedly to be pursued, for it makes a judge of the one to be judged; it makes the needy so self-sufficient that he has nothing and yet possesses all things. For him who needs a protector, it provides a defender so powerful that he has the power of receiving into the eternal tabernacles that man whose alms he here receives.

The blessed Fulgentius bears witness to this by these words: *He who has received so much virtue from the Lord despises everything in the world because of his love for heavenly kingdom. But he who has not yet such virtue should give alms of the things he has in proportion as he has them. Let him be the kind of man who may sit at judgment with the Lord. Let him be the kind of man who may stand at his right hand for judgment. Let him be the kind of man who may possess by right forever the eternal taber-*

nacles, the kind whom [the Lord] will receive. For the Lord admonishes us saying:* 'Make friends for yourselves of the mammon of iniquity that they may receive you into the eternal tabernacles'.*

Take, therefore, take the exchange which Christ offers you, as he says in the Gospel according to Mark: 'In very truth I say to you: there is no one who has left home or brothers or sisters or mother or children or father for my sake and the gospel's who shall not receive now in the present time a hundredfold as much, houses and brothers and sisters and mothers and children and lands, together with persecutions and, in the age to come, life everlasting.'*

Bede explains these words of Christ; this is the gist of his explanation: 'All those who spurn temporal things for the sake of the kingdom of God and in this life replete with trials do taste by a sure faith the joy of that very same kingdom, looking for the heavenly country, enjoy the pure delight of all those equally elected—because joined together to the brothers and the co-sharers of his own purpose by a spiritual bond —shall receive even in this life charity more delightful. And this, when compared to those things left behind, will be considered, by comparison and worth, as an hundredfold to a tiny number.*

If I, like a blind man showing the way to one with sight,† have written to you more abundant testimonies from sacred scripture than your prudence or the shortness of a letter requires, you must forgive me not only because of that reason I spoke of above (where I did not keep silent about my intention) but also because of the devout love of the one who was writing. For, according to Ambrose, 'the workman's love puts its name to the work'.*

*Lk 16:9.

*Fulgentius, Serm. 1,7; CCh 91:892 (129-132), 893 (139-144).

*Mk 10:29.

*Bede, In Marcum, 10,29-30; CCh 120:563.
†Cf. DCC, III,3; Mt 15:15, Lk 6:39.

*De officiis ministrorum, 1,30,147.

END OF THE ARGUMENT

§

NOTES TO DIALOGUE

PART ONE

1. *Sententia prolata*—the Roman legal phrase meaning a verdict rendered by a judge.
2. As a *conversus,* or late vocation, at Cluny, he would technically have been numbered among the *illiterati.* Cluny did everything possible to make them feel at home in the community, even to having them participate in the liturgy. The Cluniac *conversus* was not the Cistercian *frater-laicus.* See below, note III, 32.
3. For the conduct of Cluniac monks during the three days immediately following profession, see Udalrich (Ulrich), *Consuetudines Cluniacenses,* Book 2, chapter 28; PL 149. This ceremony is described more clearly in *The Monastic Constitutions of Lanfranc,* tr. David Knowles (Oxford, 1951) pp. 109-110.
4. *Vicem et personam gerens*—in Roman legal terms *vices gerere* or *vices agere* meant to act as deputy.
5. *Codex Theodosianus* 16.2.47: 'Clerics also, whom the accursed presumptor John the Tyrant, John the Usurper [the *Liber pontificalis,* p. 292, refers to him as Blood-thirsty John—tr.] a nephew of Vitalian, the chief tactical officer of Belisaurius had declared must be led without discrimination before secular judges, we reserve for a hearing before their bishops.'
6. *Patrona . . . auctoritas*—in Roman law *auctoritas patrona (auctoritas patrum)* was the official ratification of a law.
7. This is an instance of the Cluniacs being 'hoisted on their own petard'. The Johannine Privilege (931) granted Cluny permission to receive monks from other houses into their Order, provided these monks were in search of a better way of life in religion (PL 131:1055).
8. For intellectual life at Cluny, see Andre Chagny, *Cluny et son empire* (Paris, 1938) pp. 148-63; Philibert Schmitz, *Histoire de l'Ordre de St. Benoit*[2] (Maredous, 1949) 2:117-18. See also Joan Evans, *Monastic Life at Cluny, 910-1157* (London: Oxford University Press, 1931), and Noreen Hunt, ed., *Cluniac Monasticism in the Central Middle Ages,* Readings in European History (London: Macmillan, 1971).
9. *Lectio sacra*—spiritual reading, private reading during intervals between the Hours of the Divine Office.
10. The fundamental Roman law on *falsum* (forgery, falsification, counterfeiting) was the *Lex Cornelia de falsis* (81 BC) or *Lex Cornelia testamentaria.* The uses to which this law was later put were very wide, particularly in reference to bribery, and its penalties were severe, extending even to *interdicto aquae et igni. Falsum* 'is that which in reality does not exist, but is asserted as true'; Justice is 'the desire to render to each his due'. (*Digest* 10.1) Thus *falsa justitia* was counterfeit justice.
11. *Hom. 34,2 ad Lucam 15.1-10,* and *Decret.* D. 45, c.15: 'Sed aliud est, quod agitur tipo superbiae, aliud quod zelo disciplinae.'

12. He probably refers to *De praecepto et dispensatione* (SBOp 3:253-94) and possibly to Chapter Five of the *Apologia ad Guillelmum* (SBOp 3:90-94).

13. In Pre 48 (SBOp 3:286) Bernard states that the vow of stability should prevent the disobedience which results from spiritual laxity, all the separations which have their origin in incompatibility, all the visits which have their origin in curiosity, mental upsets and uneasiness, all levity and inconstancy. But if a bad life and lack of regard for the ways of others' lives in the community are a hindrance to leading a good life in religion, 'my advice to him is to change monasteries and to do so of his own free will; to pass from his own to another community where, unhindered, he can pay God the vows he professed orally, Indeed, "with the holy you shall be holy" and with the perverse you shall be perverted, and with the innocent you shall be innocent.' (Ps 18:25-6)

14. Huygens, p. 381, remarks that this quotation from Bernard occurs only in the works of Idung and is not mentioned in the proceedings of the General Chapter.

15. According to Cottineau, *Repertoire* 1:716-17, the monks of St-Pere-en-Valle were Benedictines. This treatise was written to the abbot of Coulombs, who was to pass it on to his own former abbot at St-Pere-en-Valle. See the introduction to the Latin text, SBOp 3:243.

16. Unfortunately for the Cluniac's argument, William of St Thierry himself had become a Cistercian in 1135.

17. Cicero, *De inventione rhetorica* 1,15,20: '*Insinuatio* is that kind of speech which covertly enters into the mind of the listener by means of specious semblance and by talking all around the subject.'

18. Huygens, p. 382, recommends substituting *Ludgunensis* for the textual *Lingoniensis*. Lincoln had no archbishop. Hugh's letter is contained in the *Exordium parvum*, ed., Ph. Guignard, in *Monuments primitifs de la regle cistercienne* (Dijon, 1878) p. 69. A biography of Hugh of Lyons would help to cast new light on the Investiture Conflict and the place of Citeaux's foundation in that reform movement. This study has yet to be made.

19. *Commentarium in Danielem, libri III (IV): De Antichristo in Danielem (IV), xii, 3, p. 938,* ed. in *S. Hieronymi Presbyteri Opera, Pars 5*, CCSL 75 (Turnhold: Brepols, 1964): 'Tantamque sit inter eruditam sanctitatem et sanctam rusticitatem quantum caelum distet et stellae."

20. Egbert of Liege, *Fecunda ratis,* ed. Voigt (1889), p. 94, no. 445.

21. RB 42. The basic sources of authority for the Cistercian in this case are sacred Scripture, the Rule, the Fathers of the early church, and the canons of the church. What exactly did the Cistercian mean by 'canons'? The canons were the canon law of the Church as found in such collections as the *Liber Canonum* or the first part of the *Dionysiana*, the *Dionysio-Hadriana* (also called by Pope Nicholas I the *Codex canonum*). Gratian's *Decretum* was known as the *Corpus decretorum, Corpus canonum, Corpus juris,* etc. It is not surprising to find the Cistercian reminding the Cluniac, over the course of the *Dialogue,* that the Cluniac order contravened 'the Rule and the canons'.

22. *Consuetudines Cluniacenses* 2:20; PL 149: 'On days on which speech is not forbidden [Tuesdays, Thursdays, and Saturdays in Lent], each monk receives a book and takes a seat before he may utter a word.'

23. Ibid.: 'Under no circumstances does he talk while standing.'

24. Ibid.: 3:3: Chapter three of the Customary deals with the punishment meted out to the disobedient and other breakers of the Rule. In it is described their prison and their treatment during imprisonment.

25. This and the three succeeding paragraphs deal with legal aspects of the Rule. Note the distinction between law as a precept and the transgression of the law as embodied in the words of St James (2:10). The basis of the Cistercian's thinking is Isidore of Seville's definition of law [*Etymologiae, caput* 3] which was incorporated into Gratian's *Decretum:* 'Lex autem juris est species. Jus autem

est dictum, quia justum est. Omne autem jus legibus et moribus constat.' (*Decret.*, D. 1, c. 2)

26. Cf. Cassian, *Inst.* 2, 4, and 6, *Vitae patrum;* PL 73:242f., *Historia Lausiaca* 38; PL 73:1137C.

27. Amand Boon, 'Regula S. Pachomii,' *Pachomiana Latina* (Louvain, 1932). Cf. No. 45 of the *Praecepta.*

28. *Tractatus sive Homiliae in Psalmos: Ps. 145:7*, in *S. Hieronymi Presbiteri Opera, Pars II: Opera homiletica*; CCSL 78 (1958) 325-26: 'Dat escam esurientibus. Esurientibus dat, non ructantibus. Qui ergo non habet monachus confidenter accipiat; qui habet et ructans est, non accipiat. Scis quia esuris, scis quia non habes: si esurieris et non habes, magis das beneficium si accipias quam tribuitur tibi. Si autem habes et non esuris non debes cibum esurientium tollere ut tu accipias saturatus. Accipe quod in uentrum mittas non quod in sacculum. Accipe tunicam quae corpus tegat non quae arcas impleat.'

29. Prosper of Acquitaine is not the author of a Rule for canons. These particular words are taken from the Emperor Louis the Pious' council for the reformation of canons, held at Aachen in 816, under the auspices of Benedict of Aniane. Prosper, about whom very little is known, wrote *De vita contemplativa*, which was quoted occasionally by Chrodogang of Metz in his *Regula canonicorum* (PL 89:1059-1120) and quoted at the Council of Aachen (814). Cf. *Decret.*, C. 1, q. 2, c. 7: 'Pastor ecclesiae his, quibus sua sufficiunt, non debet aliquid erogare, quando nihil aliud sit habentibus dare quam perdere.'

30. *pauperis prebendam.* The praebenda was originally the term used for a roman military levy or imposition. In the early Middle Ages it was written as *provenda.* For example, the monastery of Corbie had one hundred fifty *provendarii (Corpus Consuetudinum Monasticarum,* ed. K. Hallinger [Siegburg, 1963] 1:365). Ultimately it was used for a portion of food or drink. Those who benefitted at Cluny were called *prebendarii (Consuetudines Cluniacenses,* 3:24). The general meaning was a monk's food portion for one day. The portion of food alloted for alms on the death of a monk was called the *praebenda mortuorum.*

31. Peter the Venerable's *Dispositio reifamilaris Cluniacensis* (PL 189: 1047-54) affords a very good documentary estimate of Cluny's revenues. Even then they were insufficient to feed and clothe three hundred monks. The result was that Cluny resorted to an old monastic evil—taxing the cell or priory out of existence for the maintenance of the mother-house.

32. This passage has not been identified. A reference to the *De divinis officiis* VIII:4 of Rupert of Deutz has been discredited. See Huygens, p. 306, n. 32.

33. The Venerable Bede, *A History of the English Church and People* III:9, tr. Leo Sherley-Price (Penguin, 1955) p. 170: 'Do not reject one of your friends, for since you accepted the property of a sinner you must share in his punishment.'

34. See Theophilus, *De diversis artibus,* tr. C. R. Dodwell (London: Nelson's Mediaeval Texts, 1961) 37-52, for the technology of glass working during the Middle Ages.

35. Cluny celebrated the liturgy with *grandeur* and *splendeur.* Cluny took the patterns set by Benedict of Aniane, whose ideas on liturgy were strongly influenced by the Irish, and extrapolated them. For example, Cluny's elaborate bows had their origin in the Irish penchant for bowing.

Depending on the liturgical importance of the feast, the Cluniac community as a whole might robe in albs, copes or capes. Special chalices might be used. In contrast to the sparse use of lighting and candles at Citeaux, lighting was a special feature at Cluny: cartwheel candelabra (*coronae*) behind the main altar, seven golden candlesticks around the crucifix. Carpets covered the sanctuary floor, tapestries hung on the walls, everything in the dining room would be in white. At Christmas and Easter a huge *corona* bearing 493 candles was lighted in the church and on the altar were placed two golden candlesticks and three golden chalices. (Rose Graham, 'Relations of Cluny to some Movements of Monastic Reform,' in *Journal of Theological Studies* 15 (1914) 186. On monastic observance at Cluny, see also Joan Evans, *Monastic Life at Cluny, 910-1115*, 79-97; and Noreen Hunt, ed., *Cluniac Monasticism in the Central Middle Ages*, esp. pp. 44-6. St Bernard poked good-natured fun of what he regarded as ostentation and bad taste in his *Apologia* SBOp 3:81-108; CF 1: 33-69).

36. Ep 52, 10, ed. Isidorus Hilberg, *S. Eusebii Hieronymi Epistolae, Pars I, Epistolae I-LXX*; CSEL 54 (Vienna-Leipzig, 1910) p. 433.

37. Probably Berno, Cluny's founder, did not write a Customary for his foundation. We get a glimpse into his thinking by reading his last will and testament, in which he urged his monks to observe silence strictly and to observe his new regulations in charity; food and clothing were to be held in common (PL 133:852-58). Cluny's foundation charter lists some details about the recitation of the Office, food, clothing, obedience, silence, hospitality, poverty (Gerd Tellenbach, *Neue Forschungen uber Cluny* [Freiburg/br., 1939] 85-95). Abbot Odo ordered the monks to chant each day one hundred thirty-eight psalms—the remaining fourteen were omitted for the alleviation of the weaker brethren (PL 133:57,67,71). He recalled the example set by the Desert Fathers. To him, silence was all-important, hence the need for an elaborate sign language. It is fair to say that every abbot added to and subtracted from the Customs of Cluny, but it was not until the eleventh century that these Customs were given official status and put into written form.

Bruno Albers has published three tenth-century versions of Cluny's Customs. To a large extent they are an elaboration of, and accretions, to, their spiritual foundation document—the reforming decrees of the Council of Aachen. There are other versions extant from 1030 and 1042 (*Consuetudines monasticas*, 4 volumes [Stuttgart, 1900]). In 1068, Bernard of Cluny undertook a redaction of his Order's Customary. Then years later, abbot William of Hirsau sent his friends and prior Ulrich (Udalrich) to Cluny with the mission of procuring an official copy of its Customs. Ulrich discovered such a version did not exist and somewhere between the years of 1082 and 1084 he began to write, in three books, his own Customary of the Order.

38. *Campanae:* large bells, originally made in the roman Campagna. They were used by monasteries, towns, communes. The possession of such a bell was of extreme legal importance to its proprietor: its ownership was at once proof and formal notification to all that it belonged to a corporate body which had won its charter of incorporation—hence the presence of *campanae* at Cluny. Other bells were the *squilla (skilla)* and the *nola*, both small bells.

39. Apparently, Citeaux had its own problems with chant. See Canivez, *Statuta* 1:30 (AD 1134): 'vivos decet vivili voce cantare et non more femineo tinnulis vel ut vulgo dicitur falsis. Vocibus veluti histrionicam imitari lasciviam.' Welsh monks tried to introduce three and four part singing into their recitation of the Office (Canivez, *Statuta* 1:472 [AD 1217]). See Chrysogonus Waddell, 'A Plea for the *Institutio sancti Bernardi quomodo cantare et psallere debeamus*,' in *Saint Bernard of Clairvaux* (Cistercian Studies, 28 [1977]).

40. Honorius of Autun, *Sacramentarium* (PL 172). A sacramentary contained the liturgical books that went to make up the later *missale plenum*. It contained the ritual and directions for the administration of the sacraments.

41. *Sacrae scripturae tractatores*. Cf. Augustine, *De doctrina christiana* 4, 34, 91: 'The commentator and teacher of Holy Scripture, being the defender of the faith, the victor over wrong doctrine, has the duty of teaching what is correct on the faith and of rectifying what is incorrect.'

42. This refers to Jerome's famous *Letter 22*, which he himself referred to as a *libellus* rather than as an *epistola*. His words on virginity and continence

had a remarkable effect on Christian teaching and living. See P. Antin, 'Le monachisme selon saint Jerome,' *Recueil sur saint Jerome*. Collection Latomus 95 (Brussels, 1968) 101-103.

43. Huygens cites Hildemar's commentary c. 55 (ed. R. Mittermuller [Regensburg, 1880] p. 521). Cf. *Regula magistri*, ed. A. de Vogue, *La regle du maitre* 2:333; SCh 106 (Paris, 1964) ET *Rule of the Master*, CS 6, Kalamazoo, 1977. The words used are 'lineas . . . prohibemus'. These may well be the *femoralia* or underdrawers which were a garment for everyday wear in the ninth century according to the Council of Aachen in 817 (canon 22; PL 197: 381-94).

44. Hildemar, c. 48; ed. Mittermuller, p. 479.

45. *stare in veritate*—the real as opposed to the represented value.

46. Cf. Augustine, *Sermo* 355, 4, 6; PL 39:1573: 'I do not want to have hypocrites with me in the monastery. Who does not know that that is bad? It is bad if one falls away from the way of life he has embraced, but it is worse to pretend to keep it. As for myself, listen! He who has undertaken to live in the society of the common life which is praised in the Acts of the Apostles and then deserts it, falls away from his vow, falls away from his holy profession.' Cf. *Ennarratio in psalmum* 132:12; CSEL 40:1936. Cf. *Jordani de Saxonia Liber Vitasfratrum* (edd. Arbesman and Humphner) p. 495: 'If one of the brethren has offended another, he must ask pardon; he is in the monastery to no purpose, even though he is not expelled from it.'

47. Cf. Otto, *Sprichworter der Romer* (1890, 1965) p. 41, no. 184.

48. St Gregory did not write a Rule. In his *Dialogues*, however, he stated in reference to St Benedict: 'He wrote a Rule for Monks that is remarkable for its discretion and the clarity of its language.' *Dialogue* II, 36. Tr. by O. J. Zimmerman in FCh 39:107.

49. *Decret.* C. 19, q. 3, c. 6 & C. 17, q. 2, c. 1. Cf. Ivo of Chartres, *Panormia* 3, 183; PL 161:1174, and Ivo, *Decretum* 6, 428; PL 161; 538.

50. Peter the Venerable's reform Statutes of 1132 allowed for a novitiate of one month (PL 189:1036B). Cf. his *Letter* 28 to Bernard (ed. Giles Constable, *The Letters of Peter the Venerable* 1:58-62). See too David Knowles, 'The Reforming Decrees of Peter the Venerable,' *Petrus Venerabilis*. Studia Anselmiana 40 (1956) pp. 11 ff. For the rather strange system of profession at Cluny, see *Letters* 35 & 38 (PL 189:1035-36) and *Recueil des historiens des Gaules* 15: 628-54. See too the account of the huge meeting at Cluny in 1132 given by Ordericus Vitalis, who was present (Marjorie Chibnall, ed. and tr., *The Ecclesiastical History of Orderic Vitalis*, 3 vols. [Oxford: Clarendon Press; New York: Oxford University Press, 1969-72]

51. Cluny was the recipient of all manner of privileges and exemptions granted by Rome, as may be inferred from the several hundred entries in the papal registers published by A. Potthast, *Regesta Pontificum Romanorum* (Berlin, 1874-75) 2 vols. They vary from the Johannine Privilege (1131) to dispensations from the Rule, to different kinds of shoe-buckles, sandals, and mitres to be worn by the abbot of Cluny. Pope Zosimus' full text is: 'Apud nos enim inconvulsis radicibus vivit antiquitas cui decreta Patrum sanxere reverentiam'; *Decret.* C. 25, q. 1, c. 7.

52. *exordium*-beginning. A double meaning referring both to Cistercian beginnings and to the Cistercian document *Exordium parvum*, which the Cistercian obligingly goes on to quote.

53. *Exordium parvum*, ed. Ph. Guignard, *Monuments primitifs de la regle cistercienne* (Dijon, 1878) 61-75.

54. Molesme had begun as a hermitage and quickly become famous. When St Bruno the Carthusian was searching for his 'desert' he visited the hermits there. Gifts of land were heaped upon Molesme by the Burgundian nobility who adopted it as their own. In a short time it became their accustomed meeting

place for councils and courts. In short, it was soon—despite its first good intentions—absorbed into the local feudal milieu. Though the Cistercian refers to 'the abbot of Molesme of your Order', Molesme was not in fact a Cluniac house. It adopted Cluniac Customs but remained independent. Reaction to this adoption contributed to the departure of twenty monks and their abbot to Citeaux.

55. Apparently the brethren also spoke where others could hear them, because 'Alberic had urged the brothers to move from Molesme to this place [Citeaux] for which efforts he suffered many insults, imprisonment and beatings.' (*Exordium parvum*, in *Monuments primitifs*, p. 67)

56. This means they were firmly convinced that they had sworn falsely. Perjury was a very serious offence, both ecclesiastically and socially, during the Middle Ages, because the fabric of society was held together by sworn oaths. For the variety of punishments inflicted on perjurers, see J. T. McNeil and H. M. Games, *Mediaeval Handbooks of Penance*, Records of Civilization Series, No. 29 (New York, 1938). Some offenders had their tongues cut out, others rode around the town seated backwards on a donkey and holding the animal's tail. See also 'parjure' in DCC 6: cols. 1232-33.

57. Note the use of roman legal terms by the men of Citeaux: (1) *ordinare*, to establish legally; (2) *statuere*, to settle by agreement; (3) *tenere*, to make legally valid. As an Order the Cistercians were very conscious of their law and its codification. See Columban Bock, 'Les Codifications du droit cistercienne,' *Collectanea* (January & July 1952; October 1954).

58. Monks' clothing prescribed in the Rule of St Benedict consists of tunic, cowl, scapular (apron), stockings and shoes (RB 53). Undergarments (*femoralia*) were to be worn only on a journey. The tunic extended from the neck to the knees; it was not ample or flowing. Attached to it was a hood such as that worn by Italian peasants in the sixth century. What exactly was the Cluniac *froccus*? It was not the traditional Benedictine tunic because the *froccus* was ample, and yet Peter the Venerable refers to it as a tunic (PL 189:1053). David Knowles in his translation of the *Monastic Constitutions of Lanfranc* p. 2, translates *froccus* as *tunic*. Probably the only thing that can be said is that the Cluniac *froccus* served as their tunic, but the tailoring differed from that of Benedict's tunic. Each monk was issued two *frocci*, two cowls (choir robes), two shirts, two sets of underwear, two pairs of laced slippers, two pairs of heavy boots, three pelisses, one gown (*gunella*, which seems to have been something akin to a petticoat), three hoods for the pelisses, and five pairs of stockings. Each was also issued a pillow, bed-cover, mattress, suspenders for holding up the underwear, belts to keep the woollen shirt in place and on which to hang knives, combs, needle and thread. Priests and deacons were issued three sets of underwear.

59. The pelisse was a long loose outer coat, worn mostly in winter time. It was originally made from skins but as time went on it came to be made of cloth and quilted.

60. Combs became almost elaborate in make, size and ornamentation in the Middle Ages. Usually several were kept in the sacristy.

61. This refers to the Cluniac *generale* and *pittance*. For the monks' behavior in the refectory, see *Consuetudines Cluniacenses* 2, 23. A *pittanciae* was that portion given to an individual on an individual plate; a *generale* was given on one plate shared by two monks. A *pittance* could be one piece of cheese or four eggs; a *generale* could be five eggs plus a piece of cheese (*Consuetudines*, 2, 35). In addition to the regular issue of beans and greens (*pulmentum*), *pittanciae* were served on Mondays, Wednesdays, and Fridays, and a *generale* on the remaining days. Fish was served as a substitute for the *generale* on Thursdays and Sundays, if it could be procured. On the Feast of the Translation of St Benedict both the *pittance* and the *generale* were served; creamed onions and cakes were substituted for beans on the five principal feasts of Christmas, Easter, Pentecost, Assumption, and the abbey's feastday. In addition, a *generale* was served to

celebrate the abbot's safe return from a journey. When a *generale* of fish was served, the Grand Prior inspected the plates to make sure each monk was getting his fair share (Ibid. 3, 18). A *pigmentum*, made of choice wines and ground spices, was served on several occasions. St Bernard has described its effects in Apo 21; SBOp 3:98-99; CF 1:57.

62. *sagimen*—suet, lard. By order of the Council of Aachen, held in 817 under the reforming impetus of Benedict of Aniane: 'Brothers are to have some lard [suet, fat] in their daily diet, except on Fridays, eight days prior to Christmas, and from the Sunday before Ash Wednesday until Easter.' (Canon 77; PL 98:381-94). Cf. *Corpus Consuetudinum monasticarum*, ed. K. Hallinger, 1:515-36.

63. See R. A. R. Hartridge, *Vicarages in the Middle Ages* (Cambridge, 1930) 1-15.

64. *In altaria*—in this phrase, more than in any other single word, is summarized the problem of the relations between the church and local lords. In it is contained the origins, and actualities, of the *Eigentumskirche*. The local lord, having built the church, collected the altar dues such as tithes and donations at baptisms and marriages. The best work on this phase of church history is A. Fliche, *La reforme gregorienne*, 3 vols. (Louvain, 1924-37). See also H. X. Arquilliere, *Saint Gregoire VII* (Paris, 1934); and *L'Augustinisme politique* (Paris, 1934).

65. The best way of getting an intimate glimpse of so institutionalized a body is to read and become familiar with Book Three of the monastery's Customary. Using the *pittanciae* and *generalia* (described above, note 61), how does one feed three hundred monks daily? The task requires skill, resources, and organization. Book Three details the functions and duties of administrators, and Peter the Venerable shows us an administration struggling with a near-bankrupt institution, whose resources were hardly sufficient to meet its need in food alone. For an excellent study of tithes, see Giles Constable, *Monastic Tithes: from their Origins to the Twelfth Century* (Cambridge, 1964). Also of value is the article 'Dime' in DDC 4:1231-41.

66. Anselm of Laon and Ralph of Laon, his brother, *Sententias excerptas* . . . ed. G. Lefevre (Paris, 1895) p. 32, 18—a free rendering appears in the *Dialogue*. See G. Lefevre, 'De Anselmo Laudunensi scholastico,' (Diss. Paris, 1895) p. 91, n. 1, a reference to this passage in the *Dialogue*.

67. I have been unable to locate this quotation in the Works of St Augustine. Reference to this subject is to be found, without mention of Augustine, in *Decretalia Gregorii IX, lib. III, titulus cxxxi, canon 18* (2575), cf. *canon 10*. The question was probably not raised in Augustine's day at all. See also 'Notitia' in *Histoire litteraire de France par les religieux benedictines*, 10:170, on Idung's reference to Anselm and this passage. Cf. *Flores sententiarum ac quaestionum magisti Anselmi et Rudolphi fratris ejus;* PL 162:1183-4.

68. The *Regula ad monachos* of Sts. Serapion *et alii*, 14, hints at this issue of stricter discipline; PG 34:983. Referring to the Councils of Carthage (397) and Hippo (393), Augustine wrote: 'By it, clerics coming from anywhere at all are not to be received into a monastery . . . . If you are somewhat alarmed about privation, be assured that he has not been received by us into the monastery; he had not received his bishop's permission to leave.' Tr. Sr Wilfred Parsons in *Letters of St Augustine*, FCh 12:311.

69. *Regula ad monachos;* PG 34. See above, note 68.

70. *Regula Serapionis, Macarii, Paphnutii et alterius Macarii*, 13; PL 103: 439-40A.

71. In roman law, apostasy was regarded as a crime against the State, and hence severely punished in civil law. Apostates were 'those who had been confirmed in the faith and had turned to pagan rites and cults'. Cf. *Codex Theodorianus* 16. 7. For an excellent article, see 'Apostasie' in DDC 1:cols. 640-52.

72. This quotation, as rendered in the text, is not in the Vulgate. The closest approach is: 'Every way of a man seems right to himself' (Pr 21:2). The second clause, 'but they merge', approximates Pr 16:25: 'There is a way that seems right to men, but the end thereof are the ways of death.'

73. *Papa* was a title of affection; it also meant *admirabilis—the greatest one, guardian, little father*. Many bishops (for example, those of Constantinople and Alexandria) used the title. In *Letter 31*, St Augustine refers to 'the most blessed *Papa* Ambrose'. St Jerome addressed his *Letter 195* to 'The saintly lord and blessed *Papa* Augustine'.

NOTES TO DIALOGUE

PART TWO

1. Taken as a whole this paragraph is reminiscent of St Jerome's famous vision: 'Suddenly I was caught up in the spirit and dragged before the Tribunal of the Judge. Here there was so much light and such a glare from the brightness of those standing around that I cast myself on the ground . . . . upon being asked my status I replied that I was a Christian. And He who sat upon the judgment seat said: "Thou liest, thou art a Ciceronian, not Christian." ' (Letter 22) *Letters of St. Jerome,* ACW I: 156-166. For the Cistercian *captiose interrogat,* see Cicero's *Quaestiones academicae* 2.15. This and subsequent paragraphs have a rather Cistercian flavor to them.

2. For the Litany at Cluny, see *Consuetudines cluniacenses* 1:4; PL 149, 648-651. Book 1 deals with the liturgy at Cluny. Cistercian liturgy is found in *Monuments primitifs,* chiefly pp. 91-167, and, of course, in the *Rule of St Benedict.* The festal office at Cluny could last thirteen hours (See Lackner, *The Eleventh-Century Background,* pp. 52-61).

3. Manual labor at Cluny is described in the *Conuetudines Cluniacenses,* 1:30; PL 149: 675-676. Occasionally it consisted of shelling beans, weeding and watering the gardens as they went. 'Cum ventum fuerit ad locum operandi, versi omnes ad orientem per ordinem consistunt. Ad finem psalmi faciunt ante et retro . . . . " (676). See Evans, *Monastic Life at Cluny,* 87-8.

4. Some of this long quotation may well be termed 'St Augustine of Hippo according to the Cistercian of the Dialogue'. St Augustine's text (*De opera monachorum;* CSEL 41: 564-565) is followed faithfully from, 'I want to know what monks do' to 'singing the praises of the Most High'. Several sentences are then omitted. *Works of the Monks,* tr. Sr M. S. Muldowney in FCh 16: 363.

5. Not only *De opera monachorum* but many of St Augustine's two-hundred and seventy Letters (FCh, 5 vols, [New York, 1951, 1953, 1955, 1956]), shed a great deal of light on the troubled state of the Church in North Africa. Monastic priests played a prominent role in that seething community.

6. *Intentissimi esse debetis.* Cf. the opening lines of Virgil's *Aeneid:* 'conticuere omnes intentique ora tenebant.'

7. Short ejaculatory prayers rather than the longer *orationes.*

8. Suffrages were the anthems and prayers of the saints recited after Lauds and Vespers.

9. The Greek *litaneia* [entreaty] was a prayer of supplication. Cf. 'Litanie' in DACL, IX^2 (Paris, 1930) col. 1558-1560. For St Augustine and the singing of psalms during manual labor see *De opera monachorum* 363.

10. See Armand Veilleux OCSO, *La Liturgie dans le cenobitisme pachomien au quatrieme siecle.* Studia Anselmiana (Rome, 1968)—an excellent presentation of pachomian monastic life as lived in the *coenobium.*

11. They arose in the usual manner for Matins, recited the *trina oratio*, gradual psalms, Nocturns, Vigils and Matins of the Dead, and Matins of the Day. Between Easter and 1 November those so wishing could return to bed, to be awakened by the ringing of the bell (*Consuetudines cluniacenses* 2:10). Prime was to be sung after the interval following Lauds (2:16).

12. Priscian, *Institutes* 4, 34; *Prisciani grammatici caesariensis institutionum grammaticarum libri XVIII*, ed. Heinrich Keil, (Leipzig 1855, rpt, Hildesheim 1961) 2:137.

13. *Simplex, simplicitas, rusticus, rusticitas* are words found very early in the teaching of Christian doctrine. They denote the fall of the cultural and intellectual level of Rome. 'Unde magis simplici et pedestri sermone quem totus populus capere possit debent dominici mei sacerdotes populis praedicare.' (Caesarius of Arles, CSEL 103:16).

14. *Decret.* D. 10, q. 10. In Roman law a law was judged to have lost its binding force by abuse or disuse. This led to the abrogation (*abrogare legem, derogare legi*) of the law (*Digest* 1.3.32.1): Cf. Mansi, 22: canon 48 of the Fourth Lateran Council: 'remedium appelationis sit ad praesidium innocentiae institutum.' Cf. *Codex Juris Canonici*, (New York, 1918) canon 6: 'Leges quaelibet, sive universales sive particulares, praescriptis hujus Codicis oppositae, abrogantur, nisi de particularibus legibus aluid expresse caveatur.'

15. For the care of those near death in Cluny's infirmary, see *Consuetudines cluniacenses* 3:30.

16. 'Promitto vobis in vera fide.' In Roman law *fides* was the promissory formula by which one assumed guaranty (the medaeval *cautio*) for another. The complete formula was: 'spondeo, fide mea esse jubeo' or the shorter form: 'fide promitto.' (*Instituta* 3.20, *Digest* 46.1)

17. This was one of the many ways of sealing a bargain: such a handshake was often referred to as 'earnest'.

18. As a *conversus* he would have had no reason for formal probation in the novitiate and very likely had never had the *Rule* read to him. His was a *professio ad succurrundum*. There is no mention of a second ceremony of profession in Cluny's *Customary* (2:28). All it says is: 'He does everything for three days as the others do, so that what was omitted in the beginning is made up'. There must have been some irregularity in the first profession ceremony. If there were, our Cistercian is silent about it—at any rate, he does not supply a reason.

19. After a reader read the appointed chapter of the Rule, the superior might expound the chapter or deliver a sermon. St Bernard delivered many of his sermons in the assemblies called, for this very reason, 'Chapter'. This could be followed by the words: 'Let us speak about our Order' (i.e., about matters of discipline) See RB 66.

20. Evidently this particular Cistercian was unaware of the canons of the Council of Aachen, 817: 'Neither the abbot nor any brother is to eat at the monastery gate with guests, but the abbot is to extend to them all the amenities of food and drink in the dining room,'—canon 21, Hallinger, *Corpus Consuetudinum monasticarum*, 1:521. In the PL edition of the same canons, it is canon 27. The *Regula ad monachos* of SS Serapion *et alii* ordered abbots to eat with their monks (r. 11; PG 34:892).

21. *Legem judicare—Judicare*, a judgment given by an official acting as a judge in civil or criminal actions. *Judicare legem*, to render a decision on the law itself.

22. In Roman law *honor* was the dignity and power attached to an official in office; *honorem tribuere, exhibere, debere*. The same legal concept is carried over into the *Rule* and into the office of the Abbot of Cluny, or any other abbot.

23. This is the truth but not the whole truth. Apparently the Cistercian was either unaware of or ignored canon 21 (27) of the reforming Council of Aachen, 817, called by Louis the Pious at the instigation of St Benedict of

Aniane [see n. 20], the spiritual father of Cluny. This particular canon placed the refectory with his monks, despite the *Rule* which had him eating with the guests. Adequate provision was, however, made at Cluny for the abbot's absence from the guest-house. These provisions are spelled out in the *Consuetudines cluniacenses,* (3.22), redacted c. 1084 and certainly in force at Cluny when the Cistercian was a *conversus* there. A guest-master received the guests, saw to their needs and if a guest had a special need, the means to satisfy which were not on hand, he was to procure it from the treasurer. Provision was made for the proper reception of abbots and monks both of the Cluniac and of other Orders. 'But before he points out to them our customary observances . . . . he enters the church to pray.' A visiting abbot presided over the guest-house table during mealtime. Provision was also made for those who are to be received in fraternity: 'If the guest is a cleric in orders and if it is fitting that he eat in the monastery refectory, he must wear clerical dress for the occasion. When led to the door of the cloister he waits until invited by the Lord Abbot, or in his absence, by the Grand Prior, who gives him water to wash his hands . . . . No matter what the monastic fare the guest receives a generous serving.'

Technically, the abbot who observed the canons was in violation of the Rule. But when the sorry state of monasticism in the eighth century is taken into account Benedict of Aniane and his council co-abbots decided that the abbot could be of more spiritual benefit in the refectory than in the guest-house.

24. *Tunica.* This seems to be a variation on the proverb, 'My tunic is nearer than my cloak'. The tunic was the undergarment worn alike by men and women.

25. 'et quia hoc putant justum esse . . . . sequitur ut praeceptum regulae existement injustum esse.' Properly speaking, the use of *justum* as opposed to *injustum* means *rights* and a violation of rights.

26. For the problem of the *obedientiarius* who, for hospitality sake, has to entertain ladies at the *obedientia,* see *Consuetudines cluniacenses,* 3.5.

27. Canivez, *Statuta* 1:14 (Statutes of 1134, c.7). This rule was strictly enforced. For example, the abbot and cellarer of Beaulieu (England) were suspended for permitting Queen Eleanor to remain for three weeks in the monastery nursing her very ill son, the future Edward III. See J. F. O'Sullivan, *Cistercian Settlements in Wales and Monmouthshire* (New York, 1947), p. 97.

28. Qualities somewhat remindful of Adam's state of original justice.

29. Much of this is 'off the top of the head' rhetoric. Take the opposite page of the ledger: 'We have a tradition from our forefathers: when Lent comes, no matter how great the number of the poor who come along, all receive a portion of flesh meat. Great as may be the treasurer's worry about the brothers' clothing, it is not nearly as great as his worry about his alms. To make up that alms, neither our piggery nor our fat rendering plant—which is never filled—give adequate return. Subsidization must come from the treasurer's petty cash accounts. Let me not say anything further about events of this year [c. 1084]. A certified estimate of the poor gives the number as 17,000, among whom, in Christ's name, two hundred and fifty pigs' carcasses were divided.' (*Consuetudines cluniacenses,* 3.12)

On the other hand, if the Cistercian had in mind the taxes (of money and produce) levied on her dependencies for the upkeep of Cluny's three hundred monks, then he could very well have a stronger case for his charge of robbery of the poor. Cf. Peter the Venerable, *Dispositio reifamiliaris Cluniacensis* (PL 189: 1047-1054).

30. Sister M. Alfred Schroll, *Benedictine Monasticism as reflected in the Warnefrid-Hildemar Commentaries on the Rule* (New York, 1941), p. 48: [By the eight century] 'the guest house was an extensive department. It is desirable, our commentators say, to have a cloister for the noble guests arranged like that of the monks; another for the poor arranged like that of the infirm, and still another, also like that of the infirm, for the guest monks, so that the needs of all classes be

204   *Notes to Dialogue, Part Two*

taken care of.' For the function of the Almoner in relation to guests at Cluny, see *Consuetudines cluniacenses,* 3.24; the functions of the guest-master, 3.22.

31. All were dressed in albs when in procession to welcome back the Lord Abbot from a journey (*Consuetudines,* 3.3); for Easter and Christmas, the five solemn Sundays and the five principal feasts, see *Consuetudines* 10.21; for the celebration of the Eucharist from the offertory to post-communion, 2.30. A monk who was in grave fault wore an alb as did the other monks on feast days (3.3).

32. *Scarlet.* In English, scarlet also originally referred to a kind of cloth.

33. *Et notata in sinum tuum misisti.* In Roman law the *notata* or the *nota censoria* were the censures incurred for misdemeanor in office and usually ended by removal from office. The *notatus* was branded with *ignominia* (ignominy) or the loss of his good name. The same distinctions were carried over to canon law, i.e., *notatus, ignomania,* and *infamia,* in reference to accusations and trials. Cf. Ex 4:6.

34. St Bernard and the Cistercian's quotation vary on the limits of obedience:

The Cistercian	St Bernard
Nec ultra, nec citra	*Ergo praelati jussio vel*
multo minus vota sua	*prohibitio non praeterreat*
quae distinxerunt	*terminos professionis:*
labia sua quando	*nec ultra extendi, nec*
professus est, jure	*contrahi citra.*
potest cogi	
monachus.	

35. Italics mine. This is a departure from the Roman concept of Law. According to the *Digest* 50.17.1: 'a rule is that which briefly expounds a matter'. Rules were concise formulations extracted from the law then in being. Law was derived from Rules, but Rules were derived from existing Law. *Decretum,* D. 1, cc. 2-3: 'Lex autem juris est species.' 'Quid sit lex?' 'Lex est constitutio scripta.'

36. Pre X, 23-4, SBOp 3, 270; CF 1:122-24, where he quotes Matthew four times, Luke twice, John twice, and Paul twice. The idea of balanced similies is carried on to the words: 'Just as all good living Christians do not observe all the Gospels' contents and yet live in accordance with it.'

37. *Monasterii personae: Personae monachorum* or *personatus in monasterio* [*iis*] were the officials or dignitaries [*dignitates*] of that particular house, e.g., the abbot, grand and claustral priors, cellarer, cantor, treasurer, etc.

38. *Consuetudines cluniacenses,* 2.20. 'On leaving chapter—should it be a day on which speech is not forbidden [Tuesdays, Thursdays and Saturdays in Lent—in summer, speech was allowed after None when the signal therefor was given by an oblate ringing the clappers (3.8). Speech was also allowed in a separate cubicle in the infirmary (3.25).] he receives a book and sits before he utters a word. Under no circumstances whatsoever does he talk while standing. When he does talk, his speech is in a low tone. His own speech and that of others to whose speech he listens must deal with spiritual matters or about those things which this life on earth can do without.'

39. *Rule of St. Augustine,* 9.6; ed. Schroeder, *Archiv fur Urkundenforschung* 9 (1926) 288; ET, Thomas A. Hand, FCh 21:13; 'Books should be requested at a fixed hour each day; if a brother requested it outside the appointed time, it should not be given to him'.

Cistercian [Dialogue]	Rule of Augustine
Extra horam qui codicem	*Codices certa hora singulis*
petierit, non accipiat.	*diebus petantur: extra horam*
	qui petierit, non accipiat.

Much useful and scholarly information on the Rules of St Augustine may be found in the Introduction to *Jordani de Saxonia, Liber Vitasfratrum* edd. R. Arbesmann and W. Humphner (New York, 1943). See Appendix B (p. 491) for the *Regula S. Augustini prima;* Appendix C (p. 491) for the *Regula S. Augustini.*

40. As we saw in the preceding note (39) St Augustine did write a *Rule* for his own community, one of monks; his *Letters* have many references to his monks [See above n. 110]. He did not actually write the *Rule* for the Canons Regular of St Augustine. Their *Rule* is a composite of the *Regula Canonicorum* of Chrodogang of Metz (PL 89:1097-1120), the *Institutio Canonicorum* of the Council of Aachen, 817 (PL 105:805-854) and excerpts from the Regula S. Augustini and the early Fathers.

The origins of the Canons Regular have yet to find their own historian. Three worthwhile pieces of scholarly research are a good beginning in that direction: J. C. Dickinson (*The Origins of the Austin Canons and their Introduction into England,* [London, 1950] devotes the first 90 of 285 pages to origins; C. Dereine, "Vie commune, regle St. Augustin et chanoins reguliers au XII siecle," RHE 41 (1946) 365-406; Francois Petit (*La spiritualite des Premontres au XII–XIII siecles* [Paris, 1947] 11-20) deals in chapter one with the *ordo canonicus* prior to St Norbert.

41. *De nullo ordine sunt.* The orders of society were monks, clerics, and laymen. The Cistercian is evidently arguing that St Augustine's was a community of monks at Tagaste and that, because his *Rule* was a *Rule* for monks then, it remained such later. The *ordo monasticus* or monastic state and the *ordo canonicus* were the two *ordines,* i.e., of men living according to the *Rule* for Canons and the *Rule* for Monks.

42. There are two kinds of canons: (a) those who live in common in a monastery or priory under obedience to an abbot or prior, (b) those who also live in common but owe direct obedience to the bishop. There was a third, short-lived group who lived under abbots and were probably Benedictines who had tampered with the *Rule of St Benedict* in the eighth–tenth centuries.) This two-fold (a) and (b) distinction was recognized by mid-eighth century, when the Council of Vernon decreed (Canon XI) that all clergy live either 'under the hand' of the bishop or in a monastery where they observe a rule. Henceforth, those who were tonsured, 'in monasterio sint sub ordine regulari, aut sub manu episcopi sub ordine canonico' (Mansi 12:579). The main feature of the *ordo canonicus* was life in common. Canons are mentioned in the fourth century Council of Laodices (Hardouin, *Conciliorum Collectio,* 1: col. 783) and in the Council of Clermont, 535, where canon XV decreed that a priest or deacon who was not a canon or attached to the episcopal residence to a parish, but who lived and ministered in private houses, should return to the bishop's church for the celebration of the principal feasts (Hardouin, 2:1182). These are the clergy who originally constituted the *ordo canonicus* (episcopal clergy) as opposed to the *ordo regularis* (monks). It was for the episcopal clergy that Bishop Chrodogang of Metz drew up his *Regula Canonicorum* in 756 (PL 89:1057-1096) and which was amended in 816 (PL 89:1097-1120). According to his Rule, the canon-clerics (*clerici canonici*) should live in cloisters, with admittance granted neither laymen nor women. The cloister should be vigorously guarded and after Compline the porter was to bring the key to the archdeacon or person charged with keeping cloister. Dormitory and refectory were in common, but the bishop could allow private dwellings within the enclosure. Each day all were bound to attend chapter. They were to chant the *Opus dei* daily, with details for its performance given in the *Rule.*

The general tendency was to make all clergy canons, except those who were monks, and there was much legislation on this point during the reign of Charlemagne. The canon tended to become more like the monk, so much so that there was much confusion on the exact differences between the two states. The Council of Metz (813) tried to define the *ordo canonicus* by decreeing (canon 9) that canons live the canonical life, observing the teachings of Holy Scripture and writings of the Fathers, eating and sleeping at the same time where facilities exist for so doing. They might receive stipends for things ecclesiastical. They had to remain in their cloister and be obedient to superiors (Mansi 14:67). The Council of Tours of the same year (813) distinguished between three kinds of religious communities: (a) canons living with the bishop (canon 23); canons living under an abbot (canon 24); (c) monks following the Rule of St Benedict (canon 25). (Mansi, 14:86-87.) The essential difference between the two classes of canons seems to be that one was obedient to a bishop, another to the abbot. The rule of life for both was the same. Probably the canons living under an abbot had their origin in Benedictine monasteries in which the Rule of St Benedict had ceased to be observed.

The Council of Aachen, 816 (817), defined the lives of canons. Canons could use linen clothes, eat meat, give and receive private property, all of which was wholly forbidden monks, 'quod monachis . . . . paenitus inhibitum est.' MGH *Leges,* section II, pt. 1, p. 397.) Where convenient, each monk was to receive five measures of wine per day or three of wine and two of ale or one of wine and five of beer, depending upon the resources at hand. (ibid., pp. 401-403) This gave rise to the daily distribution of wine, wheat, food, etc., to which were added the gifts of the pious. Canons were not to wear the *cuculla* (cowl or hooded choir-robe) which is even today a distinguishing feature of the choir-monk (p. 405). During the chanting of the *Opus dei,* the monks were to stand, not sit, not to lean on a stick, and not to chant with others. (pp. 406-410.) Another feature of the Council was the formulation of a penal code or the beginning of the 'statutory penalties'; the *maranciae* of later times. The canon who time after time made his entrance to the Office *pompatice et incomposite* was to be punished on bread and water. Like penalties existed for going out without permission (pp. 410-12). Women could enter the church, but not the cloister (p. 418). The canons were the cathedral chapter in many cases.

Ordinarily, the canons did not take vows and were not bound to personal poverty. Soon so many abuses crept in that the *ordo canonicus* came under severe criticism during the gregorian reform period. In 1067, there appeared for the first time, in Reims, canons who followed the Rule of St Augustine (PL 147:1330-1332). They had the blessing of Pope Alexander II but were an isolated case. Twenty years later, another house appeared at Soissons and soon houses came into being in Germany. The Rule was in force in the West by the middle of the twelfth century, when, in 1153, Pope Anacletus confirmed the *Institutes of the Canons Regular* or *Institutes of the Canons of St Augustine* (Mansi 21:778-80). Thereafter there was the distinction between the *canones saeculares* attached to a cathedral and the *canones regulares* who followed the Rule of St Augustine. One of the best known orders of Canons regular are the Premonstratensians (Norbertines), founded by St Norbert and still in existence (*Vita S. Norberti, archiepiscopi Madgeburgensis,* ed. R. W. Pertz; MGH SS 13:665ff).

The question of the habit was seriously debated by St Norbert and his followers. That their habit is white is due largely to their close association with the Cistercians, from whom they also took verbatim many items in the Customary. (On the question of habit, see Petit, *La Spiritualite,* pp. 35-6.) Their choir-robe pelisse was of skins. The Premonstratensians are known from the color of their habit as the White Canons. See H. M. Colvin, *The White Canons in England* (Oxford, 1951). His first chapter (pp. 1-25) deals with the Order's foundation.

43. The central meaning of this whole passage turns on the sentence: 'What does the divine oracle tell me to discuss now?' (*tractare:* to discuss). In roman law *tractare* refers to treatment of criminals. It also means the discussion

of a legal problem, hence *tractatus*, a treatise on a legal matter. By the twelfth century the word begins to appear in both secular and ecclesiastical documents with the meaning 'to discuss', 'to treat of'. By the next century, *tractare* was much in use in reference to affairs in Parliament, with 'to treat with', 'to negotiate', as its principal meanings (e.g. *tractare de negotiis regni*).

44. *Cauterio infamiae*. Primarily, *infamia* was the stigma of an evil reputation. In addition, condemnation as 'infamous' carried with it certain legal disabilities: loss of the right to appear in court as a lawyer in a suit or as a representative for either plaintiff or defendant. The most common reasons for branding with *infamia* were malpractice in business, flagrant cheating, bankruptcy, discharge from the army for bad conduct. One of the worst consequences was the loss of the right to hold public office. The same concepts carried over into canon law. In this instance the Cistercian is referring to his *Argumenta*, q. v.

45. *Decret*. C. 36, q. 2, cc. 1-11 enumerates medieval conciliar legislation on rape. See 'Rapt' in DCC 7:454-60. See also *Passio sanctae Luciae*, ed. Mombritius, *Sanctuarium* 2 (1910) p. 108.

46. *Actio causae*—roman formula for 'to plead a case'.

47. *Monas* (Latin), μονας (Greek), plural *monades*: a single-celled organism. This became the *monad* of Leibnitz, an indivisible cell which was the basic constituent element of reality. Cf. *monas* in biology, a single-celled microscopic organism, and *monas* in chemistry, an atom or radical with a valence of one. Cf. Jean Leclercq, *Etudes sur le vocabulaire monastique du moyen age*. Studia Anselmiana 48 (1961) 22-23.

48. This thought is not original with the Cistercian. Cf. Apo X, 24-5; SBOp 3:101-102; CF 1:59-61. Cf. Anselm of Havelberg, *Epistola apologetica pro ordine canonicorum regularium*; PL 187:1119ff. Much of the Cistercian's *canonicus canonicorum, regularis regularis* terminology (below, II, 42) can also be found in this letter. See too, *Glossa ordinaria*; PL 113:941B.

49. This is also a quotation from Possidius' *Life of St. Augustine*; FCh 15: 78. Cf. Aug., *Sermo* 355; PL 39:1568-74 and Lambot, ed., *Sancti Aurelii Augustini sermones selecti duodeviginti* (Utrecht, 1950) pp. 124, 126, 385.

50. The Cistercian's antipathy for Norbertines is rather strange. The two orders enjoyed very friendly terms and because they did the Praemonstratensians took advantage of Citeaux's good will to spread throughout Europe almost as quickly and numerously as the Cistercians did.

51. St Norbert's first inclination was toward evangelism. Because he preached without having the right to wear the monastic habit in which he was dressed, he was accused at the Council of Fritzlar of several misdemeanors, chief among them being that he was dressed as a monk without having taken monastic vows. The desire to preach remained strong within the Order. With this in mind the Norbertines went to Palestine where they became almost the official preachers in the Latin Kingdom of Jerusalem, to which the first missionaries of the Order in 1136 went from the abbey of Floreffe (See *Annales Floreffienses*; MGH SS 16:618-31. L. Goovaerts, *Ecrivains, Artists, et Savants de l'ordre de Premontre. Vita S. Norberti*; PL 170:1250-84. G. Madelaine, *Histoire de S. Norbert* (2 vols.: Tongerloo, 1928). C. Kirkfleet, *History of St. Norbert* (St Louis, 1916).

52. There are so many grains of truth in this estimate of Norbert that assessment of its value is quite difficult. Norbert was born into the german imperial nobility. His father was an imperial vassal and a cousin of Emperor Henry V. When quite young he was appointed a canon at Xanten. After an illness he realized the futility of his life till then, put away his rich clothing and trappings, and used a hinny for transportation. There are two separate parts to Norbert's life: (a) founder of the Premonstratensian canons in France, and (b) Archbishop of Magdeburg in the Empire. He seems to have lost some interest in the destiny

of Premontre and to have devoted his energies to his archbishopric, mainly to the evangelization of the Slavs. By the very nature of contemporary society, he, as archbishop, had to work in close collaboration with the emperor and his court. It would have been a breach of etiquette to ride a hinny, trotting side by side with the imperial mounted charger. It is interesting to note that, later on, many Cistercian abbots were rebuked in the General Chapter for coming to Chapter on horses bedecked with ornamented bridles.

53. *Canon, regula.* Canon is derived from κανών, a rule, a list. Canons were originally clergy whose names were inscribed on the list of cathedral clergy. Regulars were those, clerical or lay, who followed a rule of life. Canons regular were characterized by being priests and following a rule. They differed from cathedral canons in that the latter did not live under a rule; they differed from monks in that monks until the eleventh and twelfth centuries seldom proceeded to the priesthood. Norbertines in Germany performed parish work while those at Premontre followed a way of life very much like that at Citeaux.

54. From the viewpoint of etymology the Cistercian is correct, but from the viewpoint of the contemporary canon law to which he so often appealed he is not correct. See above, n. 41 on canons, the *ordo canonicus,* the *ordo monasticus,* and n. 48 on his sources.

55. *Mansiones,* a word derived from *mansa,* the amount of land, with a house, necessary for the maintenance of one family. He refers here to the famous Rule of Canons produced at Aachen under the auspices of St Benedict of Aniane (816); PL 105:815ff & MGH *Concilia* 2:pp.312ff.

56. The *ordo canonicus* began with the *Regula canonicorum S. Chrodogangi Metensis Episcopi;* PL 89:1057-95. Chrodogang redacted this Rule in 756, when Louis the Pious was not yet king in Acquitaine. The Cistercian has in mind the Synod of Aachen (816) which drew up legislation for canons under the auspices of Benedict of Aniane. Legislation for monks was drawn up the following year, 817.

57. This is chapter one of the *Regula S. Augustini,* but it is not a faithful reproduction of the Rule in either of the Appendices in *Jordani de Saxonia Liber Vitasfratrum* (pp. 485-504) or of the translation of T. A. Hand; FCh 12:359.

58. *De sacramentis christianae fidei, pars tertia: De ecclesiasticis ordinibus, cap. IV;* PL 176:422: *Quomodo ordines sacri in monachis sint.* 'Quidem volunt coronam aliquando pro signo accipiendam poenitentiae quemadmodum in ordine monachorum quibus est ceteri ordines sacri qui in clero sunt proprii secundum indulgentiam conceduntur.'

After his debates with Abelard, William of Champeaux retired to the Paris suburbs to a chapel dedicated to St Victor. He and his companions organized themselves in 1108 into a community of canons following the Rule of St Augustine. William's successor, Gilduin, wrote the community's Customary. To this group came a young Saxon named Hugh, who became one of the great intellectual lights of the twelfth century. Not only was he a great scholar, he was also one of the great contemplatives of his age (*De arrha animae;* PL 176: esp. 953-55). Among his best known works are the *Didascalion* (tr. Jerome C. Taylor, *Didascalicon: The Guide to the Arts,* Records of Civilization Series [New York: Columbia Univ. Press, 1961], *De sacramentis christianae fidei* (PL 176:174-618), *Expositio in regulam beati Augustini* (tr. Dom Aloysius Smith [London, 1911]).

Hugh speaks in the *Expositio* about the Rule of St Augustine: the precepts according to which a community of religious has its being are the *regula,* the Greek κανών. Thus they who live in this manner are called either *regulares* or *canonici. Vivunt juxta regularia praecepta sanctorum patrum canonica atque apostolicae* (PL 175:xxiv–xxvii).

59. Cf. *Decret.* C. 14, 1. 3, c. 1: 'Nullus abbas vel monachus canonicos regulares a propositio professionis canonicae revocare et ad monasticum habitum trahendo usurpare audeat ut monachi fiant, quamdiu ordinis sui ecclesiasm

inveniri queant in qua canonice vivendo et animam suam salvare possint.' For the prohibition of Pope Urban II, see *ibid.*, canons 2-3. No regular canon was to leave his house for another *sine patris et totius congregationis permissione,* and no professed canon could be professed later as a monk *nisi publice lapsus fuerit.*

60. The passage in Gregory's works has not been located. Gregory had in mind the duty of preaching. For further information, see 'Cure' and 'Curé' in DCC 4:889-931.

61. For processing and working gold in the Middle Ages, see Theophilus, *De artibus diversis,* tr. Dodwell, pp. 84, 96-102, 127-8, 142.

62. St Bernard's Sermon on the Feast of St Benedict tells of land reclaimed and yielding an hundredfold, which would seem to refute the Cluniac's claim that thirty Cistercians worked to feed one (SBOp 5:3).

63. Cassian, *Inst.* 3, 2: 'These Offices which we are taught to render to the Lord at separate hours and at intervals of time . . . are celebrated continuously throughout the whole day, with the addition of work, and that of their own free will.' (NPNF 11:212-13). For the synaxis at Pachonian monasteries, see A. Boon, 'Regula S. Pachomii' in *Pachomiana Latina,* 3-74. For an excellent study on the pachomian rule, see Veilleux, *La Liturgie dans le cenobitisme pachomien au IV siecle.* On psalmody in early monasticism, see 'The Long Rules of St Basil', tr. Sr. M. Monica Wagner in *The Ascetical Works of St Basil,* FCh 9:306-11. On the Cistercian recitation of the Office while monks were at work, see Guignard, *Les monuments primitifs,* p. 179.

64. Hugh of St Victor was a canon regular, not a monk. See above notes 53, 58.

65. He seems by 'slit tunicle' (*linguata tunica*) to mean the dalmatic, which symbolizes the deacon's office of proclaiming the Gospel.

66. This is the 'Letter to Consecrated Virgins' which Augustine wrote to his sister and her bickering community (Letter 211; CSEL 57:356-71; ET by Sr Wilfred Parsons, FCh 32:38-51). This *Rule of St Augustine for Women* served as the mirror of conduct for attendants in hospitals (Jean Imbert, *Les hopitaux en droit canonique* [Paris, 1947]), for Canons Regular, for friars, and for military orders.

67. Isidore, *De ecclesiasticis officiis,* II,1; PL 83:777, says nothing particularly about them being *imitatores apostolorum*; he talks about the derivation of the word. *De regulis clericorum* (II,2:777-9) discusses their behavior, but again there is no specific reference to the imitation of the apostles. His *Etymologiae, cap.* XII, has the same information. On the imitation of the Apostles, see Cassian, *Inst.* 10.9, and 2 Thes 3:8-9, where St Paul sets the example of work for all to imitate him: 'When preaching the Gospel, I preferred to be supported by my own hands and work, that I might open up the way of perfection to you who wish to walk in the path of virtue, and might set an example of good life by my work.' See also *Decret.* C. 12, q. 1, c. 7 on the meaning of cleric.

68. Cf. John Chrysostom, *Hom. in Matt.* 43:23, in *Decret.* D. 40, c. 12.

69. Both St Jerome and his brother Paulinus were ordained to the priesthood but neither ever said Mass other than their ordination Mass. Jerome took Holy Orders willingly, but Paulinus resisted with all his physical and moral strength. St Jerome's monasteries had been caught in a quarrel over Origen's doctrines between Bishop Epiphanius of Salamis and Bishop John of Jerusalem, and Bishop John had denied Jerome the use of priests for services. Thereupon Bishop Epiphanius ordained Paulinus to the diaconate and priesthood, intending to solve Jerome's problems. Epiphanius wrote a letter of justification to John in which he gives details: 'I saw that the monasteries contained a large number of brothers and nuns and that the reverend presbyters, Jerome and Vincent, through modesty and humility, were unwilling to offer the sacrifice permitted to their rank' (i.e. were unwilling to celebrate the Eucharist). Then follows an account of Paulinus' ordination. Paulinus appeared before the bishop not suspecting what was in store for him. Epiphanius wrote: 'While the *Collect* was being

celebrated in the church of the villa which adjoins the monastery [of Besandue, of which Epiphanius had been abbot for thirty years before becoming Bishop of Salamis] —he being quite ignorant and unsuspicious of my purpose—I gave orders to a number of deacons to seize him and to stop his mouth, lest in his eagerness to free himself he might abjure in the name of Christ. I ordained him deacon, setting before him the fear of God, and compelled him to minister; for he made a hard struggle against it . . . . And when he had ministered in offering the holy Sacrifice, once more with great difficulty I closed his mouth and ordained him presbyter.' Paulinus never did minister. (ET, NPNF 6:83-4).

70. Physical disability was an impediment to priesthood.

71. *Laici monachi*: a reference to the *conversi*, who on feast days dressed in albs as did the professed monks.

72. *Papa* was a title of affection. It also meant *admirabilis*, 'the greatest one', 'guardian', 'little father'. Many bishops, e.g. of Constantinople and Alexandria, used the title. In Letter 31, to Paulinus and Therasia, St Augustine says: 'I believe that your sanctity has the books of the most blessed *papa* Ambrose.' (FCh 12:116). In Letter 195, Jerome addressed himself to 'The saintly lord and blessed *papa*, Augustine' (FCh 30:332).

NOTES TO DIALOGUE

PART THREE

1. The Cisterican is quoting from memory:

St Bernard	Cistercian
'Una quidem oris ubique promissio sed quia non una est omnibus cordis intentio potest indubitanter sine detrimento salutis, et sine damno professionis, operis quoque non una ubique observatio celebrari.'	*'una quidem oris . . .* . . . . *intentio non aliud proculdubio quisque promittit, quam quod habere pia illorum vita videtur, cum quibus deinceps vivere disponit et elegit.'*

2. *Affectu—effectu:* a favorite Cistercian balance. Cf. William of St Thierry, *De contemplando deo;* SCh 61:104: 'et sanctificans amamus te, vel amas tu te in nobis, nos affectu, tu effectu . . . ; 108: 'justitiamque multi volunt affectu, a qua procul sunt effectu . . . ' ; 126: immo O anima enitere quantum potes non tam rationis, effectu quam amoris affectu.'

3. Cf. Amedee Hallier, *The Monastic Theology of Aelred of Rievaulx,* CS 2 (1969) p. 13 n. 55: The word *virtus (habitus anim.)* is here used in the sense in which it is used by the Fathers: participating in the Virtue par excellence, the Word of God.

4. See Anselm of Canterbury, *Liber de similitudinibus,* Ch. 79, in M. Rule, ed., *Chronicles and Memorials of Great Britain and Ireland,* Rolls Series (London, 1884): 'Ipsi jam probati sunt in omni humilitate et obedientia, et patientia, et observatione omnium quae *ordo* exposcit.' Italics mine.

5. On the relationship existing between Cistercian nuns and abbeys of men, see Sr Michael [Elizabeth] Connor OCSO, 'The First Cistercian Nuns and Renewal Today.' CSt 5 (1970) 131-168.

6. *ad fenestras earum,* which implies a 'talk-window' or separation between the nuns and their spiritual guide.

7. *Regula monachorum* 3, *Sancti Columbani Opera,* ed. G. S. M. Walker in *Scriptores Latini Hiberniae* (Dublin, 1957) 2:124-5.

8. 'A pittance is what is given in one plate to be shared by two.' *Consuetudines Cluniacenses,* 2:35. See above I, n. 61. People in secular society ordinarily ate two to a single dish at this time.

9. This was the 'before and after' bow which Cluny taught its novices with care. *Consuetudines Cluniacenses* 2:2.

10. *Aristolelica regula:* deductive system of logic, especially the syllogism.

11. Our thanks to Professor E. A. Synan for help in unravelling the Cistercian's complicated—and unconvincing—logic. —ed.

12. Six yards = *Sex alae: ala* = wing, the length of a man's arm and shoulder.

13. See Ardo, *Vita Benedicti Anianensis;* PL 103:353-383; and DHGE 8: cols. 177-188. According to Ardo (*Vita,* col. 357): 'There were many things which were done according to local custom and about which he remained silent. But above all, henceforth the monks' habits were to be furnished with clasps: without them, the habit was in complete disarray, loose and disorderly.' (Col. 367) 'He likewise legislated for the monastic habit which by then had become customary and was of all varieties—benedictine habits, irish habits, Caesarian [of Arles] habits, augustinian habits, basilican habits, and bits and pieces of all the habits on one monk were on hand. Some had choir robes which reached as low as the ankles. Because of this, the man of God instituted a uniform choir-robe to be worn by all; it was not to be more than two cubits in length, but it could even reach the knees, *Capitulare monasticum* (817); PL 103:381-394: 'Should the abbot find it necessary to issue an order increasing the size of the choir-robe in a particular case, he is impowered to do so.' (ibid., canon 21) 'The size of the choir-robe is to be two cubits.'

14. For an account of the origins of Cistercian convents, see, Jacques de Vitry, *Libri duo quorum prior orientalis sive Hierosolymita; aliter occidentalis historiae nomine vocatur* (Douai, 1597). St Bernard's sister, Humbeline, entered the benedictine house of Jully-les-Nonnains and later became its prioress. The first convent of cistercian nuns was founded c. 1132 at Tart, near Dijon, and was an off-spring of Jully-les-Nonnais (PL 185:1387).

15. Although this is not in Urban's Register in Jaffe's *Regesta Pontificum Romanorum* (2nd edition) 2 vols. (Leipzig, 1885-1888), nor among his 304 letters, most of which deal with privileges to monasteries (PL 149:961-1018), Huygens located this passage in 'Gerhoch von Reichersberg und die Regularkanoniker in Bayeon und Oesterreich', ed. P. Classen, in *La vita commune del clero nei secoli XI e XII* (Miscellanea del Centro di Studi Medioevali III, Septembre 1959 [1962], vol I:337 (339)-340: Beilage 3: *Ein unbekanntes Mandat Papst Urbans II. fur Rottenbuch*).

16. *Decret.* C. 19, q.2, c.2: The same Pope, Urban II, deciding the case of the Canons Regular of St Rufe: 'Si quis horum in ecclesia sua sub episcopo populum retinet, et saeculariter vivit, si afflatus Spiritu Sancto in aliquo monasterio vel regulari canonica alvare se voluerit, quia lege privata ducitur, nulla ratio exigit, ut a publica lege constringatur.'

17. Cassian, *Conf.* 17,8-9. Hildemar, *Commentary on the Rule* c. 61; ed. Mittermuller, pp. 565-7. The matter was discussed at the cistercian chapter general of 1134.

18. These sentences are the essence of the *Carta Charitatis;* Guignard, *Les monuments primitifs,* pp. 79-84.

19. *acephali:* this has a double meaning: simply leaderless (Greek, *akephalos:* headless) and also leaderless in the sense of being heretical.

20. Cluny was located in the diocese of Macon but the monks called in other bishops and archbishops (usually the archbishop of Besancon) to bless and install their abbots. There are many papal bulls and papal privileges allowing them to do so (for a list, see Guy de Valous, *Monachisme clunisien,* I, p. 99, nn. 1,2). The abbatial history of Cluny was especially troubled during the abbatial tenure Ponce [Pons] de Melgueil, who was made a cardinal by Pope Calixtus II during his stay at Cluny for the canonization of St Hugh. The community revolted against Ponce who then went to the Holy Land. Claiming the abbatial chair of Cluny on his return, he succeeded in recapturing the abbey and more or less pillaged the abbey of its treasures. He died in prison in 1125, and was succeeded by the last of Cluny's great abbots, Peter the Venerable. [For a recent evaluation of the Ponce scandle, see J. Leclercq, A. H. Bredero, P. Zerbi, 'Encore sur Pons de Cluny et Pierre le Venerable', *Aevum* 48 (1974) 134-49—ed].

21. Citeaux's refusal to have attached peasants was formally legalized in *Instituta monachorum cisterciensium de molismo venientium;* Guignard, *Monuments primitifs,* 71-72. Cluny's serfs numbered in the hundreds. They owed labor, they planted and reaped, did vine culture, etc. The most reliable document on Cluny's demands on its serfs is Peter the Venerable's *Dispositio reifamiliaris;* PL 189:1048-1054.

22. The matter of boon days occasionally led to strikes which usually took the form of sit-ins on the headlands, an act which prevented the ox-teams from turning. On Holy Saturday the spring gifts of eggs were due at the manor house, as were hens and roosters at Christmastime. In time these gifts became customary, that is, fixed by custom, and this resulted in grumbling and mutual bad feeling. See G. G. Homans, *English Villages of the 13th Century,* (Cambridge, 1941), C. Verlinden, *L'esclavage dans l'Europe medievale,* I (Bruges, 1955), P. Bernard, *Etude sur les Esclaves et les serfs d'Eglise,* (Paris, 1919).

23. Cluny derived revenue of various kinds from many towns and cities, e.g., '20,000 herring from the city of Poitiers'; 'the cheeses which are either obligatory levies or come from the food stocks of the town of Cluny or Massy': see *Dispositio reifamiliaris;* PL 189:1052.

24. *Seniores:* those who had entered the community before he had.

25. *Jordani de Saxonia, Liber Vitasfratrum,* edd. Arbesmann and Hempfner, p. 496.

26. Cf. S. Jerome, Ep 125; *CSEL,* 56, p. 126: 'Vas electionis in cujus Christus ore sonabat macerat corpus suum et subjicit servituti . . . .'

27. *Corona:* a crown, a ring, a garland (*korone, koronos*) of hair around the head, below and above which the hair was cut close or shaved: Cf., 'Tonsure' in *DACL,* XV/2:2430-2443.

28. Jerome, Ep 125; *CSEL,* 56:124: 'Tu vero, si monachus esse vis . . . sordes vestium candidae mentis indicio sint, utilis tunica contemptum saeculi porbet ita dumtaxat ne animus tumeat, ne habitus sermoque dissentiat.'

29. The mark of the monastic and clerical office was the tonsure or *corona.*

30. *Carinna (Carrina, Carena)* was a fast of forty days imposed publicly by the bishop on both clergy and laymen for serious crimes. It was also used in monasteries and imposed by the abbot for serious breaches of discipline.

31. Notice here the emphasis on the *tonsure* as the distinctive mark of the cleric. In the first centuries of the Church—and probably until the twelfth century—tonsure was not a condition for the rite of admission to the clerical state. It was of very early use in the Church but was regarded as a preparation for, rather than the initiation to, Holy Orders. Gregory the Great does not include the tonsured among the clerical Orders (*Decret.* C. 11, q. 1, c. 38). Nor is it included in Isidore of Seville's enumeration of clerical orders (*ibid.,* D. 21, c. 1). Its primary significance was that it marked those consecrated to God. The precise date at which it became the distinctive mark of those in clerical status is not known but, in this Dialogue, the Cistercian gives the impression that it was in current practice by the late twelfth century.

32. Two distinctions are being made here. *Clerics* in the Middle Ages meant clergymen and, because only clergy could read, literates. A man who could prove his ability to read, for example, was exempt from secular justice. *Lay brothers* among the Cistercians were not considered *monks,* a term reserved to the choir monks who were literate and ordained.

33. The research of Veilleux, *La liturgie,* should be studied carefully and fully on this point. He has shown quite conclusively the identity of the pachomian monasteries with the local parish churches. The monastery was a part of the parish, its spiritual needs cared for by the local priest. Hence, there was no necessity for many priests

34. Actually Epiphanius was Bishop of Salamis in Cyprus.

214   *Notes to Dialogue, Part Three*

35. · *Epistola Epiphanii Cyprii missa ad Johannem Episopum, a Sancto Hieronymo translata,* Ep 51; CSEL 54:395-412. This is Jerome's monastery in Bethlehem. The central point of this letter is the Origenist controversy. Jerome had become embroiled with his own ordinary over origenist teachings. Since Jerome and Vincent, though priests, would not function as priests, the monastery was without a priest for its spiritual cares. Bishop Epiphanius ordained Jerome's brother, Paulinian, without John's permission. This, plus the fact that Epiphanius wanted the monastery of Bethlehem to be independent of his adversary, Bishop John of Jerusalem, culminated in the forced ordination of Paulinian, who although he was then almost thirty years of age, is referred to in the bitter controversy between the two prelates as 'a mere boy'. (See above II, n. 69)

36. Cf. St Ambrose, *The Holy Spirit;* FCh 44:110 ' . . . and carried about the world the sweet-smelling fruits of the holy religion.'

37. Those who had committed serious and public sin had to perform public penance. They appeared at the church door on Ash Wednesday, dressed in sackcloth and shoeless, and prostrated themselves on the earth. Those who were to be absolved were led within the church; those refused absolution at that particular time were chased away by the bishop. (Cf. Regino, *Libri duo de ecclesiastica disciplina;* PL 132:245-6)

38. The supply of grain for horses, either those of Cluny itself or those of the guests, became critical in the twelfth century. The following is an excerpt from Peter the Venerable's document on his final reorganization of Cluny's finances: 'Those who are to read these arrangements should know that after I made them I ordered the obedientiary of Massily to provide enough oats for all the guests' horses and, if perchance their normal sureties for covering advances on oats are not enough and they must pledge their own money, he is to accept it as collateral.

'Prior to the issuance of this order, the above-mentioned obedientiary returned only 1,200 measures of oats annually to the procurator [of Cluny], on the basis of my first reorganizing regulations. The oats were distributed haphazardly to the guests' horses, to those of the Lord Abbot, the Grand Prior, and the cellarer and procurator. Since everybody grabbed what he could from this pile of oats, bickerings were frequently heard and the guests' horses neglected. Accordingly, I have ordered that the abbot's, prior's, and the cellarer's claims are to be discarded and that the procurator should be given oats sufficient for the guests' horses only, and make provision for them no matter how long they stay, As I have already stated, he should have their guaranteed promise to pay, especially from those who are complete strangers. [A list of priors of houses who are not charged for horses feed follows] . . . .

'As regards the Grand Prior of Cluny, I am ordering that he receive from the obedientiary of Ecuselle three-hundred measures of oats for his horses' feed.' (*Dispositio reifamiliaris Cluniacensis;* PL 189:1052-3).

39. The passage, 'vir fidelis et ferventis fidei cautam distributionem genus infidelitatus putat', is not a direct quotation from Jerome. It expresses the thought of both the following passages:

Ep 66, 7; CSEL 54:656: 'Do you want to be perfect? There is no compulsion laid upon you. If you are to win the prize, it must be by the exercise of your own free will. If therefore you want to be perfect and desire to be as the prophets, as the Apostles, as Christ himself, sell not a part of your substance, *lest the fear of want become an occasion of lack of faith* and so you perish with Ananias and Sapphira, but sell all that you have.'

Contra Vigilantium 14; PL 23:366: 'As for his [Vigilantius'] argument that they who keep what they have and distribute among the poor the increase of their property little by little [i. e. make a *cauta distributio*] than they who sell their possessions and once and for all give everything away, not I but the Lord shall make answer: "If you want to be perfect, go, sell all you have and give it to the poor, and come, follow me" ' (Mt 19:21).

Huygens refers to the probable source as Jerome, *Ep ad Nepotien* 52 (16).

AN ARGUMENT CONCERNING FOUR QUESTIONS

Notes by Joseph Leahey

1. The statement of the question is perhaps as important as the answer. *Persona* refers primarily to legal personality. The significance of *una eademque* is found first of all in the principle of identity, and secondly in the maxim *bis de eadem re ne sit actio* and the clause *bis idem exigere*.
2. *Voluntas* (wish, a desire, a will, an intention) was an element essential to a legal act.
3. I have translated *sanctimoniales feminae* as 'cloistered nuns', although strictly speaking, this is redundant. This is in keeping with the distinction made by Idung in the third question. On the growth of Cistercian and Premonstratensian nuns and new forms of religious life, see Ernest W. McDonnell, *The Beguines and Beghards in Medieval Culture* (New York: Octagon Books, 1969) 101f., 320-340.
4. The edition of the Rule used throughout is *Commentary on the Rule of St. Benedict* by Paul Delatte, trans. Justin McCann (London: Burns Oates and Washbourne Limited, 1921). Hereafter cited as RSB.
5. Herbord was a *scholasticus* at Bamberg and the author of a *Life* of Otto of Bamberg.
6. On the term *pauperes Christi*, in use after Augustine of Hippo, see Huygens, p. 343, note. See, Bede Lackner, *Eleventh Century Background of Citeaux*, CS 8 (1972), pp. xviif; 150f; 210, 271. To the excellent references to *paupertas Christi, pauperes Christi* may be added Glenn Olsen, 'The Idea of the *Ecclesia Primitiva* in the Writings of the Twelfth-Century Canonists,' *Traditio* 25 (1969) 61-86, and Giles Constable, *Monastic Tithes from their Origins to the Twelfth Century*, Cambridge Studies in Medieval Life and Thought, New Series, No. 10 (New York: Cambridge University Press, 1964) 169-170; 185-186; 262-263.
7. The meaning of thoughts (*sententia*) is that of the schoolroom rather than of the cloister. See Leclercq, p. 209. The basic meaning is that of the language of law.
8. *Past. Care* I, 11; ACW 11:41: 'But there are some who, disliking to be considered dull, often busy themselves with a variety of inquisitions, more than is needful, and fall into error by their excessive subtlety.' *Ibid.*, II, 4; pp. 51, 55. Cf. DCC I, 15; II, 29, 27, 40, 34.
9. Cf. DCC, I, 47. Idung's language has reminiscences if not parallels with Roman law. While his reasoning is clear enough, the terminology which he employs makes it more precise. The infinitive *intelligere* means 'to understand'. Understanding is requisite for effective, valid, action. If the liberally educated people to whom Idung refers have not read the orthodox fathers, their ignorance is perhaps culpable. Yet it is the *insensata sententia et indocta doctrina* of these people that the monastic profession destroys the office of cleric. They stupidly

opine precisely because they lack understanding. More so, in Roman legal usage, *sensus* refers to 'the capacity of understanding the significance of one's own doings, in particular, whether they are wrong or right.' Therefore, an *insensata sententia* results in a non-judgment, for it was based on a lack of knowledge. Likewise, their *indocta doctrina* is not a teaching at all, for they never learned.

10. 'ignorant of letters and of law' (*qui litteras et legem ignorat*) can refer to three things: (1) ignorance of the existence or ignorance of the meaning of a legal norm or both; (2) error regarding the existence or the meaning of a legal norm or both; (3) both ignorance and error. In either of the cases, ignorance of the law 'does not afford an excuse and the person who acts from lack of knowledge of the law has to bear the consequences of his ignorance.' *DRL*, 491. Decret. Pars II, C. 1, q. 4, c. 12, 3, 1: 'Notandum quoque est, quod non omnis ignorantia aliquem excusat. Est enim ignorantia alia facti alia iuris. Facti alia, quod non oportuit eum scire, alia, quod oportuit eum scire.' *Ibid.*, pars 2: 'Item ignorantia iuris alia naturalis, alia civilis.' D. 1, c. 3: 'The law is a written constitution.'

11. Cf. 1 P 3:20-21. Hugh of St. Victor, *Summa Sententiarum, Tractatus Quintus: De sacramento baptismi;* PL 176:130, recognizes the distinction between the matter and the form of the sacrament. *Ibid.*, PL 176:136. On Marriage, he writes: 'Constat enim conjuges fieri quicunque ex communi consensu se invicem recipiunt.' *Ibid., Tractatus VII: De sacramento conjugii,* I: PL 176:155. This is continued in greater detail in the *De sacramentis,* II, XI, iv; PL 176:483.

12. The reliable history may well be *Historia Monachorum in Aegypto sive de Vitis Patrum;* PL 21:388-462.

13. Mutilation was a bar to ordination. This self-mutilation may be compared to CT 7, 13, 5, 10. See *The Paradise of the Fathers*, cited in RSB, p. 426 n. 3. DCC, II, 57.

14. The absurdity is that Idung, like Hugh of St Victor, did not want to have the efficacy of the sacrament depend on the spiritual state of the minister. Cf. *De sacramentis,* II, VII, xiii; PL 176:459.

15. 'evil in his heart'. See the notes on *moechus* in Jerome Taylor, *The Didascalion of Hugh of St. Victor,* Records of Civilization Sources and Studies, No. 64 (New York: Columbia University Press, 1961) p. 191 note 64. Cf. Mt 5:28.

16. On the lapsed and the need for penance, see Cyprian of Carthage, *The Lapsed,* XV-XXIII; ACW 25:24-32. On the restoration of office, *ibid.*, ACW 25:84-85 notes 66-67. See Decret. D. 50; *Sirm* 15.

17. Cuno was bishop of Regensburg (1126-1132).

18. Associated closely with the principle of identity are two other principles, namely, that of contradiction and that of the excluded middle. According to the principle of contradiction, "It is impossible for the same thing to be and not to be at the same time." According to the principle of the excluded middle, "A thing either is or is not." The latter implies that to affirm one thing is to deny its contradictory. Likewise, to deny one thing is to affirm its contradictory. See Celestine N. Bittle, *The Science of Correct Thinking,* rev. ed. (Milwaukee: Bruce, 1950) 133. The point that Idung makes regarding predication is connected with the problem of universals. See David Knowles, *The Evolution of Medieval Thought* (New York: Vintage Books edition, 1962) 107-130. See DCC, III, 40.

19. A man having had two wives in succession, not (as in our day) simultaneously, for medieval law did not recognize the validity of the second of simultaneous marriages. DRL. 373-4, 693, 765. CT 3, 7, 1-3; 1-2. Decret. D. 23, c. 2; D. 26, c. 2.

20. Decret. D. 26, c. 1 (quoting Jerome *ad Oceanum,* Ep 83): A *monogamus* is a man who after baptism has one wife. If indeed he had a wife before

baptism, who has died, it will not be imputed to him . . . .
21. CT, 3, 1-2; DRL, 676, DCC, II, 57, 59.
22. In 378 A.D., Valens, a Christian emperor, forbade clerics to inherit. See CT 16, 2, 11, 20, 27, 28.
23. This may have been a reminiscence of Cicero, *De divinatione,* 1, 6, 10.
24. Ermine (*peregrini muris* = foreign mouse).
25. On monastic sufficiency, see Decret., C. 1, q. 2, c. 7. Cf. DCC, I, 31, 32.
26. This reference to Bernard of Clairvaux as a 'contemporary writer', is one clue that the Argument was written about 1153.
27. Huygen, p. 349, says 'Cette anecdote n'est connue que par Idung'. It is interesting to compare with a passage in Gregory the Great, *Pastoral Care,* II, 4; ACW 11:53-54: 'The little bells are fittingly described as fixed to the vesture; and indeed, what else is to be understood by the priests' vestments but his righteous works? The Prophet witnesses to this when he says: 'Let thy priests be clothed with justice.' " Therefore, little bells are fixed to the vestments, that even the works of the priests should loudly proclaim his way of life in the sound of his speech.'
28. *Suessionensium* instead of *Senonensium* as in the text. The correction has been made in the notes of Professor Huygen's critical edition, p. 349 note 1.235. Cf. DCC, I, 17.
29. *in cameris:* This is a play on words. *In cameris* literally means 'in chambers'; hence, in secret. However, here it refers to the papal *camera* or chancery. The *camerarius* was the chancellor.
30. *non gregarius sed hereditarius:* On *gregarius,* see CT, 7, 13, 8; on *hereditarius, ibid.,* 16, 2, 6. In the twelfth century, *hereditarius* could also mean 'knight': OCD, 526, s.v. *honestiores.*
31. The tonsure was a mark of the clergy. Long hair was considered barbaric by the Romans and a sign of nobility by the barbarians. See CT, 16, 10, 4. On the considerable confusion over the monastic and clerical *corona,* see DCC, III, 36. On the *corona* (tonsure) and martyrdom, see Cyprian of Carthage, *The Lapsed,* II, ACW 25:14, note 9, IV (ACW 25:15), X (ACW 25:21); *The Unity of the Church,* XIV (ACW 25:57).
32. *non in angaria sed paupertate voluntaria.* Professor Huygen offers as a comparison, Ps.-Augustine, *Sermo* 247, 7; PL 39:2204; *Qui vero in angaria Christi crucem portat.* I am not sure whether this is the source, for the text continues: *poterit plura de ejus virtute experimenta cognoscere, quam possit sermo retexere, vel humana cogitatio comprehendere.* It would seem that here *angaria* has a more positive connotation than is in Idung. A more proximate source of the phrase may be Ep 258 of St Bernard, cited in DCC, I, 15: *Immolavi de sinu meo cari pignioris hostiam; et non in angaria fateor; sed in voluntate mea parui voluntati, quae quos vult angariat.* Cf. CT 8, 5, 4.
33. This thought is reflected in Roman law. CT 12, 1, 107: 'Decurions who prefer to serve the church . . . shall hold in contempt those goods which they stealthily withdraw . . . Indeed, it is not seemly for spirits bound by divine worship to be occupied by desire for patrimonies.'
34. See above, note 10.
35. On tax farming, see CT, 12, 1, 92, 97. DRL, 372, 642, 702, 746, 405, 346; regarding the *rustici,* DC, VII, 246-247; DRL, 686.
36. 'Secular' has three basic meanings: a worldling; a canon living without a rule; anyone who is not bound by a (monastic) rule. It is quite possible that Idung is referring to the canons secular.
37. This part of the argumentum may indicate that the *argumentum* was a response to Herbord.
38. *Subtilitas* as opposed to monastic *simplicitas.*
39. On modesty *formulae,* see Curtius, pp. 83-85; 278-280. For a definition

of *facultas,* see Cicero, *De inventione,* 1, 27, 41. For a definition of *intelligentia, ibid.,* 2, 53.

40. *cui ei tradiderat versum: Tradere* has been translated as 'to teach', but *traditio* contains a wealth of tradition *(paradosis)* as well as connotation.

41. The *locus,* the topic of discussion. Cf. *loci communes,* general arguments which could be applied to a number of cases.

42. Cf. DCC I, 48. 1 Co 1:20. Huygen traces the phrases to Ps-Augustine [Fulgentius of Ruspe], *De fide ad Petrum* 47(IV)-86(XLIII); CCh 91A:744-59. See Huygen's notes, pp. 355-6 for instances of its use.

43. Does this two page digression lead one to think that Idung's scholastic career was intruding?

44. *Comm. pro virgine mart:* ... *etiam in sexu fragili victoriam martyrii contulisti* .... *(Missale Romanum* [New York: Benziger Brothers, 1962] p. 29). On the 'fragile sex', see Cyprian of Carthage, Ep 4; FCh 51:11-13.

45. See Hugh of St Victor, *Didascalion,* II, 28-30, and Taylor, ed., *Introduction,* pp. 15-16 and note 48, p. 112.

46. Cf. Quintilian, *Institutio Oratoria,* trans. H.E. Butler, (4 vols.; Cambridge, Mass.: Harvard University Press, 1959-1963) 5, 9, 1, 2.

47. *in adulta virgine:* During the Roman republic and empire, one was an *impubes* up to about the age of fifteen years. From fifteen to thirty years old, one was an *adulescens.* However, one could also be an *adulescens* from thirty to forty years of age. However, have we here the 'old woman and girl' topos? See, Curtius, pp. 101-105. See Gregory the Great, *Dial.* II, 2 (FCh 61).

48. In another context, 'In wine there is severity, in oil there is compassion.' See *Homilies of St. Jerome,* Homily 42: On Psalm 127 (128); FCh 48:323.

49. On *lectio divina,* see *Dial.* II, 3: FCh: 67.

50. The *telas* in question would seem to have been finished cloths as one would find displayed in mideastern bazaars. She should reject cloths made out of silk. Arabian silk seems to have been considered the best. There was also Assyrian silk. 'Chinese silks' would not seem to be accurate for 'the mulberry silkworm *(bombyx mori)* was not bred in the Mediterranean world before the 6th century A.D.' OCD, 990.

51. See Quintilian, *Institutio Oratoria,* 4, 4, 2; 9, 2, 103.

52. See note 13B to Jr 13:22; *The Jerusalem Bible* (New York: Doubleday and Company, 1971).

53. St Ambrose, for example, wrote several works on virginity, the most famous of them, the *De virginibus ad Marcellinam sororem suam libri tres;* PL 16:197-244.

54. The *De lapsu virginis consecratae, liber unus;* PL 16:383-399, 'was not composed by St. Ambrose, and should probably be attributed to Nicetas of Remesiana'—F. Cayre, *Manual of Patrology and History of Theology* (2 vols; Paris: Desclee & Co., 1935) I, 532.

55. *sacrarium Dei:* See Ps 79:1; 1 Co 3:16-17. Gregory the Great, *Dial.* II, 2 (FCh 39:61): 'It is a well known fact, Peter, that temptations of the flesh are violent during youth, whereas after the age of fifty, concupiscence dies down. Now, the sacred vessels (Nb 8:24-26) are the souls of the faithful. God's chosen servants must therefore obey and serve and tire themselves out with strenuous work as long as they are still subject to temptations. Only when full maturity has left them undisturbed by evil thoughts are they put in charge of the sacred vessels, for then they become teachers of souls.'

56. At the time Idungus was writing, the Cistercians were beginning to become involved with the direction of nuns. Cf. DCC III, 12, 13.

57. On the question of monks preaching and exercising pastoral functions, see Usmer Berliere, 'L'exercise du ministere paroissial par les moines dans le haut moyen age,' *Revue Benedictine,* 39 (1927), and Jean Leclercq, 'The Priesthood

for Monks,' *Monastic Studies,* 3 (1965).

58.   *partes dei.* See DC, VI, 182-183, and Alfons Dopsch, *The Economic and Social Foundations of European Civilization* (London: Howard Fertig, Inc. by arrangement with Routledge and Kegan Paul Ltd., 1969) 135-146.

59.   This is an interesting use of Jerome given the return to the desert characteristic of eleventh and twelfth century monasticism. 'Stationed', *constitutus,* is borrowed from military language and means 'to station or to post troops'. Also, 'vast desert' (*solitudo*) can be translated as 'solitude'. It is clear though, that with geographical solitude went an emotional barrenness and deprivation.

60.   Jerome's source for this may be Terence, *The Eunuch,* 2, 25 (trans. John Sargeant [Cambridge, Mass.: Harvard University Press, 1939]). There are many references to Ethiopia and to Ethiopians in the homilies of Jerome. See *Homilies of St Jerome,* No. 3: On Ps 7: No. 18: On Ps 86 (87): (FCh 48:28, 140).

61.   A very interesting mental, emotional, and physical process is being described here. It is that of a man arguing with himself, standing up to himself, and abandoning himself to and for God. This passage is a reminiscence of the entry into the desert by stages. The use of *conscia* by Jerome calls for a brief comment. Jerome describes himself as being in a state of spiritual and physical anxiety. He was not only alone but he feared to be alone with his thoughts; or worse, what he thought in delusion to be his thoughts. The use of *cella* is not exclusively monastic nor hieronomian. Seneca, the great Stoic, also uses *cella* as a place of self-denial. *Select Letters of Seneca,* ed., Walter C. Summers (London: Macmillan and Company, 1940) Ep 18, 7, p. 20.

62.   It is difficult to pin-point Jerome's source. See, Vergil's *Aeneid,* I, 105; Cicero, *The Verrine Orations,* trans. L.H.G. Greenwood (Cambridge, Mass.: Harvard University Press, 1960) II, *Verr.* 2, 5, 56 No. 145. Since Suetonis was 'St. Jerome's source and model for literary history' perhaps it would not be incorrect to cite Suetonis, *Tiberius,* 40, in *The Twelve Caesars.* See H.J. Rose, *A Handbook of Latin Literature* (New York: E.P. Dutton and Company, 1960), p. 511. *Praerupta rupes* is attributed to Suetonis. See *Harper's Latin Dictionary* (New York: American Book Company, 1907), 1427.

63.   Equivocation, one of the several fallacies of language, is the basing of an argument on 'words used in different meanings'. Division, another fallacy, is the 'taking separately what should be taken jointly'. Celestine N. Bittle, *The Science of Correct Thinking* (Milwaukee: Bruce Publishing, 1950) 361-368.

64.   This is an appeal to shame or to modesty (*argumentum ad verecundiam*) where one does 'not argue a question on its intrinsic merits, but strives to convince a person by pointing out the *dignity* of those who adhere to a certain view'—Bittle, p. 375.

65.   Idung uses *presbyter* as a synonym for priest. In the letter of Jerome, Ep 14,8, the meaning is 'bishop'.

66.   The doctrine of the anthropomorphites was that 'God has the same human form and members that we have.' *Homilies of St. Jerome,* No. 22: On Ps 93 (94); FCh 48:177.

67.   This passage makes clear the conscious use of the new logic. According to the law of contrariety 'Contraries cannot be true together; contraries may be false together.' There is also a law of sub-contraries: 'Both subcontraries cannot be false together; but both subcontraries may be true together.' See Bittle, p. 146. This paragraph and the next two form a kind of syllogism or at least indicate a mode of reasoning according to the rules of logic. Part of the orator's task was to 'invent arguments'. Here is an example of an 'internal argument' *ex contrario.* See Cicero, *De partitione oratoria,* II, 5, 7, and *De fato,* trans. H. Rackham (Cambridge, Mass.: Harvard University Press, 1960), XVI, 37. Idung refers here clearly to inference, of which there are two kinds: immediate and mediate. The practical application of this rhetorical-logical-legal heritage may be seen in

DCC, II, 16.

68. Lanfranc (1005-1089) had been a pupil of Fulbert of Chartres, as well as a lawyer and teacher of literature, before becoming a monk at Bec, and later Archbishop of Canterbury. For an excellent account of Lanfranc and Berenger, see R.W. Southern, *The Making of the Middle Ages* (New Haven: Yale University Press, 1965) 196-201. For the basic information regarding the teaching of Lanfranc, see F. Cayre, *Manual,* No. 2: 387-389, 393. The work in question is *De corpore et sanguine domini adversus Berengarium Turonensem liber;* PL 150: 407-442.

69. In the translation of *episcopus monachus,* Idung is concerned not with monastic bishops but with episcopal monks. In a way, episcopal consecration is an addition to monastic profession.

70. 'Invested', that is, 'clothed in'.

71. The form of the syllogism is as follows:
Major Premise: Clerics are ordained by grade and receive 'something'
Minor Premise: Monks are ordained in the same way.
Conclusion: Monks receive the same 'something'
See DCC, I, 13; II, 46. As to how a priest is ordained, see Decret. Pars I, D. 23, cc. 8, 9. On the proper sequence of grades and the interstices to be observed, see, *ibid.,* D. 77, cc. 1-4. As applied to monks, *ibid.,* cc. 8, 9.

72. St Wolfgang (934-994) was a student at both Reichenau and Wurzburg and a teacher at Trier. He became a benedictine monk at Maria Einsiedeln Abbey. Ordained to the priesthood in 968, he became the bishop of Ratisbon in 972. His *Life* was written by Othlo, monk of St Emmeran, about 1050. See, *Othloni, Vita Sancti Wolfkangi Episcopi,* ed. G. Waitz, MGH SS (Leipzig, 1925) IV:521-525 (Introduction); 525-542 (text). See 1 Co 12:31.

73. Pannonia was the mid-Danube region.

74. Idung's comments would seem to indicate that Wolfgang was not yet a bishop, that is, the date is between 968-972. However, *parochia* can and does often refer to a diocese. See Gratian, Pars II, C. 6, q. 3, which deals with this problem of jurisdiction and uses the same metaphor of scythe and harvest, but in a different context.

75. See Gregory the Great, *Dialogues,* III, 14. While Idung writes of monastic humility, the virtue proper to monks, he actually means the holding of an immunity, a benefice or benefices proper to the monastic *ordo.* On monastic humility in the sense of a benefice, see DC IV:263. See Gratian, *Decret.,* Pars II, C. 16, q. 1, cc. 19-25.

76. *inhumana:* removed from the common lot of humanity.

77. See Jerome, *Homilies of St. Jerome,* No. 38: On Ps 111 (112): (FCh 48:281): 'Fear is the mark of beginners; love, indeed, of proficients since "perfect love casts out fear.' (Jn 4:18)'.

78. See Gregory the Great, *Past. Care,* II, 7 (ACW 11:71): 'Doctrine taught does not penetrate the minds of the needy, if a compassionate heart does not commend it to the heart of the hearers; but the seed of the word does germinate promptly, when the kindness of the preacher waters it in the hearer's heart.'

79. This would seem to refer to the gift of tears. See Gregory the Great, *Dial.* I, 13; III, 33; IV, 49 (FCh 39:51; 171, 173-175; 259).

ABBREVIATIONS

ACW   Ancient Christian Writers series. Westminster, Maryland, 1946–

Apo   Bernard of Clairvaux, *Apologia to Abbot William of St Thierry*

CC   *Corpus Christianorum* series. Turnhout, 1953– .

CF   Cistercian Fathers series.

Conf.   John Cassian, *Conferences*. Edited M. Petschenig, CSEL 13 (1886). English translation: NPNF 11.

CS   Cistercian Studies series.

CSEL   *Corpus scriptorum ecclesiasticorum latinorum* series. Vienna. 1866– .

Csi   Bernard of Clairvaux, *Five Books on Consideration*.

CT   *The Theodosian Code and Novels and the Sirmondian Constitutions*. Translated by Clyde Pharr. Princeton: Princeton University Press, 1952.

DACL   *Dictionnaire d'Archéologie chrétienne et Liturgie*. Paris, 1924–53.

DCC   *Dialogue between a Cluniac and a Cistercian Monk*

Decret.   Gratian, *Decretum*. Edited Emil A. Friedberg, *Corpus juris canonici*. Leipzig, 1879.

DHGE	*Dictionnaire d'histoire et de géographie ecclésiastique.* Paris, 1912- .
Dial.	Gregory the Great, *Dialogues. (Gregorii Magni Dialogi)* Edited U. Moricca. Rome, 1924. English translation by O. J. Zimmermann. FCh 39.
DRL	Adolph Berger, *Encyclopedic Dictionary of Roman Law,* Transactions of the American Philosophical Society, 43, Part 2, New Series. Philadelphia, American Philosophical Society, 1953.
Ep(p)	Epistola(e) / Letter(s)
FCh	Fathers of the Church Series. New York and Washington, 1947- .
Inst.	John Cassian, *Institutes.* Edited by Petschenig, CSEL 17 (1888). English translation: NPNF 11.
Interr.	Basil the Great, *Interrogationes [Regula sancti Basilii].* PL 103:487-554.
Mansi	J. D. Mansi, *Sacrorum conciliorum nova et amplissima collectio.* Florence-Venice, 1759-98. Paris, 1900-27. Graz, 1960-61.
MGH	*Monumenta Germaniae Historica.*
Mor	Bernard of Clairvaux, *On the Habits and Duties of Bishops.*
NPNF	The Nicene and Post-Nicene Fathers of the Church series. Reprinted Grand Rapids: Eerdmans.
OCD	*Oxford Classical Dictionary,* 2nd edition. London: Oxford University Press, 1970.
Past. Care	Gregory the Great, *The Pastoral Care.* English translation by Henry David, ACW 11 (1955).
PL	J. P. Migne, *Patrologiae cursus completus, series latina.* 222 volumes. Paris, 1844-64.

PP	Bernard of Clairvaux, *Sermon for the Feast of SS. Peter and Paul*
Pre	Bernard of Clairvaux, *On Precept and Dispensation (De praecepto et dispensationis)*
RB	Saint Benedict's Rule for Monasteries
RSB	Paul Delatte, *Commentary on the Rule of St Benedict.* Translated by Justin McCann. London: Burns, Oates, Washburn, 1921.
SBOp	*Sancti Bernardi Opera,* edd. Jean Leclercq, C. H. Talbot, H. M. Rochais. Rome: Editiones cistercienses, 1957- .
SC	Bernard of Clairvaux, *Sermons on the Song of Songs (Sermones super cantica canticorum)*
SCh	Sources chrétiennes series. Paris: Editions du Cerf.

Scriptural citations have been made according to the enumeration and nomenclature of the Jerusalem Bible.

A SELECTED BIBLIOGRAPHY

Albers, Bruno. *Consuetudines monasticae.* 4 volumes. Stuttgart, 1900.
Antin, P. 'Le monachisme selon saint Jérôme'. *Recueil sur saint Jérôme.* Collection Latomus, 95. Brussels, 1968.
Arquillière, H. X. *L'Augustinisme politique.* Paris, 1934.
———. *Saint Grégoire VII.* Paris, 1934.
Augustine, Saint. *The Letters of St Augustine.* Translated by Sister Wilfred Parsons. Fathers of the Church series, 4 volumes. 1951-56.
———. *The Work of the Monks (De opere monachorum).* Translated by Sister M. S. Muldowney. Fathers of the Church series, 16 (1952).
Baldwin, Charles Sears. *Medieval Rhetoric and Poetic (to 1400).* Gloucester, Massachusetts: Peter Smith, 1959.
Bede the Venerable. *A History of the English Church and People.* Translated by Leo Sherley-Price. Hammersworth-Baltimore: Penguin, 1955.
Bittle, Celestine N. *The Science of Correct Thinking.* Revised edition. Milwaukee: Bruce, 1950.
Boethius. *The Consolation of Philosophy (Philosophiae consolatio).* Translated by H. F. Stewart. Cambridge: Harvard University Press, 1953.
Boon, A. *Pachomiana Latina.* Louvain, 1932.
Buckland, W. W. *A Textbook of Roman Law from Augustine to Justinian.* 3rd edition, revised by Peter Stein. Cambridge: Cambridge University Press, 1966.
Canivez, J. M. *Statuta Capitulorum Generalium Ordinis Cisterciensis ab anno 1116 ad annum 1786.* 8 volumes. Louvain, 1933-41.
Cayre, F. *Manual of Patrology and History of Theology.* Translated by H. Howitt. Paris: Desclée, 1936.
Chagny, André. *Cluny et son empire.* Paris, 1938.
Chibnell, Marjorie, ed., tr. *The Ecclesiastical History of Orderic Vitalis.* 3 volumes. Oxford: Clarendon Press; New York: Oxford University Press, 1969-72.

Codex Juris Canonici. New York 1918.

Colvin, H. M. *The White Canons in England.* Oxford, 1951.

Constable, Giles, ed. *The Letters of Peter the Venerable.* Cambridge: Harvard University Press, 1967.

———. *Monastic Tithes, from their Origins to the Twelfth Century,* Cambridge Studies in Medieval Life and Thought, New Series, Nbr. 10. New York: Cambridge University Press, 1964.

———. ed. *Petrus Venerabilis, 1156-1956: Studies and texts commemorating the eighth centenary of his death,* Studia Anselmiana, 40. Rome: Herder, 1956.

Cottineaux, L. *Répertoire topo-bibliographique des abbayes et prieurés.* Mâcon, 1939-70.

Dickinson, J. C. *The Origins of the Austin Canons and their Introduction into England.* London, 1950.

Evans, Joan. *Monastic Life at Cluny, 910-1157.* London: Oxford University Press, 1931.

Fliche, A. *La reforme grégorienne.* 3 volumes. Louvain, 1924-37.

Graham, Rose. 'Relations of Cluny to some Movements of Monastic Reform'. *Journal of Theological Studies,* 15 (1914).

Guignard, Ph., ed. *Monuments primitifs de la règle cistercienne.* Dijon, 1878.

Hallier, Amédée. *The Monastic Theology of Aelred of Rievaulx,* Cistercian Studies Series, 2. Spencer, Massachusetts: Cistercian Publications, 1969.

Hallinger, Kassius. *Corpus Consuetudinum Monasticarum.* Siegburg, 1963.

Hardouin, Jean. *Conciliorum collectio regia maxima . . .* Paris, 1714-15.

Hartridge, R. A. R. *Vicarages in the Middle Ages.* Cambridge, 1930.

Hugh of St Victor. *Didascalion. The Didascalion of Hugh of St. Victor.* Translated by Jerome Taylor. Records of Civilization Sources and Studies, 64. New York: Columbia University Press, 1961.

Hunt, Noreen, ed. *Cluniac Monasticism in the Central Middle Ages.* Readings in European History. London: Macmillan, 1971.

———. *Cluny under Saint Hugh, 1049-1109.* South Bend: Notre Dame University Press, 1968.

Jaffé, Philipp. *Regesta Pontificum Romanorum.* 2nd edition. 2 volumes. Leipzig, 1885-88.

Jerome. *The Select Letters of St. Jerome.* Translated by F. A. Wright. Cambridge: Harvard University Press, 1954.

Jordan of Saxony. *Jordani de Saxonia, Liber Vitasfratrum.* Edited by R. Arbesmann and W. Hümphner. New York, 1943.

Knowles, David. *The Evolution of Medieval Thought*. London: Longmans; Baltimore: Helicon, 1962.

——. *The Monastic Constitutions of Lanfranc*. Oxford, 1951.

Lackner, Bede. *The Eleventh-Century Background of Cîteaux*, Cistercian Studies Series, 8. Spencer, Massachusetts: Cistercian Publications, 1972.

Leclercq, Jean and R. Foreville. 'Un débat sur le sacerdoce des moines au XIIe siècle'. *Studia Anselmiana*, 41 (1957) 8-118.

McNeil, J. T. and H. M. Gamer. *Mediaeval Handbooks of Penance*, Records of Civilization Series, 29. New York: Columbia University Press, 1938.

Olsen, Glenn. 'The Idea of the *Ecclesia Primitiva* in the Writings of the Twelfth-Century Canonists'. *Traditio* 25 (1969) 61-86.

O'Sullivan, J. F. *Cistercian Settlements in Wales and Monmouthshire*. New York, 1947.

Pennington, M. Basil, ed. *Saint Bernard of Clairvaux: Studies Commemorating the Eighth Centenary of His Canonization*, Cistercian Studies Series, 28. Kalamazoo, 1977.

Petit, François. *La spiritualité des Premontrés au XII–XIII siècles*. Paris, 1947.

Potthast, A. *Regesta Pontificum Romanorum*. 2 volumes. Berlin, 1874-5.

Regula sancti Augustini. Edited by Schroeder, *Archiv für Urkundenforschung* 9 (1926). Translated by Thomas A. Hand, Fathers of the Church, 12. Westminster, Md., 1956.

Schmitz, Philibert. *Histoire de l'Ordre de St. Benoît*. 2nd edition. Maredsous, 1949.

Schroll, Sister M. Alfred. *Benedictine Monasticism as reflected in the Warnefrid–Hildemar Commentaries on the Rule*. New York, 1941.

Southern, R. W. *The Making of the Middle Ages*. New Haven: Yale University Press, 1965.

Storm, J. *Untersuchungen zum* Dialogue duorum monachorum Cluniacensis et Cisterciensis. *Ein Betrag zur Ordensgeschichte des 12. Jahrhundert*. Diss. Münster, 1926.

Tellenbach, Gerd. *Neue Forschungen über Cluny*. Freiburg im Breisgau, 1939.

Theophilus. *De diversis artibus*. Translated by C. R. Dodwell. London: Nelson, 1961.

Veilleux, Armand. *La liturgie dans le cénobitisme pachômien au quatrième siècle*, Studia Anselmiana. Rome: Herder, 1968.

Williams, Watkin. 'A Dialogue between a Cluniac and a Cistercian'.

The Journal of Theological Studies 31 (1930) and Williams, *Monastic Studies*. Manchester, 1938, pp. 61-74.

Wilmart, Andre. 'Une riposte de l'ancien monachisme au manifest de saint Bernard'. *Revue Bénédictine,* 46 (1934) 296-344.

Yvo of Chartres. *Decretum.* PL 161:47-1022.

———. *Panormia.* PL 161:1041-1344.

CISTERCIAN PUBLICATIONS

Cistercian Publications publishes in the following areas:

MONASTIC TEXTS IN ENGLISH TRANSLATION

- Sermons and treatises by twelfth & thirteenth-century cistercian spiritual writers
- Classic texts from the monastic wisdom of both the eastern and western Churches

MONASTIC LIFE, HISTORY, SPIRITUALITY, ARCHITECTURE, AND LITURGY

- For those with a personal interest in contemplative prayer and monastic lifestyle
- For students exploring monastic tradition
- For scholars specializing in aspects of monastic history, art, liturgy, or theology

- Reflections by contemporary monks and nuns
- Specialized studies by scholars
- Overviews of patristic & medieval doctrine
- Cistercian music and retreat addresses on CD and audio-cassette
- Video / DVD visits to contemporary abbeys

Editorial Offices & Customer Service

- Cistercian Publications: Editorial Offices
  WMU Station, 1903 West Michigan Avenue
  Kalamazoo, Michigan 49008-5415   USA

  Telephone 269 387 8920
  Fax   269 387 8390
  e-mail   cistpub@wmich.edu

- Cistercian Publications: Customer Service
  Liturgical Press
  Saint John's Abbey
  Collegeville, MN 56321-7500

  Telephone 800 436 8431
  Fax   320 363 3299
  e-mail   sales@litpress.org

Canada

- Bayard-Novalis
  49 Front Street East, Second Floor
  Toronto, Ontario M5E 1B3   CANADA

  Telephone 800 204 4140
  Fax   416 363 9409

UK and Europe

- Alban Books
  14 Belford Road   West End
  Edinburgh EH4 3BL

  Telephone 0131 226 2217
  Fax   0131 225 5999
  e-mail   sales@albanbooks.com

Website

- www.spencerabbey.org/cistpub

To explore the range of titles in our series of texts and studies in the monastic tradition, please request our free complete catalogue from customer service or visit our website.

www.ingramcontent.com/pod-product-compliance
Lightning Source LLC
Chambersburg PA
CBHW031242290426
44109CB00012B/400